SERIALS MANAGEMENT
IN ACADEMIC LIBRARIES

Serials Management in Academic Libraries

A GUIDE TO ISSUES AND PRACTICES

Jean Walter Farrington

THE GREENWOOD LIBRARY MANAGEMENT COLLECTION

GREENWOOD PRESS
Westport, Connecticut • London

Library of Congress Cataloging-in-Publication Data

Farrington, Jean Walter, 1948–
    Serials management in academic libraries : a guide to issues and
practices / Jean Walter Farrington.
      p.   cm.—(The Greenwood library management collection, ISSN
0894–2986)
    Includes bibliographical references (p.) and index.
    ISBN 0–313–27378–2 (alk. paper)
    1. Academic libraries—United States.   2. Serials control systems—
United States. I. Title. II. Series.
Z675.U5F37   1997
025.17'32—dc21   96–37648

British Library Cataloguing in Publication Data is available.

Library of Congress Catalog Card Number: 96–37648
ISBN: 0–313–27378–2
ISSN: 0894–2986

First published in 1997

Greenwood Press, 88 Post Road West, Westport, CT 06881
An imprint of Greenwood Publishing Group, Inc.

Printed in the United States of America

The paper used in this book complies with the
Permanent Paper Standard issued by the National
Information Standards Organization (Z39.48–1984).

10 9 8 7 6 5 4 3 2 1

In memory of Erich and Erich A.
and
for Tim and Greg

Contents

Introduction

The librarian is a middleman [who] neither produces "information" nor consumes it; he merely transfers it in the form in which it is made available to him and in which the user wants it.

Dix (1968, 39)

This professional reference is a guide for serials librarians in academic libraries and for librarians in academic libraries whose responsibilities include serials. It deals with the principal areas of serials management in an academic setting and highlights some of the key issues of the time: namely, access versus ownership, electronic dissemination of text and document delivery, standards for electronic transfer of data, and cataloging locally versus outsourcing. In the decade ahead, one of the themes that will be played out is that "less is more." Fewer journal titles owned by each institution, less detailed cataloging, and fewer staff may become givens as academic libraries across the nation cope with reduced budgets. The stringencies in funding will be felt by all areas of the academic enterprise. Serials management, in particular, will require a greater degree of flexibility and adaptability, but will be aided by automation. The means to achieving the greatest flexibility in tracking spending, monitoring staff productivity, and adapting work flow is automation, automation, automation.

Many serials managers will be faced with the task of organizing the serials processing work flow to maximize efficiency and productivity yet, simultaneously, minimize the cost and eliminate duplicate effort. Libraries that have engaged in the luxury of a second check-in of serial material when it arrived in the holding location may find that automation and a leaner staff make this an unaffordable and unnecessary extravagance. Likewise, more effort will be put into identifying the best bibliographic record at the time of ordering so that this record becomes the basis for cataloging. More cataloging will be done upon receipt by what is presently acquisitions staff. In addition, academic libraries will continue to see an increase in the availability of electronic materials, particularly journals, and this will transform the work of the serials staff. As one writer put it, "The next chapter in the history of publishing may not yet be written, but it is being created, keyed and transmitted today by a multitude of companies and individuals. Publishers are rapidly realizing the cost of not having an electronic presence and publishing electronically, and electronic commerce is developing rapidly" (Rush 1995, 2). It is becoming second nature to find the Web address for arts organizations, companies, and community organizations included as a part of their print advertising and information. Serials librarians will be called upon to demonstrate an even greater measure of adaptability and a willingness to work within a changing environment.

The traditional serials department's relationship to interlibrary loan (or document delivery, as many of these units have been renamed) will also change as electronic delivery of text increases. Whether this relationship is a fusion of functions, an integration of staff, or a symbiotic working partnership is not yet clear. Basic questions, such as who owns the journals, how are they acquired, and who receives them and provides access will need to be addressed and will have an impact on serials processing as we know it. The separate serials department is already undergoing a metamorphosis and, in some cases, becoming subsumed or absorbed by super-acquisitions/cataloging departments. What percentage of paper journals will be received in each academic library five to seven years hence is also a question, and if the serials are not in paper, what form are they? Who does the receipt, and is traditional receipt necessary? What is evident is that the patterns of receipt and access are already changing and will continue to change; serials librarians will find themselves entangled in these developments whether they wish it or not.

If it is true that there is a major shift in librarians' roles not just in the library, but on campus, so that "the issue now is not nearly so much one of how we work with media and computing specialists, but the collegial bonds we form with faculty" (Hubbard 1992, 707), then all librarians, including serials librarians, must be prepared for a major upheaval in how serials exist, how libraries provide access to them, and what their new roles will be. Or to put it another way, "either librarians realize they are in the information-providing business and move into networks, CD-ROMs, and electronic databases, or they stay in the paper world and become extinct" (Montgomery 1993, 26). The academic library itself is evolving from a print-based, locally sited physical collection to becoming the gateway to collections that are local, but also materials that are electronic in form only and resident on a remote computer; in short, we are witnessing the creation of the digital library. "Although most contemporary digital libraries are being built to manage digitized versions of things that were already available in analog formats (e.g., books, periodicals, and video and sound recordings), a steadily increasing number now on the drawing boards are being built to manage 'digital' rather than 'digitized' information" (Peters 1995, 11). Serials management has never been for weak types; in the future, it will, to an even greater extent, require vision, flexibility, good humor, and the courage to deal with change of a seismic nature. This book, then, is meant to be a guide to current serials management practice with an emphasis on the options and the choices that can be made by the librarian and the library for the decade to come.

REFERENCES

Dix, William Shepard. 1968. "The Librarian of the Uncertain Future." *Wilson Library Bulletin* 43: 39.

Hubbard, Willis M. 1992. "Shifting Paradigms for Librarians." *College and Research Libraries News* 53, no. 1: 707–708.

Montgomery, Margot J. 1993. "Document Supply in a Changing World." *Interlending and Document Supply* 21, no. 4: 24–29.

Peters, Paul Evan. 1995. "Digital Libraries Are Much More Than Digitized Collections." *Educom Review*, July/August: 11–15.

Rush, James E. 1995. "Electronic Publishing—The Future Is Today." *PALINET News*, no. 112: 2, 6.

1

Serials Automation: The Last Frontier

Automation is a part of everyday life for academic libraries in the late 1990s, and in many libraries, all processing is done in the online environment. Despite this, serials processing has usually been the last module to be developed in most library management systems and often the last activity to be implemented by any given library. This is probably due to a combination of factors: the difficulty of programming serials processes and the complexities of the serials work itself. The latter have made some libraries reluctant and hesitant about making the transition to online serials processing. In 1984, in what now appears like pre-science, Dick Boss made the following observation: "The present [computer] systems will have to develop sophisticated serials control software before there is widespread adoption of integrated automated systems in special libraries" (Boss 1984, 1184). Although he was referring to special libraries, his remark could have applied equally well to academic libraries.

We are now at a time, however, when trends in system architecture have shifted away from mainframe computing, and a host of libraries are preparing to leave their mainframe automated systems and migrate to the next generation of automated systems, the new (or at least, newer) world of client/server architecture and relational databases. Many libraries are in the process of evaluating the new UNIX-based library management systems and are rethinking and re-evaluating how serials and other functions play out in this new arena.

In the world of paper, which still remains the dominant format for most serials titles, the receipt and processing of serials are detailed tasks with many steps and the possibility for a wide range of variation in how these steps are carried out and by what level of staff. Serials functions were among the last to be tackled by the automation vendors, and it was not until the late 1980s, and well into the 1990s, that significant numbers of academic libraries had fully automated their serials operations. The benefits of serials automation, particularly the ability to track missing issues and to claim them promptly, more than compensate for the more tedious aspects of making the transition from manual records to automated ones. Some serials systems have now evolved to second or third versions and there is a wide variety of newer library management systems from which to choose. Some of the new client/server, UNIX-based systems offer easier ways to create prediction records for serials receipt, and they fully support the MARC format for display of serials holdings, at the same time that they are evolving into fully mature products. This chapter will address the issues involved in selecting a system for serials, including how to evaluate functionality, and then, once the system is selected, review considerations in making the transition as well as the actual implementation.

There are a number of sources of evaluative and market information for the serials systems currently available. Recent issues of *Library Technology Reports*, published by the American Library Association, included an in-depth look at virtually all of the integrated system vendors. Each spring *Library Journal* publishes a survey of the automated system marketplace, including trends, sales highlights, and brief annotations for those vendors having the largest market share (Bridge 1993; Griffiths and Kertes 1994; Barry et al. 1995; Barry et al. 1996). Another source of information is the *Library Systems Evaluation Guides* volume on serials control (1983), which although dated in terms of the specific system information, nonetheless provides a context or a framework of considerations within which to conduct a system evaluation. It is also informative to visit vendors' booths at the American Library Association exhibits during the midwinter and annual conferences, and at the smaller, division-level conferences and state and regional association meetings where some vendors also exhibit. Talking with a vendor at a conference gives the librarian the opportunity to get an overview of that vendor's product in a neutral setting and to see a number of systems at one time. Follow-up visits by the vendor to the local library can then be scheduled before any serious negotiations for purchase of a given system take place.

CONSIDERATIONS FOR SELECTING AN AUTOMATED SYSTEM

Work Flow Issues

If a library is planning to automate its serials processing for the first time, then it has a unique opportunity and, this author would add, "an obligation" to assess in detail the existing work flow patterns. Most libraries' procedures for doing a particular task, checking in and labeling a journal issue, for example, have developed over time; extra steps may have been added or the precise order in which the steps are done may be a reflection of which staff member is doing it. Trying to totally rethink how tasks in a serials operation are apportioned and what tasks or steps may no longer be necessary forces one to imagine a more streamlined work flow and should lead to a process of automation that makes the most of its potential. It is far easier to take an existing work flow and make it fit the automated system than to look at the automation first and determine how it will facilitate doing the tasks that need doing.

In order to do this, the serials manager should evaluate each process that is currently being done step-by-step, and ask at each step why that step is being done, could it be done another way if it is necessary, and is there anything in the automated system that would eliminate the need to do it. Finally, is it most appropriately being done by the particular staff person who is now doing it, or does it fit better with some other person's duties or at some other point in the work flow? A desirable outcome of automating for the first time, or of migrating from one system to another, would be if the serials manager were to realign the work flow and reconfigure or modify the duties of one or more of the serials staff. If the existing work flow seems not to need modification, then the serials unit is either very efficient already or is not taking full advantage of the economies of processing computerization should allow. If the serials manager implements online functions in a thoughtful way, then he or she is forced to contemplate and reevaluate all the steps of every job as it is now being performed.

Effects of Automation

In making the transition from a non-automated, most likely Kardex or other card file environment to online processing, the most noticeable impact for patrons and library staff probably will be the immediacy with which check-in information becomes available: most systems display current periodical information in the online catalog upon receipt. This instantaneous access to serials information has a potentially greater effect on how the serials department functions than almost anything else. From being a "backroom" function, quite often out of sight of, and most likely out of mind of, the patrons, the serials department's "goods" or check-in data are now on display in the front window. Online check-in of current periodicals issues has ramifications for the timely shelving of issues in a main collection and, if check-in is being done centrally, for their delivery to other branch or department libraries. The serials manager needs to have an accurate sense of what the real delays are between when a particular periodical issue or serial volume arrives in the serials unit and when it leaves the area for its shelving location. Questions about when a particular issue is truly available for a patron to use become of paramount importance. In some cases, the individual library may need to make changes in delivery schedules to branch libraries or in shelving procedures in order to reduce the time that an issue is checked in on the system and appears to patrons, but is not yet in its rightful place.

Types of Systems

The computing world is always in a state of change, but the changes, at least as they apply to hardware and overall system design for libraries, seem to be occurring at a more rapid pace as we approach the year 2000. Specifically, these changes relate to a rethinking of the size of machine that is necessary for certain applications, the cost implications of these various types of hardware, and the widespread adoption of client/server architecture. Client/server architecture, or the combination of smaller machines called servers which hold the database itself with powerful desktop workstations (called clients), has gained in popularity in the library market. One of the advantages is that some of the work of the system is done at the desktop machine with certain software and processes residing there instead of on the larger, server machine. This increases system efficiency, allows for pieces of the database to be spread across multiple machines, and allows for hardware redundancy at less cost. The client/server approach makes it possible ''to stretch computer resources'' and also ''leverages the investment in microcomputers for running client processes. While the client/server model is the way to do computing, it is also a very 'seductive' technology in which the disadvantages, risks, and additional costs are often hidden.'' (Barry et al. 1995, 47). Any library contemplating the client/server model should insist that the vendor explain the advantages and should understand the gains in computing power and any cost benefits as well as the potential trade-offs. There are, at the time of this writing, some unanswered questions about how well the client/server model scales for very large libraries with databases of several million records, and whether or not there are response-time trade-offs in such an architecture and size. Several of the system vendors are actively investigating these scalability and performance issues and working with hardware vendors to test response time with sample databases.

For academic libraries preparing to automate serials functions, there are choices to be made both in the type of serials system and in the hardware on which it will run. Sometimes the two are inextricably linked, but often they are just related issues. Serials systems initially were developed as a part of integrated systems operating on large, mainframe computers, as modules on or separate systems on smaller, minicomputers, and as standalone systems based on a personal computer (PC). More recently, with the growing acceptance of client/server architecture, serials systems have become part of integrated systems running on UNIX-based minicomputers. There are also a few serials systems that are subscription vendor-based systems. For the most part, sales to the academic library market in 1994 were sales of minicomputer systems with less than 4 percent of academic libraries acquiring licenses for microcomputer-based systems (Barry et al. 1995, 45).

Large academic libraries, those with more than 10,000 current titles, are more likely to want to consider an integrated library management system (rather than a separate, vendor-based system) since such a system can more easily accommodate the larger volume of titles and orders. A library management system, whether it be client/server architecture running UNIX or a more traditional, host-based system running UNIX or some other operating system, has the added advantage of enabling patrons to easily view bibliographic, order, and current receipt information for serials in one look-up. This information may be all on one screen or on several screens. Current development work is on systems which are UNIX-based and can be mounted on smaller machines from a variety of hardware manufacturers. Not only can UNIX be run on smaller machines, but the ability to use hardware from a variety of manufacturers makes it more affordable to build in some hardware redundancy as well as to spread out portions of the database or individual files (journal article databases, for example) or functions over several different machines.

Systems for Academic Libraries: The Integrated Approach

There are a number of vendors marketing systems for academic libraries: among them are Ameritech Library Services, Innovative Interfaces, Geac, Sirsi, DRA, VTLS, and Endeavor Information Systems. Ameritech Library Services (the corporate entity formed by the merger of Dynix and NOTIS Systems) now markets a client/server product called Horizon in addition to its mainframe-based NOTIS LMS or Library Management System. Horizon is the formerly named Dynix Marquis system which is being further developed to meet large research libraries' needs. Most of these system vendors have in development or are contemplating a change to UNIX and client/server architecture. The Geac ADVANCE system runs on UNIX, and the company is beginning to develop and offer client/server products for its OPAC and for cataloging and technical services in general (Farley et al. 1994). The Sirsi Company, with ten years of experience with UNIX, markets its UNICORN client/server system to academic, special, and other libraries (Young et al. 1994). Sirsi uses the powerful BRS search engine for its OPAC and was one of the earliest, if not the first, of the large system vendors to offer a World Wide Web–based version of the catalog with its WebCat product. The ubiquity of the Web and the ready adoption of Netscape and other browsers by many academic faculty and students makes a Web-based OPAC a very appealing option for those libraries whose campuses are already networked. As of this writing, most of the other major vendors (Ameritech, DRA, Innovative, Endeavor) have just presented their own Web clients or have them in active development. Innovative Interfaces was an early pioneer in providing sophisticated automated acquisitions and serials functions in its earlier INNOVACQ system. Today it offers the INNOPAC system that is a host-based, rather than client/server, system that can be run on UNIX. INNOPAC was selected by the libraries of Ohio as the basis for the OhioLINK project, a system that links the state library with all of the state universities and facilitates the sharing of bibliographic information as well as interlibrary lending (Kohl 1994). Also of potential interest to academic libraries are systems offered by DRA, VTLS, and Endeavor. DRA markets its Data Research System, which is based on VMS and offers a great deal of functionality and flexibility; DRA is in the process of migrating its system's functions to a UNIX platform also. VTLS offers both mini- and micro-based systems and has sold heavily in the international market; its systems are also UNIX-based. VTLS recently announced that over the next several years, it will develop a new client/server system with three-tiered architecture (applications software is separated from the database and the clients are the third tier) called Virtua. Endeavor, a company founded in 1994, purchased the Voyager system software from MARCorp of California, and is marketing Voyager as its management system for large academic libraries. It is a client/server UNIX-based product which employs multitiered architecture; applications software is separate from the database on the server which allows for greater efficiency of operation and easier modification of software to change or improve functionality. Voyager initially ran under Ingres as its relational database management software, but as of fall 1996 has ported to the Oracle relational database management system.

Some of the earliest library management systems were so-called "turnkey" systems; the library staff had only to "turn the key" and the system ran. There was no local programming required, there was no need for a large cadre of systems staff in the library, and the systems were intended to be straightforward to operate. Although the term "turnkey" is used less frequently today than ten years ago, there is a difference in what the library staff is or is not able to do in the way of programming on the newer system products. At the opposite end of the spectrum from the "turnkey" systems are those mainframe systems which arrived complete with the system code. The library staff had the opportunity, if they had the in-house programming expertise, to make major modifications to the code. These changes, then, had to be noted and the library was then obligated to carry them forward every time a new software release was added. Sometimes these local changes were not easily accommodated with a software upgrade and considerable effort was necessary to make all of the new features work, while at the same time retaining the library's customizations. The days when the library received a copy of the system source code are now in the past. Many of the new library management systems are closer to being "turnkey" in the sense of being low maintenance for the library and for not requiring a sizable systems staff; some vendors will configure all tables as part of the installation process, while other vendors assume complete responsibility for loading any and all software upgrades and new versions. As some of these vendors install more client/server systems to large libraries, however, they have begun to rethink the issue of who does what and larger libraries that have systems staff in-house may be able to be more involved with installing software releases, and so on. With the newer system design and the client/server model, there is generally more flexibility for the library in determining how records display, what fields are part of an order record, what menu choices a user sees at the point of log-on, and what the text of overdue and other messages is, for example. Many of these newer systems are table-driven and utilize relational databases, rather than the traditional hierarchical file structure; this makes it possible set up all sorts of parameters and combinations of values which give the system a great deal of power and flexibility for the individual library. This means that two different library OPACs may look quite different, even though both libraries have installed the same system. In addition, at least one system vendor provides the library the opportunity to do further customization by writing local programs which do not affect the basic system code, but which add to the ability to meet local needs. This kind of approach is called "applications programmable interface," or API.

Systems for Academic Libraries: The Subscription Vendor Approach

While the integrated system is an appealing option for large libraries in particular, there are also advantages to a vendor-based system for just serials. This is particularly true if all, or nearly all, of the library's serials orders are handled through one vendor. Usually, the vendor will provide the initial bibliographic records for all the titles currently received by the library; this saves the library the task of having to key or otherwise create its basic record file. Claiming is made simpler by virtue of the fact that there is only one vendor to deal with, and claims can be transmitted by disk or more likely, electronically over the Internet. Furthermore, the equipment investment for a vendor-based system is a lot less for libraries with a small title file, since the simplest vendor system requires only a dedicated terminal or a personal computer with a modem. Examples of vendor-based serials systems are Faxon's MicroLINX and Readmore's REMO system.

Readmore's REMO system is microcomputer-based, rather than PC-based, and runs on IBM or IBM compatible hardware. There are minimal telecommunication costs and a title file up to 10,000 titles can be accommodated (Geyer and Botta 1989). Network costs for five, ten, or more than ten users of the software are in addition to the software package prices. MicroLINX runs on an IBM or compatible PC, can handle up to 5,000 titles, and offers predictive check-in and electronic claiming as well as routing and management reports. Both MicroLINX and REMO offer the advantages of local control over serials functions along with the ability to communicate electronically with the subscription vendor for the purposes of claiming and querying the vendor's title files. Communication with the vendor is fast and frequent, yet the library is printing and handling its own reports. The chief disadvantage of vendor systems such as these is that the receipt and claiming information exists only in that system and is not readily available to patrons in the local online catalog. As an alternative, some smaller libraries print out weekly lists of current issues received.

The particular kind of system that will best meet a given library's serials functions depends on a variety of factors, most particularly on what other automation the library already has in place and how serials information fits into the library's and the college or university's overall information picture. Issues of cost, of what other computer hardware the library and the campus currently support, and whether or not the serials system is to be separate or part of an integrated system are all part of the total picture. A microcomputer system, for example, usually requires only a modest investment in hardware and often, the hardware and software are purchased as a package. This kind of system, whether it is subscription vendor-based or not, may be a good choice for small libraries. In the new world of Z39.50, it may also be possible to provide a link from the standalone serials system to the library's OPAC in order to show serials holdings to patrons. Deciding to purchase an integrated system that includes a serials module is something that needs the active participation of staff at multiple levels within the organization up to and including the serials manager, department heads, support staff, and the library director.

The decision to select an integrated system rather than separate modules from different vendors (the "mix and match" approach) is generally predicated on a desire to link all the functions in the library from acquisitions to the online catalog. In the ideal, an integrated system provides for one access point for all the records for staff and patrons. Integrated systems require a larger expenditure for hardware and may well involve some local programming or additional cost for customization of the software. Newer systems provide the local library with more options and more choices for setting up library locations, default values for new orders, and the like. Given the fact that automated systems are always evolving and new software is always being written, there is always the possibility that the integrated system selected for the library as a whole may not have all of the features one would like for serials. At no matter what point in time a library purchases a new system, all modules or functions will not be created equal; past history, early customers, current market demands, and ongoing contract obligations will all have had an impact on where the product is in terms of overall maturity and refinement. A good system is one that is continually evolving and improving. Any potential customer will want to see the active list of development projects, talk to current users to assess their satisfaction with system performance and features, ascertain whether the vendor delivers software upgrades in a timely fashion, and gain a clear understanding of the role of the customer base in determining the system vendor's future development priorities. For most of the existing mainframe systems, staff operations are performed at a dumb terminal; with the advent of client/server architecture, the terminal has been replaced by a computer workstation, which means it is more capable in terms of how it performs the library system functions, and it probably also includes software for other tasks such as word processing and spreadsheets as well as communications packages to allow for e-mail and other Internet access. To date, the client software for most of the newer systems is either Windows or Windows NT, and in one case OS/2. There has been little or no support for Macintosh clients on the staff side (some on the public clients), but this is changing somewhat as a couple of vendors are now indicating that public Macintosh clients will be available once the Windows versions are fully ready across all modules. It will be useful to track how the even newer Web clients roll out and whether or not they overtake the Windows clients as the public client of choice for OPAC access. On a large campus, the prospect of keeping the Windows clients current for thousands of users is a daunting proposition compared to the relative ease with which each faculty, staff, or student can keep his or her copy of Netscape up-to-date.

Functions of the System

Receipt. The high-volume activity of most serials processing units remains the checking in or receipt of periodical issues; and consequently, serials managers are most likely to want to automate check-in followed by claiming and binding. The heart of serials control in any system is the check in process. Therefore, looking closely at how an issue is checked in is a necessary first step in evaluating any serials system or module. Some key considerations are:

How is the check-in record accessed?

How many screens does it take to get to it?

Can the record be easily retrieved by title, ISSN, SICI code, or library purchase order number?

Are the fields on the check-in screen labeled?

Is it easy to interpret?

Is the next expected issue shown (predictive check-in) or does all the information regarding the issue in hand have to be keyed?

How many keystrokes are required to receive one issue?

Does the system support check-in by scanning of the SICI or UPC bar codes?

If issues are received out of order, does the system automatically rearrange the order of public display of the current issues?

Does the system record the date the issue was received and if so, is this receipt date retained indefinitely?

How are multiple copies of the same title received for the same location?

How are multiple copies for different locations handled?

Will the system prevent the operator from checking in two copies of an issue on the same record (instead of on two different records)?

What are the general security provisions regarding checking in on different orders? If check-in is decentralized, can the check-in be limited in functionality either by staff members' log-on or to a particular location?

What kind of flexibility exists for handling special issues, unnumbered supplements, and other extra issues?

How many issues can a trained staff member check in in an hour?

Does the check-in screen show the location of the received copy as well as the call number?

How is routing information handled?

Is there provision for binding information and does the vendor have now or intend to provide a binding module with lists of titles ready to be pulled for binding?

What happens to the check-in data for individual issues when a volume is bound?

How do the checked-in issues display to the public and does the display include both enumeration and chronology?

How many current issues display in the OPAC?

Is the format clear and easy to interpret and is it possible to distinguish between unbound periodicals and bound volumes?

Generally, the more data an individual has to enter per issue, the greater the likelihood of keying errors and also, the more time it takes per issue. Several years ago, the then NOTIS company did a comparative study of check-in times for issues received by straight keying of title or ISSN and issues with SICI codes. Not surprisingly, the time per issue was less when the issue information was able to be scanned in. It is also desirable that the staff members receiving issues have to access the fewest number of screens; generally, the expected issue, its location and call number, its frequency, and any special processing instructions or routing information should all be present on one receipt screen. It should also be possible to easily link to the source of the title (vendor, fund being paid from, and most recent payment) by toggling to another screen or moving directly to another screen without having to leave the serials control portion of the system.

Claiming. If check-in is the heart of serials control, then one can argue that the claiming function is the conscience. Despite serials librarians' best efforts and publishers' best intentions, not all issues of every title will arrive when and where they should. Therefore, a good claiming function is critical to the success of any serials system. In fact, for many serials librarians, the desire to have better control over claiming is one of the strongest incentives to automate serials processing. It is also, unquestionably, the area where the results will have the greatest potential impact on the serials department's performance, and, on patron satisfaction with the library. Claiming in the manual environment is tedious and slow, takes a lot of time for what may seem to be little return, and often is just not done systematically, due to a lack of available staff time. For any serials system under consideration, the following questions address some of the key issues related to the claiming function:

What is the mechanism for claiming gaps in receipt?

What governs the interval for determining that a claim is needed?

Does the system automatically prompt the staff member for a claim when a later issue is received and the expected issue has not arrived?

Are claim letters generated automatically by running a batch claim program?

How does the system handle claims for new orders that have not started coming?

Is there an online review process before claims are produced?

Does the system vendor support online transmission of claims between the library and the subscription or standing order vendor, using the X12, EDIFACT, or some other generally accepted standard for Electronic Data Interchange (EDI)?

Is there support for receiving and logging publisher and vendor claim responses electronically in the appropriate receipt record?

Some systems produce a list of titles that need to be reviewed for possible claiming; serials staff look at each record and then make a judgment and, by some action, issue a claim request. In this author's experience, review of titles before the claims are generated is worthwhile, since it eliminates unnecessary claims for foreign or other titles that may need more time. Electronic claiming will be a must in the near future; several vendors, including Faxon (with Ameritech) and EBSCO (with Sirsi), are involved in testing electronic claiming using the X12 standard. In the initial tests, the claim was sent to the vendor electronically, but the claim responses were returned to the library in the usual nonelectronic way. Another vendor, Endeavor Information Systems, has begun development work to support the EDIFACT standard for transmitting claim, order, and invoice data between the local library and a variety of system vendors. In fact, there is now a general agreement among system vendors that the X12 standard should be abandoned in favor of the EDIFACT standard, which has already undergone significant testing in Europe. It is quite reasonable for a library to expect the system vendors to support some form of EDI in the not-too-distant future for claiming, ordering, and invoicing.

Binding. The area of binding control has developed much more slowly than other serials functions, perhaps, in part, because a number of commercial binders have developed their own automated programs which they are marketing to libraries. Consequently, some serials systems do not yet include a binding control function. Several systems that do handle some aspects of binding are: IN-NOPAC, VTLS, Ameritech's Horizon, and Unicorn (Sirsi's system). Most serials librarians would deem it essential that any binding module be able to produce a list of all the periodicals that are ready for binding based on the library's locally defined criterion of what constitutes "ready." For example, "ready for binding" may be (1) after the last issue of the volume, (2) after the first issue of the next volume has been received, or (3) after some portion of the year's issues have been received (every two months for *Time* magazine, for example), or any of these plus some interval of delay to allow the patrons access to the last issue before it is sent for binding. Other considerations for a binding module are:

Can the system produce a binding slip to accompany the issue to the bindery?

How are the volumes that are out for binding monitored or noted in the system for staff viewing? What does the public see?

What happens when the volume is returned?

Is there a straightforward way to check in the volume from the bindery and have it simultaneously added to the bound volume holdings?

If the serials system in question does not currently have a binding function, what are the vendor's plans to provide it?

In an integrated system, one would also expect to find the binding function feeding into the circulation charge and discharge functions. This then would allow for tracking of a particular volume's whereabouts from the time it leaves the building until it returns as a bound volume.

Electronic Data

Work is also underway to provide for the transmission of delivery information from subscription vendors to libraries. B.H. Blackwell, for example, currently receives the dates certain publishers have mailed particular issues of a journal to their subscribers and is passing this information on to libraries through its online Connect service. Blackwell's Connect is just one example; other vendors are also working to make this information available to their customers. In time, this data may be transmitted using EDI (Electronic Data Interchange) directly from the subscription or serial vendors to the library's system, thus enabling library staff to better inform their patrons about when particular issues should arrive and be available for use.

Holdings Display

Holdings information is detailed, may be entered into the library's records in several different styles reflecting input at different points in time, and may be incomplete. For libraries with large collections and many branch libraries with multiple copies of titles in several different locations, and possibly the combination of centralized and decentralized check-in, holdings data is very important. The serials manager will want to pay close attention to how this data is loaded from any existing machine-readable records as well as how new holdings data will be presented in the system. He or she should thoroughly investigate how current issues are displayed (is there support for the most detailed level of the MARC holdings format, for example) and determine if multiple copies of the same title can have separate holdings statements.

What is the public display of current issues? An issue-by-issue list? Or is there a summary holdings statement that shows the unbound issues with gaps noted?

If a gap is filled in by a subsequent receipt, will the system automatically update the summary holdings statement?

Serial holdings information is complicated and can be fraught with complications for the system vendor. Some of the newer versions of systems may not, in fact, handle holdings displays as well as the earlier mainframe systems. What is generally expected in an integrated system is that the patron will see in one record a summary of the bound volume holdings as well as the currently received unbound issues of a journal. This display should clearly distinguish between current issues (which are usually unbound) and bound volume holdings and clearly indicate the location and call number of both types of holdings. If a subset of either type of holding is shelved in yet another location, then this should be apparent with clear notes or messages. The display should also provide for public notes regarding limited retention of a title (''latest two years only,'' for example) or retention until a microform copy is received. While much of the emphasis here has been on the handling of periodical titles, other serials (such as annuals and monographic series), loose-leaf services which are checked in like periodicals, and depository items (which can be of all types) also need to be accommodated in an acceptable fashion. In evaluating serials systems, it is advisable to request examples of how to treat these other serials.

The issues related to the display of holdings to the patron are somewhat different in a standalone system than in a vendor-based system. Since standalone systems are often not linked in to the online catalog, separate provisions need to be made for providing holdings information to the patron as well as to the serials staff. With a standalone system, the library may wish to make a terminal available to patrons to call up the records in order to provide access similar to what would be the case in an integrated system. Another option is for the library to print a daily or weekly listing of all the new issues that have been received. A third option is to investigate an electronic link between the serials system and the OPAC whereby the holdings information from the serials system displays in the public catalog; with all that is being done with the Z39.50 standard, this may be a real possibility. In a small academic library, a weekly printed list might be feasible, but it immediately sacrifices some of the currency of an online system, since such a list will be out-of-date as soon as it is printed. If a direct linkage is not possible, it may reasonable to offer limited information in the online catalog for patrons, such as that the title is currently received from a certain point. Library staff would be the ones to access the actual receipt data from a non-public terminal or workstation, or one located at a reference or service desk, and give it to patrons orally. This is more workable if all of the patrons are coming into the library for their serials' holdings information; with the current tendency to perform a lot of searching and look-ups remotely from home, a dorm room, or an office, this is a less satisfactory solution.

For microcomputer or vendor-based serials systems or modules in which the serials holdings information will be self-contained and not necessarily a part of the library's online catalog, the library needs to weigh the desirability of having all of the relevant holdings information about a serial in one record display in the OPAC, for example, against the staff time and labor involved in doing it. It may be possible to enter retrospective holdings for serials into the vendor-based processing system on a one-time basis and, from that time forward, to build the holdings data from the ongoing receipt of current issues and volumes. In this instance, it is possible that the most current serials information will be in the serials processing system rather than in the public catalog.

Online Fund Management

It is possible to receive serials online without ordering or paying for them there, but it severely limits the library's ability to track costs by discipline, to see price increases, and to monitor budget expenditures on a monthly and yearly basis. A comprehensive online fund-accounting package ought to allow serials staff to link payments by invoice and title, to generate vouchers for payment, to set up fund codes by discipline or gift, to track expenditures within a fund code by type of material or type of order, and to know immediately the status of each fund in terms of money expended, money committed, unexpended balance, and percentage expended. Monthly and year-end accounting reports ought to be easy to produce and well designed. Likewise, a good fiscal package should enable the production of standard as well as locally designed reports on demand such as: lists of orders by specific vendor (useful for monitoring vendor performance and for facilitating cancellation projects or the transfer of a one vendor's orders to another), a summary of dollars spent per vendor in a given time period, total number of open orders with specified foreign vendors with the dollar value for each vendor, and counts of the number of open orders by material type, based on a subdivision within the fund code (all microforms, all CD-ROMs, for example). A sophisticated fund-accounting module should also compute currency conversions based on values the library staff enters on a regular basis. With the development of the UNIX-based client/server systems, many system vendors are able to offer commercial report-writing software packages that utilize SQL (Standard Query Language) protocols. This generally means the system comes with a suite of standard reports which can then be customized, and also new reports can be created once staff are comfortable with how to use SQL. The relational database structure of these newer systems allows for virtually any field in a record to be pulled out for reporting purposes. As a result, the reports capability of the client/server systems is, in general, superior to what exists today in many of the older mainframe systems.

In addition, other aspects of fund accounting to be considered include:

What are the steps involved in creating and paying on an invoice record?

What is the maximum number of items allowed on a single invoice?

How are credits handled?

How many levels of fund codes are possible?

How many access points are there for retrieving fund and order records?

Does the library have local control over fund types, vendor types, and order types?

Can default values be set for funds as part of an individual staff member's session preferences?

Are fund management reports customizable?

Can these reports be produced without system staff intervention?

Finally, does the system allow for tape loading or electronic transfer of large renewal invoices either via EDI or FTP (File Transfer Protocol)?

Electronic Invoicing and Other EDI Capabilities

Currently, EBSCO, Faxon, B.H. Blackwell, Harrassowitz, and other vendors are able to produce computer invoice tapes or files for many of the library management systems including: the NOTIS LMS system, Innovative Interfaces, Geac, and others. All the titles to be renewed are billed by the subscription vendor as output to a computer tape or FTP file (with a paper copy to the library as well). A program on the library's management system then creates invoice records and writes pay statements for each title in the appropriate order record as well as on the invoice record. The appropriate fund codes are debited for the titles. The benefits of this feature to the library are significant in terms of time saved in the keying of individual pay statements and in having more accurate payment information. Generally, reports that result from this invoice load process include not only a list of items that did not post and why, but also summaries of charges to each fund, excessive price increases (all titles that increased more than a percentage determined by the library), and the like. The initial preparation does require some investment of serials staff time. For most automated systems, the library needs to add some unique piece of vendor information to its order record which then functions as the match point for the incoming invoice data; this can be the vendor's title number or some other piece of data. Usually, the library provides the vendor with an extract tape or file of all of that vendor's titles. The vendor then picks up the library's system order number for its files. The two numbers, the vendor's title number and the library's system order number, are match points. The vendor's title number in the library system's order record is a hook which the vendor will use to get into their system to add the library order number. With some vendors, it may also be possible to transmit invoice data over the Internet using FTP (File Transfer Protocol), instead of sending it on magnetic tape. The library then takes this file and loads it using the appropriate library management system software to insert the prices in the order records and create the online invoice records.

This use of computer-produced invoice tapes, although in use for more than five years, is just the beginning of a whole new era of electronic data transfer from vendor to library. Vendors and libraries are now planning and working toward other types of interfaces, called EDI or "electronic data interchange," for the online transfer of orders and claims (McKay and Piazza 1992). It will be interesting to see if these computer services continue to be free, that is, offered as part of the library's basic subscription vendor service charge, or whether there will be additional costs associated with their use. In the future, perhaps invoice data will be able to be downloaded directly into the individual library's system from the vendor or publisher, making use of X12 or some other data exchange standard, without any other software intervention.

Advantages of Online Ordering

New orders that are placed online and thus appear in the library's online catalog reduce the chance of duplicate orders being placed and give patrons the added benefit of being able to see what is on order. In many libraries, the patron can also request that that book or serial be processed for them when it is received. Producing new orders in an automated serials environment will vary, depending on whether or not the library is on a vendor-based system or an integrated system. If it is the vendor's system, ordering new titles from that vendor may well require only some keying of information into an online order template which is then sent via telephone dial-up or over the Internet to the vendor's computer, where it is processed. Ordering on an integrated system most likely still will involve the creation of a paper order form, at least for the near future. An order record is generally attached to some sort of bibliographic record (this may be imported from a utility or keyed) and usually consists of a vendor name or code, ordering and receiving addresses or codes, the fund code to which the item or subscription is to be charged, what issue or volume the order is to start with or to include, and a follow-up date for action if the material has not been received at that point. Orders should be able to be modified and reprinted or resent if errors are made. Any good system will include a template or session preferences feature that allows the library staff member to set default values for a number of fields in the order record; this way, if multiple orders are being placed with the same vendor, the vendor and other standard information does not have to be keyed for each individual order. This is both more efficient and reduces the number of errors. The system should also include a provision to code or note the type of order: paid, exchange, depository, or gift, for example.

Standards

The library world runs on standards and has been standards-conscious for several decades, but especially since the 1960s, when the MARC (MAchine Readable Cataloging) format was introduced. The MARC bibliographic format has long been accepted as the basic format for coding and transmitting bibliographic information, and most systems have adopted it as the basic record format. There may, however, be a few remaining systems that do not use MARC and for any academic library, this would be a serious drawback. The other standard that is increasingly being implemented by serials vendors is the MARC format for holdings and locations, referred to in some circles as MHFL. This relatively new standard (1992) provides a systematic approach for the display and communication of serials holdings information (volumes and years held) at several different levels of detail and complexity. Use of this standard can facilitate the sharing of holdings information in local and national union lists of serials. It also sets up a structure for holdings data within one's own serials environment that can provide for greater consistency in how holdings information displays to the public.

To keep fully informed on the latest developments in the area of library standards, the National Information Standards Organization (NISO) publishes a useful publication called *Information Standards Quarterly*, which regularly reports on standards in development, standards being reviewed and revised, as well as those that have been discontinued. In evaluating library management systems for how well they deal with established library standards, the following should be considered:

MARC bibliographic record formats

Are all of the currently existing MARC bibliographic record formats supported by the system?

Has the systems vendor implemented format integration (this was implemented in two stages with the variable fields integrated in January 1995 and the fixed fields in March 1996)?

Is it possible to limit staff and OPAC searches by primary format type?

MARC standard for holdings and locations

How is the MARC holdings format accessed?

Are staff able to input data directly into a holdings template or a MARC tagged display?

Can the user request the tagged display if that is not the default display?

Can creation, update, and deletion of MARC holdings records be controlled based on user log-on or some other form of security control?

Is the formatting of existing holdings information preserved in any migration from one automated system to another?

EDI (Electronic Data Interchange)

What work has the vendor done in the area of electronic transmission of claim data, claim responses, orders, and order responses?

Is the system vendor committed to implementing these within a specified time frame?

What standard for EDI will the vendor be supporting: X12, EDIFACT, or some other?

Z39.50 Standard

Although the Z39.50 standard for linking disparate computers does not apply directly to serials, it has the potential to increase the use of the local serials collection when used in combination with local system software to link the library's holdings to citations in journal articles and other bibliographic databases. Z39.50 is a standard that enables one computer to exchange data with another; to access a foreign system, the home computer must have a server that is Z39.50 compliant. To receive data from an outside source, the local library client (the workstation or PC) must be a Z39.50 client. Some system vendors currently offer software to provide these links between citation databases that are mounted locally and the local OPAC (Caswell et al. 1995). The field most often used for the linking is the ISSN or ISBN, and this argues for inclusion of the ISSN in all serial records and the regular updating of this field as changes to it become known.

IMPACT OF AUTOMATION

Serials Information More Available

Automating serials functions makes serials information more visible and hence, available to staff and patrons. A library using a Kardex for check-in information could be compared to a company privately held by a family; all of the financial information and business dealings are private matters. With the introduction of online check-in, the library becomes more like a corporation with public stock that reports to a large group of investors, investors who are keenly interested in what transpires in the corporation. Holdings information suddenly becomes public information and the staff, particularly if they have not had exposure to the patrons previously, may well feel on view and vulnerable in a new way. Their work and its timeliness will become matters of public concern. This frequently leads to questions regarding the timeliness of the receipt of individual issues and how long it takes these issues to reach their final destinations. It also raises the issue of centralization verses decentralization of check-in (one site or many sites), the need for a delivery van or runners to branch libraries, and the frequency of such delivery (daily or several times a day). A side effect of the greater visibility of serials information is that it may result in an advisory or instructional role for serials staff that they may not have had before. They may be called upon more frequently to interpret receipt information in the online catalog to their colleagues and to patrons and to provide status information regarding claimed or missing issues and titles that are delayed in publication.

Centralized versus Decentralized Check-in

As one might expect, some large libraries have taken advantage of serials automation as an opportunity to decentralize their check-in; moving the location of the receipt process to the branch library gives that unit greater control over its own collections and over the claiming process. This works well particularly if there is adequate staff in the individual sites to be able to handle both the technical work of receipt as well as the public service work they may already be doing. In other cases, automation has strengthened the concept of centralized check-in. Some of the branches for which the main library does receipt may have very few staff; having check-in done online centrally frees branch staff from doing a duplicate check-in when the issues are received, and does away with the necessity of intensive training for lots of additional staff. For branch libraries to comfortably accept centralized check-in and not feel compelled to do a second local check-in, however, there needs to be both a high degree of trust in the competency of staff in the main library's serials unit and a consistent level of accuracy in the work the central staff is doing. One without the other will not suffice. It is also critical that the staff in branch libraries who rely on the centrally updated records have an understanding of the central serials unit's work flow to enable them to comfortably and accurately interpret the check-in records for themselves and for their patrons for information on receipts, claims, and payment.

Local Systems Environment

A final consideration in which and what type of serials system is selected for an individual library is the local computing environment, both within the library and on the college or university campus. If the library were contemplating a mainframe computer system, which serials system to select could well be influenced by the institution's existing commitment to a particular hardware vendor or to considerations such as who will operate the computer and whether or not it will only be used for library applications. In some institutions, the library may purchase the mainframe, but it will be housed in an existing computer center and operated by computer systems staff and possibly be used for some non-library operations. In the latter arrangement, a computer housed outside the library and operated by non-library staff, it is essential that the library establish its place in the priority of computer jobs in order to ensure smooth operation of library functions. Operating costs for mainframe computers can be very high, and many colleges and universities are looking to migrate as much of their

computing as possible to smaller machines (often UNIX-based) or to sophisticated workstations or to a combination of both. The library as a whole, and the
serials librarian in particular, need to take into account the overall campus computing environment (is there a hardware vendor of choice for the campus, for
example?) and be knowledgeable about how remote users as well as in-house
patrons will be accessing the library's catalog and what impact this has on
hardware requirements, software design, and the future look of computing at the
institution five years hence. Even in the world of UNIX minicomputers, there
may be a campus preference for a particular type of hardware or for a particular
operating system (the campus may already have other applications running on
Oracle or Ingres which would make one preferable over the other); also there
may already be campus support for certain hardware and some well-developed
expertise in working with particular operating systems.

Even as the campus computing environment is changing, the mix and format
of the material received in the serials department has also shifted as print is
joined by CD-ROMs, diskettes, and other formats. As these formats are supple-
mented, and in some cases, supplanted by the influx of electronic journals and
enhanced document delivery, the serials processing workload of paper journals
to be received may begin to diminish to a trickle of what it once was. These
trends in serial publishing ought to be borne in mind as the serials manager and
others contemplate future automation and the specific advantages and disadvantages of particular systems.

PREPARATION FOR ONLINE PROCESSING

Bibliographic Files

Preparation for online serials processing is a multiphase process that begins
as soon as (if not before) the particular system is selected. The basis for any
serials system is the bibliographic record. A key question, therefore, is whether
this record will be supplied by the system vendor or whether the library needs
to create the database. If the library is creating the database, then any serials
records that are already in machine-readable form such as RLIN, OCLC, or
WLN records, or bibliographic records from some other system or utility ought
to be able to be loaded into the new serials system. If the library is in the
position of migrating from one automated system to another, then the issue
becomes one of getting the bibliographic records (and their associated holdings
and item records) out of the existing system and into the new system. Bibliographic records generally present the least number of problems for this kind of
conversion since MARC is a standard. But, even though the MARC format is
the MARC format is the MARC format, there are some differences in the way
in which the various utilities have implemented MARC and how they handle
local fields; OCLC MARC is different from RLIN MARC, and therefore, the

earlier one starts working with the vendor on its requirements for dealing with whatever form of MARC record is being loaded, the better.

It is also extremely important to map out very carefully the treatment of local or holdings fields from these records, especially the 950 and 955 fields on RLIN and the 049 field from OCLC. These contain the library's unique location, call number, and volume holdings information as well as other local notes relating to special shelving locations and limited retention periods. Understanding how this information will be mapped over to the new system is critical to how the library proceeds with additional holdings information (Farrington 1990). If all of the local note information cannot be captured by the tape load program, then it will have to be rekeyed. This can be a time-consuming and long, drawn-out process, especially if the note information has to be added as the record is updated and not imported or added in some systematic, comprehensive way. For those libraries that have not maintained specific holdings information in their cataloging records, it may be a worthwhile investment of time to undertake a special project to add summary holdings information to the bibliographic records after they are loaded.

Order and Fund Records

The cornerstone of most online serials systems is the check-in record, which may also be the ongoing or open order record. To create such a record in most systems, it is necessary to first establish vendor codes and address files as well as library fund codes. Knowing the parameters of the system, library staff can proceed to build these codes and files. Before creating a file of library serials and book vendors from scratch, the library may want to investigate trying to purchase an already existing file from the system vendor or another library. This saves both decision-making time and keying time that would be required if one were to create vendor records from scratch. If the library is setting up its own vendor file (and not inheriting one or only using one vendor so that it is not really an issue), it is worthwhile to include codes for the various depository programs the library participates in (US, UN, and European Union, for example) as well as for special programs such as PL-480 and state depository programs. Even though depository items are not paid items, most libraries will either be required to or wish to track their receipt and claim them when appropriate. A good rule is to create a vendor record whenever there are more than five or six titles handled by a particular source. Doing that will save time keying and re-keying the address many times. If a library is changing systems, then one would expect that the vendor file could be migrated from the existing to the new system.

Each library has its own idiosyncrasies for how its serials money is allocated and how it deals with operating budget monies and outside gift monies. Nonetheless, a system of fund codes will be needed to track how money is expended. It is possible, of course, to carry over whatever system of funds is already in use, and just transfer it to the new system. The installation of a new automated system, however, may be an auspicious time to reexamine the fund codes and perhaps refine how they are defined and used. In an online environment, there should be the opportunity for multiple levels of codes and more detailed information on exactly how the serials money is being spent. Serious thought should also be given to when in the fiscal year the switch over to the new system takes place. For most libraries, it is very desirable, if not essential, to move online fund accounting just before the beginning of a new fiscal year. It may be possible to start using a new system mid-year, depending on the library's local accounting practices and whether or not fund accounting was previously automated. In general, it is easier to start online accounting mid-year if the library is not moving from one online system to another.

There are several approaches to serials fund codes, and large libraries may well want to use a combination of approaches. Allocations may be made broadly by large programmatic areas such as health sciences, humanities, social sciences, and so on. Or allocations can be done simply by subject matter, regardless of location. Another approach is to allocate by location as well as subject. This is fairly easily done if the subject matter and location are practically the same, as in a chemistry fund for the chemistry library. Sometimes a branch library covers several disciplines and it may be desirable within the math-physics library, for example, to separate out expenditures for mathematics from those for physics. The other way to approach fund codes is to allocate or, in some way, separate out by format. It is generally accepted practice to separate out monograph expenditures from serials expenditures, but there may also be categories within each of these areas that need to be monitored. Examples are: microforms, newspapers, backfiles, replacements, periodicals, true serials, and CD-ROM and other computer formats. It is to be expected that any reasonable fund accounting package will allow for this kind of flexibility. Provision should also be made for funds to keep track of postage, service charges, bank charges, deposit accounts, and prepayments to serials vendors. Within a central library, it may be useful to break down funds quite narrowly by LC class numbers or according to the responsible subject bibliographers. Reference materials also merit a separate fund or account

Some systems, such as the NOTIS LMS system, provide for expenditure class or type codes which can be used for type or format breakdowns within each fund code. The class codes are the same across the system, but they can be applied to any fund code. Therefore, the library monitors what it spends on microforms, for example, in each fund or subject area. Figure 1.1 illustrates the categories that one library wished to track within each fund or discipline. The numbers were arbitrarily determined, but within this system, all of the serials codes begin with zero, the monograph ones begin with one, and when there are equivalent codes for both monographs and serials the base number is the same; thus, "general" is 0140 for serials and 1140 for monographs. With this type of

Figure 1.1
Examples of One Library's Expenditure Costs for Serials

0010	Periodical
0020	Continuation
0030	Microform periodical
0040	Microform continuation
0050	Replacement issue or volume
0060	Microform replacement
0070	Exchange item
0090	Membership
0100	CD-ROM subscription
0105	CD-ROM backfile
0110	Print backfile
0130	Audio-visual material
0140	General
0160	Microform backfile
0170	Electronic databases and computer tapes
0185	Electronic access or use fee
0000	Electronic journal

categorization, the serials librarian would know how much money was being spent on just CD-ROM subscriptions for chemistry, for example.

Once the bibliographic database is loaded, and a set of fund codes and one or more vendor codes has been established, the library is ready to begin creating order records. Depending on how the system works, the easiest approach may be to begin by creating all new orders online. The advantage of this is that one begins from scratch with this title and the records for it are only in the new system. Another option is to start by transferring order information for all the currently received periodicals, working from the Kardex or other file. This type of project can be segmented alphabetically (all the Js in the Kardex will be done first), by vendor (all of the Nijhoff titles will be converted first), by location (the math library has a small collection of periodicals so theirs will be converted first), or by type (all the periodicals on display or all the newspapers or all the microforms). It is helpful for reference staff and, indirectly, the patrons, if one is able to state which portions of the orders have been converted. A third option is simply to transfer the order information to the online system when the next issue of a periodical is received. This is a more random approach and probably works better when the creation of the order record is linked to converting the check-in information at the same time. In a large collection, however, separating creating the orders from converting the check-in data makes sense and gives the library the opportunity to get a sizable number of orders online before check-in is converted. In a small collection, there are advantages to doing both the order creation and check-in transfer together, since it means checking the old records only once instead of twice. Also, the smaller number of titles means that a greater percentage of the total will be available to the public faster and so there will not be the frustration of just a handful being checked in online. All of the above discussion presupposes that the library has chosen a system that is not vendor-based and, therefore, that the library is handling the record creation itself or hiring additional staff to do it. It is quite clear in this area that there are advantages to having a subscription vendor's system. The agent provides the bibliographic record and probably much of the order information as well, such as order number, previous year's cost, and so on. However, some subscription vendors may be able to provide the library with assistance in doing this conversion in the form of barcode labels that contain all of the titles the library purchases from that vendor along with the ISSNs, the vendor's title number, the library's order number from its manual environment or previous system; scanning this information can facilitate the process of getting this information online in the new system.

Holdings Information

It is not enough to just add order information to the online bibliographic record; staff and patrons will need to know about existing holdings for these titles. If the extent of the library's holdings is already a part of the bibliographic information (i.e., it was a part of the cataloging record and so is loaded when that is loaded), then the information about each title displayed to the public will be complete, showing back holdings plus current issues. If that is not the case and the bibliographic record is supplied by the vendor, then the library will have to consider some way to get the holdings information added, either as a separate project or as part of creating the order record. In a small collection, it is also possible to do a shelf inventory of the bound volumes before adding the holdings information to the record. Having the staff resources and the time to carry out an inventory is a definite advantage, since one can clean up old problems and be sure that the holdings information is truly accurate. Again, the serials staff should inquire what services may be available from the system vendor to migrate holdings data from one online system to another. Customizable conversion programs may be available to migrate current receipts and other holdings information from the old to the new online system.

In a subscription vendor-based system, the library should consider how and if access to current issues received is made available to patrons. It may be that a public workstation just for serials look-ups is available. Perhaps a patron using the online catalog for the library switches from one system to another at the same terminal for current serials receipts, or lastly, the library may make some arrangements to upload vendor system holdings information to the library's online catalog, or do some sort of tape load weekly to update current issue information. Or, perhaps, the current issue information is only readily available to staff who then access it, upon request, for patrons. This whole question of patron access to single-issue receipt is a significant one and, in selecting a subscription vendor-based serials system, merits careful study.

TRAINING

Staff training for any new online system is critical to the successful introduction of the system. It is critical to introduce the idea of the new system long before it is a reality and critical to get staff to begin thinking about it in an accepting way. Sharing information along the way, involving staff as much as possible in the selection process by including them in vendor presentations and demonstrations, and scheduling frequent meetings and in-house workshops to introduce system concepts are all essential steps in making for a smooth transition. If the library and the serials staff, in particular, are making the transition from manual records to online processing for the first time, then the process will be more difficult. Most individuals, including serials librarians, derive a great sense of security from having paper files and paper records. It requires a leap of faith for some, and for others is a demonstration of trust in the library management, to give over their work to a computer screen and not to retain paper files. A manager who recognizes from the start that weaning staff away from paper files is an ongoing, time-intensive process will make the implementation easier for him or herself.

Even with the ubiquity of computers such as the automated bank teller machines in daily life, some staff who have not had a lot of exposure to computers are fearful that something they do will in some way destroy the database, or will undo everyone's work as well as their own, or will permanently break the system. It is most useful, in the training process, to reiterate again and again that there is little they can do to cause any lasting harm. To support this contention, it is important to show staff how to get out of situations; for example, a case in which, if they proceed, they will delete something that should not be deleted, or create an order that they suddenly realize should not be created. For the individual staff member, knowing that there are ways out of possible errors provides some measure of psychological comfort in approaching work at a computer terminal. The manager should also recognize that individuals learn at very different rates and that some people will need more hand-holding and reassurance, while others will pick up the new routines quickly and be breezing along happily very soon. Nonetheless, the manager should be prepared to invest a significant amount of time in one-on-one training, initially and each time a new function is introduced to the staff. Every system has its own logic and if the manager is aware of how the system works, then it is possible to put an individual staff member's tasks in the context of the system design. For many people, appreciating that there is some sort of logic to how the computer system functions helps them to understand the steps in their own jobs. Other people will not want to be bothered with those kinds of explanations and will prefer simply to know the steps they do when, but not particularly why. It should be noted that most vendors will also provide formal training on how to use their systems. Usually, a certain number of hours of training is provided at the library as part of the purchase agreement. After that, the library may well wish to contract for more specialized training from the vendor at an hourly or daily rate, or take the approach of having the vendor train the trainer who then is responsible for training staff in a particular area. Many of the newer systems have a graphical interface and some have chosen to support Microsoft Windows conventions in their staff interfaces. This use of Windows can make the transition to serials processing online smoother if the staff have already used Windows for word processing or other functions. Having mastered Windows, then the learning curve for specific serials functions that use Windows or Windows conventions is much less and the manager can focus on teaching the serials processes and not the navigation.

GOING ONLINE

The expectation is that most libraries will decide to begin serials processing online with ordering and receiving. For this reason, the starting point here is converting order records from the Kardex or whatever manual file and then beginning to receive online. The other piece of this, of course, is the generation of orders for new titles, backfiles, or replacements. If the library has selected a subscription vendor's system, then placing a new order may be as simple as finding the title in the vendor's files, if one is using a dial-up mode to access the vendor, or keying some brief information and then uploading it to the vendor's computer. In either of these cases, there is no paper produced and the order is easily created and transmitted. If another kind of system is being used, the library may well create an order online and then print it and mail it to the vendor. Initially, details will have to be worked out as to the frequency of printing orders, sorting them (if several different locations are doing ordering), and then stuffing them for mailing.

If the library both catalogs and orders on its serials-based system, then the order record may well become the cataloging record when the title is received. This is most desirable, since the order is created once in one place and all the work is done on one record. Some libraries have software and hardware that enable the downloading or importing of records from the bibliographic utilities to the library's local system. As part of the downloading process, the incoming record may or may not be overlaid onto an existing record; if overlaid, the local call number and holdings information in the previously existing record will usually be retained. Downloading records from the utility allows the library to take advantage of the bibliographic resources of its utility and yet still be able to provide on-order and receipt information in its own local system. Also, for the library that does not want to do its cataloging on the local system, whether for contractual reasons or for not wanting to print shelflist cards (some libraries still want or need these in the automated age), downloading also holds the potential for providing the best of all possible worlds: contributing records to a shared bibliographic database, yet simultaneously meeting the needs of the local patrons for immediate information on status and availability of materials.

The newer client/server systems are often Z39.50 compliant, which enables them to easily access remote databases and present an interface that looks like the local or home system. Z39.50 also offers the possibility of easy import and export of records from one database to another. For cataloging, being able to seamlessly import bibliographic records from RLIN or OCLC is a must; being able to access these records on one's own workstation immediately without waiting for any intervening batch processes or indexing updates is a gift and holds out the promise of greater efficiency in the work flow. At least one automated system already has such an import feature. A record is passed from the utility to a file on the individual user's disk drive, and then the cataloger or other staff is able to access it, modify it if desired, and then save it to the library's local online catalog. This capability coupled, with multi-tasking (the ability to have several programs or databases open simultaneously), offers opportunities for cutting and pasting portions of records back and forth between the utilities and the library's local catalog, and may well result in increased efficiency and an overall reduction in the processing time required to get a serial from receipt to the shelf.

Deciding when to begin check-in of serial issues online will depend on some local variables, such as size of the collection, how many of the titles have order records online, whether or not to wait until all orders have been created or set up, and what staff are available to do the check-in. If the system requires the staff member to key the issue information, rather than to just acknowledge which issue has been received, then there need to be explicit instructions on the format to be used for this issue information. This will provide consistency in input and will enable patrons and staff to more easily interpret the holdings information.

One approach to online check-in is to decide that, at the point of transferring issue information from the Kardex or manual file to the online system, all the unbound issues, or anything that is not already reflected in the bound volume holdings, will be shown in the current issue area. This is especially important in an integrated system where patrons should be able from one record display to determine the complete holdings of a title from bound volumes to latest issue received. While moving all of this information over to the online system adds to the initial conversion times for each title, it does mean that the Kardex for that particular title can be considered closed and never again be added to. On a vendor-based system, there may be very good reasons not to be concerned about unbound issues, but rather to just begin checking in at a certain point such as the beginning of a calendar year or at the start of a new volume. It is not as simple, nor probably as essential, to transfer all previous billing information from the manual files to online. In this situation, it may be necessary, particularly if there are questions about payment, to check the old Kardex file before claiming missing issues. If this is not acceptable and the library is not dealing with a vendor system which already includes the library's payment information, then it may be worthwhile to include some sort of note regarding the extent of the most recent billing period. A note such as "Paid through Dec. 96" could suffice. For a library migrating from one system to another, deciding when to begin which functions on the new system is perhaps more complex than just moving from manual files to online; since everything in an automated system is already interrelated and intertwined, there may well be merit in determining a "day one" when all functions go into production in the new system. This is quite a contrast to the more leisurely pace many libraries took in bringing up various functions sequentially (ordering, then receipt, then cataloging, then circulation, for example) when they moved from manual processing to the online system.

Serials functions online are all linked to one another, and it quickly becomes apparent that as soon as a library begins performing one function online, there are logical reasons to add other functions. The one function that can be more easily divorced in many systems is payment of invoices. The disadvantage of not paying online is that the library loses the online tracking of allocations, commitments, and expenditures as well as the individual subscription information right with the title. However, it is still possible to check in online without also processing invoices online. If one does process invoices online, then generally payment is shown in the order record or somehow linked to it; payment for a title can also be viewed in an entire invoice record with all of its line items.

Reports

Production statistics, the number of items processed, the number of orders placed, for example, are important for a library to evaluate how much work it is doing now and compared to past years. Statistics that help indicate the library's ranking compared to peer institutions, how many serials are received currently, how many volumes are cataloged each year, for example, determine the library's status in the academic arena. Mainframe-based library systems provided some of this statistical data to a greater or lesser extent, sometimes through the use of SAS programming. Newer systems are more likely to have a separate report-writing package, which may be a commercial package that the vendor has integrated. Ideally, it should be relatively easy for the serials manager to obtain the following basic statistics: the number of orders placed, the number of claims generated, the number of issues received, the number of invoices processed, and status of all the funds—what has been spent to date, how much has been encumbered, and in what subcategories were the expenditures. Some systems provide these statistics by individual terminal or workstation, which can be one part of evaluating an individual staff member's performance. Monthly statistical reports should give the serials manager and the library administration quantifiable measures of how much work the serials staff are actually doing. Sophisticated report writers are more and more a part of the client/server system environment, giving the library staff a wider range of both standard and custom reports. In these times of intense scrutiny and greater accountability for all of higher education, libraries, too, have a greater need to demonstrate what their staff are doing and how they are spending their resources.

CONCLUSION

Certainly, the automation of serials processing was the most significant development in the serials world in the 1980s and early 1990s. Automated processing enables a library to process more material more quickly (or perhaps with fewer staff) or to be more current in its processing with the same number of staff. The serials arena of the late 1990s is changing shape with the growth in electronic publishing and the pervasiveness of the Internet, the heavy use of the World Wide Web, the proliferation of electronic journals, and cheaper, easier electronic document delivery of journal articles and other text. Serials are taking on new forms; the next ten years could be very exciting, challenging, and even a little frightening as the print world evolves to a multimodal environment. During this transition, however, the serials librarian will need to straddle both worlds—the paper one and the electronic one—and work to bridge them, all with the intent of best serving the information needs of the library's students, faculty, and researchers. Even if the serials processing unit ceases to exist as a separate unit, the expertise and experience of serials librarians will be needed to help guide users to the serial material they need, whatever the format.

REFERENCES

Barry, Jeff, Jose-Marie Griffiths, and Gerald Lundeen. 1995. "Automated System Marketplace 1995: The Changing Face of Automation." *Library Journal* 120 (April 1): 44–54.

Barry, Jeff, Jose-Marie Griffiths, and Peiling Wang. 1996. "Automated System Marketplace 96: Jockeying for Supremacy in a Networked World." *Library Journal* 121 (April 1): 40–51.

Boss, Richard W. 1984. "Technology and the Modern Library." *Library Journal* 109 (June 15): 1183–1189.

Bridge, Frank R. 1993. "Automated System Marketplace 1993: Part I: Focus on Minicomputers." *Library Journal* 118 (April 1): 52–64.

Farley, Charles, Susan Beck, and Julia Miller. 1994. "Geac: A Formula for the Future." *Library Hi-Tech*, no. 47: 7–30.

Farrington, Jean Walter. 1990. "*In Medias Res*: A Serials Department in Transition." *Serials Librarian* 19, nos. 1/2: 31–42.

Geyer, Enid, and Gail Botta. 1989. "REMO: Automated Serials Management in a Medium-Sized Medical Library." *Serials Librarian* 16, nos. 1/2: 39–64.

Griffiths, Jose-Marie, and Kimberly Kertes. 1994. "Automated Systems Marketplace 1994." *Library Journal* 119 (April 1): 50–59.

Kohl, David. 1994. "OhioLINK: A Vision for the 21st Century." *Library Hi-Tech*, no. 48: 29–34.

Library Systems Evaluation Guide. 1983. Vol. 1, Serials Control. Powell, Ohio: James E. Rush Associates.

McKay, Sharon Cline, and Charles J. Piazza, Jr. 1992. "EDI and X12: What, Why, Who?" *Serials Review* 18, no. 4: 7–10.

Young, Jacky, with Debbie Collins and Kerry Keel. 1994. "Sirsi: History and 'Vizion' of an Integrated Information Systems Vendor." *Library Hi-Tech*, no. 48: 35–57.

2

Changing Roles, Changing Shape: Organizing and Staffing Serials Operations

INTRODUCTION

Separate departments to handle the functions of serials processing have existed for more than 50 years. At one time, serials were simply part of acquisitions or some other department, particularly since the number of titles involved was generally quite small. As long as there have been separate serials departments, however, debate and discussion have waxed and waned over the best way to organize these functions in an academic library. The classic article on serials organization, "The New Serials Department," appeared in 1935 (Gable 1935). Every few years since then, the discussion has been revitalized and a new round of opinions has surfaced; in recent years the debate has become livelier with the implementation of online processing and the explosion in the amount of material available electronically. Weber was a chief proponent of a separate serials department (Weber 1979), while several others (Gorman 1985; Potter 1981; Harrington 1985) each put forth arguments for decentralizing serials functions or, as a minimum, reevaluating why serials functions are organized the way they are in a particular library. In the past, arguments were made that by virtue of their complexity and the need for constant monitoring (claiming), it made sense to handle serials in one place; these individuals favored organization based on the form of the material. With the introduction of online systems, both the form (organize by type of material) and the function (organize by type of activity rather than format) camps have declared that an automated system makes their approach the more sensible one. With automation, the decentralization of check-in has become more feasible and, in some situations, preferable. At the same time, the existence of one serial record that serves bibliographic, ordering, receipt, and holdings purposes has made it worthwhile to rethink previous separations of work flow. These separations were perhaps more justifiable before automation, and one may see again the merging and blending of serials functions with acquisitions.

At the present time (the late 1990s), there is a trend toward the creation of super- or mega-departments that combine acquisitions and cataloging functions in one department, and in some libraries there is even the merging of interlibrary loan and document delivery into technical services. These new super-departments often have large staffs, but they were created with the intention of streamlining the work flow. The expectation is that in a super-department it will be possible to reduce steps in a process; such as, for example, the number of times a particular order or item is handled between the time the order is placed and when that ordered item is delivered, cataloged, and marked, to the shelf, and to cross-train staff for more than one function or task. The organization of serials processing will certainly be affected by the trends in publishing away from paper and toward electronic formats. As more electronic journals are introduced, as government documents in fiche and paper are replaced by electronic access, and as academic libraries have the technical capability to "point to" rather than the need to purchase core journals, the current workload of serials staff may well diminish to a trickle of the former steady flow. Such a drastic reduction in the amount of material to be processed could result in staff time being freed up for other duties after an appropriate period of retraining and orientation.

Contemporaneous with the trend toward merged or mega-departments is the concept of reengineering the library. Borrowed from the corporate world, where there is a need to make business more efficient and less staff-intensive in order to continue to realize a profit (Hammer 1993), reengineering has begun to take hold in the academic arena as well. Many colleges and universities are experiencing a decline in the number of student applications and decreases in funding from the federal government at the same time as their own operating costs continue to rise. Consequently, the very structure of the organization is being reexamined to see how operations can be performed more efficiently in order to reduce costs. The library is not exempt from such scrutiny and those library directors and library staff who want to have the most influence on shaping their futures have themselves initiated the process of self-study and work flow analysis. Technical services is an area that typically includes a large proportion of the library's staff and, therefore, it is reasonable to assume that it is an area that will be examined in minute detail (Stanford University Libraries 1995; McCue 1994). Along with the need to reduce costs and to reengineer the shape and structure of the organization, there is the rapidly expanding universe of electronic materials and the movement toward what is called the electronic, or the digital library. If one accepts as a given that the digital library is the academic library of the near future, then to be equipped to function effectively in this new environment, "technical services staff members must be able to articulate the value they add to the institution—not only in the realm of the library's bibliographic database but also in the large context of building an organizational framework for electronic information and services. Technical services departments must be willing to reengineer processing activities and equip their staffs with both the hardware and the skills needed to meet these challenges" (McCue 1994, 63–64). At Stanford University, the reexamination of receipt and cataloging processes in the library resulted in "a conceptual redesign that focuses on eliminating duplicate transactions, using technology and vendor services when possible to increase efficiencies, and performing tasks at the time or location that makes the most sense" (Stanford University Libraries 1995, 6).

What follows is a discussion of the historical view of serials organization, several alternatives for organizing serials functions in the current environment, and a look at the staffing and organizational design approaches for the electronic arena of the near future.

ORGANIZATION OF SERIALS FUNCTIONS

Overview

Serials functions can comfortably reside in one or several departments or units within the academic library. A serials department that includes everything from ordering through receipt and cataloging (the complete serials department) is, in reality, a microcosm of technical services as a whole. Staff in this department may perform acquisitions and receiving functions as well as cataloging and binding functions. In addition to these technical processing functions, some serials departments also have responsibility for the periodicals services desk or the shelving and maintenance of current periodicals, making the department a hybrid of both public and technical services. At the opposite extreme from this centralization of some or all serials functions is the "splinter" approach; in this organizational model, serials acquisitions is aligned with monograph acquisitions in the acquisitions department, serials cataloging is located in the cataloging department (after all, it is cataloging), and current periodicals service is placed in the public services division, perhaps grouped with microforms or reference, or simply as one of several public services units. More recently, some large research libraries have adopted a third option, the concept of super-departments, and have reduced the number of individual departments in a technical services area from four or five to two, by combining all of cataloging and postprocessing in one department and all of acquisitions and serials receipt and billing into another department. In an online environment, this approach may make for some real economies in the work flow, while making the size of the department staff very large. Other libraries are reexamining totally all of their assumptions about where each part of the work should be done and taking more advantage of services offered by vendors and of efficiencies gained by the use of sophisticated workstations (Stanford University Libraries 1995).

The Complete Serials Department

By definition, the traditional serials department is an example of organization by form of material rather than by function. This makes the traditional serials department an anomaly, since most other technical services units are organized by function: acquisitions, cataloging, binding, and marking, for example. What is encompassed within this so-called traditional serials department is not so clearly defined and herein lies some of the reason for the debate. From this author's perspective, there are three conventional approaches to serials organization which range from (1) fully integrated to (2) completely decentralized to (3) quasi-integrated or integrated/split.

In the first instance, the fully integrated serials department, all the functions pertaining to serials are the responsibility of the serials department. The important word here is "all," since this department includes oversight of the current periodicals area or service desk. This department also includes serials cataloging. The second approach to serials processing, completely decentralized, occurs when the serials functions are distributed throughout technical services and public services and grouped with other like functions. Therefore, the acquisitions department includes serials acquisitions and receipt, the cataloging department handles serials cataloging, and the public service periodicals function may be overseen by reference or be a part of access or public services along with circulation and microforms. In this version of serials processing, there is no serials department as such, and more different staff handle serials than in the first approach. The third approach, which is something of a compromise between the others, is called partially integrated or integrated/split. The serials department may or may not include cataloging, but does perform the other functions of acquisitions, receipt, claiming, and invoice processing. It is also fairly likely in this partially integrated model that the public service function will be in another part of the organization as well. Although these three approaches demonstrate the most common instances of serials processing, in fact, there are a number of variations and refinements on these themes which will be explored further.

It should be acknowledged that serials cataloging is most frequently the function that is left out of the otherwise integrated serials department and is probably the function about which there has been the most debate. The size of the serials operation and the particular local policies regarding cataloging and classification of serials may have some bearing on how, for example, serials cataloging is treated. If there is not enough serials cataloging to keep at least one person occupied full-time, then probably having serials cataloging as part of the cataloging department is reasonable. If serials functions are divided up and located organizationally in several different departments or units, then some thought

Figure 2.1
Library A

Small to medium-sized academic library

Separate serials department

1 serials librarian

1 paraprofessional

1 clerk

Reports to technical services

Dept. includes cataloging and public service

should be given to the relative proximity of serials cataloging to the other parts of the serials operation. Is there any need for the person doing serials cataloging to be physically near the receiving location? In the non-automated environment, there were good reasons why the serials cataloger may have needed or wanted to check order or Kardex files or consult with the serials receipt staff. When, however, all the functions are being performed online and everyone, including the serials cataloger, has his or her own workstation, and all staff have online access to the order records, this proximity is probably not as important. It may still be desirable and beneficial, however, for promoting regular communication between the staff carrying out the different serials processing tasks.

Of secondary importance, but also worth noting, is that there is less consistency from library to library on where providing public service for current periodicals is placed; most often it is probably part of public or access services. Given all of this, what then are the core serials functions which are grouped together to form a serials processing unit. They would appear to be: ordering, receiving, claiming, and invoice processing.

Variations in Serials Organization

Library A: Small Serials Staff. In order to appreciate these differences in approach more fully, it would be helpful to look at three variations on serials organization in some generic libraries. The libraries will be designated A, B, and C. Library A is a small to medium-sized library and has a relatively small serials collection. Libraries B and C are large libraries whose organization illustrates the range of possibilities. The serials unit in Library A (Figure 2.1) consists of three staff members: one librarian, one paraprofessional, and one clerk, or perhaps instead of the paraprofessional, another clerk. The unit is part of technical services and handles all aspects of serials processing: ordering, receiving, entering invoices, cataloging, shelving, stack maintenance, binding,

Figure 2.2
Library B

Large academic library

Separate serials department

18 FTE serials staff

1 dept. head

5 cataloger librarians

11 serials assistants

1 secretary

Dept. includes all functions except public services

and most likely, public service. There are also one or two part-time student assistants who do the shelving. The librarian administers the unit, compiles monthly statistics, handles collection development matters, and oversees reporting to union lists of serials. Student assistants may also assist with binding preparation, correcting spine labels, and sorting gift titles. If someone is absent, other staff are expected to do whatever needs to be done. What may vary in this configuration is where the shelving of current issues and volumes is actually done and by whom (the serials staff or by regular stack staff), and to what extent collection development, in the sense of selection rather than just acquisition of an already selected title, is part of the serials librarian's responsibilities. In this kind of organizational structure, the serials librarian may report to an assistant director or head of technical services or directly to the director of the library. With the small size of the collection, there is a diversity of tasks handled by each individual and more variety in each job than is generally the case in a larger setting where staff tend to be more specialized in their duties.

Library B: Centralized Department with Units. Library B is somewhat larger than Library A and its organizational structure is more complex, but it still has a separate serials department which is recognizable on the organization chart (Figure 2.2). This kind of organizational approach might be viewed as typical throughout the 1980s. This serials department is part of a central technical services unit which reports to an associate director for resource or technical services and consists of eighteen full-time staff. These staff are divided into three units: serials maintenance, cataloging, and acquisitions and receiving. Staff consist of a department head, five cataloger librarians, eleven library assistants, and one secretary. Although this particular department has no responsibility for public service, its cataloger librarians do serve as liaisons with specific subject bibliographers. This affords the catalogers the opportunity to become familiar with the particular needs of their discipline and a particular group of users. The eleven library assistants are responsible for serials receipt, claiming, correspondence, and binding preparation. Some of the support staff also have duties relating to cataloging such as searching for cataloging copy, closing out dead titles, and the like. This staffing pattern is based on a real library model from the late 1980s, but in the context of the mid-1990s seems to be heavy in the number of catalogers. It is possible that this library receives a significant amount of material in esoteric or difficult languages, has catalogers involved in ongoing retrospective conversion projects, or simply receives a lot of new serial material to be cataloged.

A variation on the organization of Library B is another very large research library that has a serials staff of approximately 22 individuals. Once again, this department has no responsibility for the current periodicals reading room, but does include cataloging, acquisitions, and receipt sections. The cataloging section also has several part-time staff devoted to serials retrospective conversion. Departmental staffing includes a head, assistant department head, secretary, three section heads, and then other staff within each section. In this department, the units or sections have very specific tasks and the day-to-day supervision is handled by section heads reporting to the assistant department head and department head. One advantage of this organizational structure is that it frees up the department head for long-term planning and overall goal setting. One would again observe that this number of staff appears very generous in light of the more stringent budgets of the 1990s. What is significant in both variations on Library B is that serials processing is a centralized function within the technical services area, while the public service aspects are handled by other staff. One may question the number of catalogers in these hypothetical departments; suffice it to say that these are very large collections of serials in many different languages and that some of these catalogers may well have particular language or subject expertise. Over the next five years, however, it would be intriguing to watch these departments to see if the number of catalogers declines over time. One could make a convincing case that the number of serials catalogers in academic libraries may well have already dropped since the advent of the utilities in the 1970s and the ready availability of online records from other libraries. However, more recently, some libraries have ceased adding their records to RLIN and OCLC, and are only reflecting them in their local online catalogs. This has resulted in a reduction in the amount of available acceptable copy, and therefore, the amount of original cataloging required for non-English-language research titles may have increased in many libraries.

Library C: Decentralized Serials Processing. The third hypothetical library, Library C (Figure 2.3), has recently made the decision to decentralize its serials functions and locate them with other like functions in the library. Library C has about fourteen staff doing serials processing and public service, and they are scattered about on the library's organization chart. There is a serials cataloging section within the cataloging department which employs a total of seven full-

Figure 2.3
Library C

Decentralized serials operation

14 FTE staff for serials functions

Serials cataloging section

(3 librarians + 4 support staff)

Serials acquisitions section

(9.5 FTE support staff + 1 librarian)

Periodicals reading room

(3.5 FTE support staff)

time staff including three librarians (one of whom is the section head) and four support staff. Within the acquisitions department there is also a serials acquisitions section which has three units: Kardex, records updating, and exchange publications, with about 9.5 FTE. This translates to one librarian and the rest varying levels of support staff. The serials acquisitions section also oversees a serials information window. This service window is in addition to the periodical room which is part of access services in the public service division of the library. Three and a half FTE are used to staff the periodical room and these staff assume responsibility for checking in periodicals, shelving and binding, as well as assisting at the service desk. The checking in of journals in this library is done in the public area; in Library A, it was handled in technical services away from the service desk. This can be an advantage in that the staff servicing the public services desk may know more readily what issues have been received, but doing check-in the public area can be a process of constant interruptions if the total staffing in the area is not adequate.

A second variation on Library C is a situation in which the current periodicals public services area is located with the government documents unit, instead of as a separate desk or service unit. The periodicals and newspaper collections are a separate section, and their own separate staff handle shelving of their materials; binding of document serials is initiated by documents staff, but binding of periodicals is initiated by the acquisitions department staff. The actual ordering and receiving of the periodical and newspaper titles is also handled by acquisitions. Justification for this organizational grouping is based on the fact that many of the document titles that the library receives are serials and thus the handling upon receipt has similarities with periodicals. This model also has the benefit of a shared service desk for periodicals and documents which should mean fewer staff required than if two separate service desks were maintained.

It is worth considering the various factors that influence how a library decides to organize its serials processes. Among these are: the past history and practice of the organization; whether there are any currently existing staff vacancies and in which department they occur; where there are staff who can take on additional tasks; whether automation is a part of the serials work flow; and where the equipment (workstations, etc.) is located. Within a given library, it makes sense to consider which kind of organizational structure makes the most efficient use of the existing library staff. If centralizing some or all serials processes will reduce the number of times a given issue is passed from person to person before it gets to the patron, then perhaps centralizing is justified. If, however, the workstations used to handle receipt are located in the acquisitions department and the library's equipment budget is very tight, but the acquisitions department has staff who can take on added duties, then it may make sense to combine serials receipt with monographic receipt. It is important to remember, despite the strong positions taken in the serial literature, that centralization of serials functions is not intrinsically the right way and decentralization inherently wrong, or vice versa. It is also foresighted to realize that the introduction of automation to the serials process may be the ideal time to make major changes in the organization of the serials work flow. What will work and be best for any particular library will depend, of course, upon its size, its degree of automation, its level of staffing, and any particular quirks of staffing and practice that may need or be desirable to retain. Libraries A, B, and C show three different approaches on the continuum from centralized to decentralized check-in. In the middle is the option of splitting up serials functions, an approach that may offer the library the greatest flexibility and greatest range and variety of combinations of staff and service units.

Library Z: Reengineered Serials Processing. Another possibility for organizing serials processing is a serials department that is centralized for purposes of bibliographic control only; in this case, anything that relates to cataloging or updating holdings statements, title changes, setting up new titles, checking in (and perhaps shelving) is handled by serials staff. This model will be referred to as Library Z (Figure 2.4). Fiscal control of serials, which in this particular context means ordering, claiming, and invoice processing, is done in the acquisitions department or elsewhere. In this model, a separate processing department may handle binding, while the selection of new titles is performed by a standing serials committee within the collection development division. Library Z is also taking advantage of having a commercial vendor do most of its straightforward serials cataloging, an approach that more academic libraries have begun to investigate and experiment with, especially for monographic cataloging.

Reengineering Trends

''Reengineering'' and ''restructuring'' are the buzz words of the 1990s, as corporations are paring down their work forces, selling off unprofitable subsid-

Figure 2.4
Library Z

Reengineered serials operation

Serials check-in combined with acquisitions receiving

Public service handled by multifunction service desk for periodicals
+ microforms or other formats

Most serials cataloging outsourced to vendor

Support staff handle both electronic journal receipt
+ document delivery requests

iaries, and realigning themselves internally in order to arrive at more streamlined organizations. This trend has migrated to the academic world and many colleges and universities are reexamining their own organizational structures from the top down and from the center to periphery. As a component of the university, the library is often being asked to perform a similar self-analysis or is electing to initiate its own such review. A key area for close scrutiny is technical services. Some libraries are contemplating contracting out (outsourcing) portions of their cataloging and book preparation functions traditionally handled in-house. Both Cornell (McCue 1994) and Stanford Universities (Stanford 1995) have shared aspects of their processes. At Cornell, for example, "the acquisitions staff acquire networked resources and the cataloging staff help create the organizational structure to access that information. Technical services staff have reengineered processing activities while developing the skills needed for this digital world" (McCue 1994, 64). Recently, for example, the University of Pennsylvania library combined its serials and acquisitions departments for managerial purposes into one unit called materials acquisitions. Although the two departments remain as discrete units, they are being administered overall by one individual; this will allow for a close examination of the current work flow as the library prepares to migrate from a mainframe-based system to a new client/server system. In the next five years, one can expect to see more technical services operations being redesigned and reformulated to meet the economic and digital challenges of the next century.

STAFFING

Levels of Staff

In each of the sample serials departments (Libraries A, B, C, and Z), there is a combination of professional and non-professional staff and usually several levels within the non-professional or clerical staff. In addition, many libraries hire their own students on a part-time basis for certain tasks. The number of student hours and the specific duties performed by student assistants vary greatly from library to library. There are, however, some tasks that are commonly performed by student assistants no matter which library they work in. These may include opening and sorting periodicals mail, shelving periodicals, and helping patrons at the service desk. While there are libraries that use students for some aspects of periodicals receipt, other libraries may be precluded from doing this by the terms of collective bargaining agreements or may simply choose not to do this because they feel that the training time is too great for the high turnover in student positions. Other libraries use students to do straightforward check-in of certain periodical titles (English-language weeklies, monthlies, quarterlies, etc.) with complex titles, foreign language titles, and any problem titles being referred to full-time staff. Many libraries also rely on students to fill evening and weekend hours at public service desks.

The classification of clerical support staff in any given institution is generally governed by overall campus guidelines. The class or grade of the position may be determined by a central personnel office, but the library is able to make a standard job description for the various types or levels of support staff, such as clerk positions, library service assistants, and other paraprofessional positions. Within each individual department, such as serials, the supervisor or department head should formulate a particular job description that includes the duties of a specific position. When writing job descriptions for serials positions or when recruiting for new serials staff, stressing the necessity for attention to detail and the desirability of familiarity with several foreign languages will enhance one's chances of success. One library has a standard clerk job description for all of technical services included in its union contract. Some of the duties of this position are given in Figure 2.5. Although this list of duties refers to ''typing,'' rather than keying into an online system, the kinds of duties included here accurately reflect the sorts of tasks that clerks, both in serials and elsewhere in the organization, do perform. One assumes for most basic clerical positions that the tasks to be performed are routine ones, often repetitive in nature, and that the job does not require independent judgment or decision making. It is expected that there are written procedures to follow and that the employee will ask when he or she encounters a problem or something unfamiliar. These are also positions that are closely supervised by a unit or department head who is available to answer questions about those items or processes that deviate from the norm. At higher levels on a support staff ladder, there may be counterpart positions in public and technical services where the job level and extent of responsibility are the same, but the title and the specific duties reflect the particular milieu of each area. For example, a library service assistant in the public services area may be asked to do the following: ''under the general supervision of professional staff members, . . . responsible for circulation and information desk operations, some training and supervision of library clerks and part-time staff, and the maintenance of records and files established in libraries to govern the acquisition, organization, and preservation of collections'' (AFSCME 1994, 36). In technical

Figure 2.5
Selected Library Clerk Duties in a Technical Services Area

Prepare and type book purchase orders and other requests and maintain related files.

Check incoming books and other materials in a variety of languages against purchase orders, check their condition; check depository shipping lists; and prepare, check, or approve invoices for payment.

Maintain shelflist records, maintain statistics and prepare reports.

Enter serials receipts on appropriate records, prepare claims for missing issues.

Under supervision, process books in a variety of languages using catalog information, including the matching of material against the holdings of the library, and adding holdings where necessary.

Assemble materials for binding, including preparation or typing or instructions maintaining related files, and checking invoices submitted by binder.

Source: AFSCME Contract 1994, 33.

services, the counterpart staff, called bibliographic assistants, are "responsible for the creation, maintenance, and interpretation of the bibliographic records that describe library holdings and for the bibliographic processing of additions to the collection" (AFSCME 1994, 35). Beyond these two levels, there may be higher levels of support staff and even paraprofessional staff who operate fairly independently and assume responsibility for certain functions in the absence of the professional or under the general guidance of the librarian. The terminology for support staff positions varies from institution to institution and some libraries may have a specifically defined paraprofessional career track. This could be an individual who is in the process of completing his or her master's degree in library or information science or an individual who has worked his or her way up in the organization and who possesses a wealth of experience in the library and a solid knowledge of library processes. Often, individuals in these positions, whatever they are called (library technical assistant being one example), share in the supervisory responsibility for student assistants or for some of the clerical staff, or they may just be resource people for other staff when the professional staff is unavailable.

Effects of Automation

It is worthwhile to focus again on automation because it has had such an impact on work flow and staffing patterns in the technical services environment. Most technical services areas, and serials departments in particular, relied heavily on paper files until the introduction of online processing. Now, most of these files, files of orders, claim letters, vendor lists, and correspondence, have been subsumed or replaced by online records and files. This should have the inevitable effect of changing the work flow; if not, it at least offers the opportunity to dissect the work flow and, if possible, modify or eliminate steps in processing. For example, is it necessary for two individuals to handle a newly received serials volume before it is sent to binding and marking? In the manual environment, one person may have received it in the Kardex while another person added it to the shelflist record either in the card shelflist or online in the OCLC or RLIN record. Perhaps in the online system, it is possible and logical for the one person to both receive it and update the holdings information.

In an article detailing fifteen years of experience with automation, Horny cites two real-life examples of how automation brought about changes in organization and staffing at Northwestern University. The first is that serials cataloging, for many years a unit within the cataloging department, became part of a larger serials department. "The rationale for this decision was strongly influenced by the way in which the integrated system is based on use of the same record for order, check-in, and cataloging procedures. The ability to use the serials expertise of the staff efficiently was the most significant factor in merging the units" (Horny 1987, 73). The second example is the "upward reclassification of jobs." The use of the NOTIS library management system eliminated duties traditionally done at lower levels and some clerk jobs were phased out. Likewise, some work done by professionals in the past was shifted down to support staff and some clerical tasks were further shifted to student assistants. In other library settings, some staff found that the level of complexity of the work they were doing increased with automation and all the occupants of a given level job were moved to the next job class at one time.

One of the seemingly trivial, but potentially time-saving, benefits of automating serials processing is that it is no longer necessary to alphabetize periodicals in order to receive them. Most serials departments found it efficient to put the journals in alphabetical order before going to the Kardex or check-in file since it saved the time of skipping from drawer to drawer. With automation, it doesn't matter if the clerk checks in *Science* followed by *Harper's* followed by the *Atlantic*, since the clerk is using the same workstation for all three. In reality, however, many serials departments have continued the practice of assigning responsibility for certain letters of the alphabet to a specific person and having that person receive only those titles. This means that the journals will still need to be sorted by gross letter groups, but not put in strict order. The advantages of this approach are that the staff member becomes familiar with a particular group of titles and knows their publication patterns, whether or not they run late, whether they have supplements; and is sole person responsible for claiming and keeping on top of those titles. It is true that predictive check-in will simplify the receipt procedure for many journals, and perhaps some serials departments will want to consider just divvying up a given day's mail evenly among all the check-in staff instead of apportioning it by letter. Not dividing up the work ahead of time can make it easier to monitor how quickly a day's periodical mail is dealt with and to ensure that all of it is handled before the next day's receipts.

Expectations for Staff Performance

Libraries, particularly technical services operations, are statistics-oriented; many activities and transactions are counted, and productivity is measured to a large degree by the volume of these transactions. This is true in the technical services area where counts are made of the number of orders placed, titles cataloged, and volumes added each year. In the serials department, the number of periodicals issues received, while a measure of work done, probably has not been counted on a regular basis. With some automated systems, it is possible to get terminal-by-terminal statistics on all of the transactions performed at that terminal, including items received. This is one way to measure both an individual's and a department's output over a month or a year. As libraries and institutions of higher education in general deal with the stringent budgets of the 1990s, there will be an increased emphasis on productivity and getting the most out of each staff member. Having statistical measures of the amount of work done readily at hand will help serials managers assess the overall productivity of their staff and deal with individuals who are not performing up to standards. Having such statistics also enables the manager to determine benchmarks for performance in certain tasks and to justify needed increases in staff or to defend the department against proposed cuts or reassignment of staff. Even without the benefit of individual transaction statistics from the automated system, the serials manager may decide that it is useful to have staff self-report such measures of work performed each month. In order to fairly interpret each staff member's statistics, it is crucial to assess first whether or not a given staff member fully understands his or her job. Another trend in library management is the development of teams responsible for certain aspects of a job. In some attempts to flatten out the organizational structure, there are fewer departments, fewer layers, and teams with team leaders. Each team has an assigned task and individual staff may be members of more than one team as part of a total job description. For example, a serials copy cataloger may be a member of both the serials cataloging team (along with an original cataloger) and the retrospective conversion team (along with monographic catalogers). The recon team may have as its goal for the next six months the conversion of all of the literature classes and all of the titles therein, both monographic and serial.

Training and Ergonomics

No matter how the library ultimately decides to configure its serials operations, it must provide for adequate training for all staff. Most library administrations assume that the most basic training in how to do one's job will be handled by the staff member's immediate supervisor. As automation has taken hold and as libraries have continued to upgrade their system software with new releases and new functions, more attention has been paid to the desirability of providing library-wide training for all staff in addition to instruction from their supervisors. These training sessions may consist of lecture-style presentations on the basic system architecture and new features as well as hands-on sessions on such topics as keyword searching, interpreting serials records, and online journal databases; for example, *Current Contents* and *PsycInfo*. Since serials records often pose difficulty for non-serials staff members, the serials staff may wish to be closely involved in designing and leading any special staff training sessions in this area. There will also be the need to expand the skill set of most serials support staff to include training in Windows, how to navigate the World Wide Web using Netscape or Mosaic, the use of electronic mail, and perhaps basic word processing and spreadsheet programs. Gone are the days when it was sufficient for staff to merely know how to type at a typewriter or a dumb terminal; with the movement to client/server library management systems, all library processing staff are more likely to have fully equipped workstations at their desks and, consequently, will need to know how to work in the wider electronic world. Many of the newer library automation systems are based on Microsoft Windows software or a Windows-like graphical environment, and it will be beneficial for staff to become comfortable with Windows capabilities before having to learn the intricacies of their daily processing activities.

Another outcome of the proliferation of automation in libraries is an increased concern over work environment issues. As more and more staff spend many more hours sitting at a keyboard, attention has had to be paid to a seeming increase in the number of cases of carpal tunnel syndrome and repetitive stress injuries. Libraries that have not yet dealt with such matters will need to be prepared to provide ergonomically designed chairs and keyboard trays and to deal with requests to limit the time spent in one keying session so that a staff member's work day is broken up into different tasks not all requiring sitting and keying. Some serials staff positions, such as those for keying invoices or orders, deserve close inspection for ways to make them more varied.

The Future

What will the serials department, if there is one, look like five years from now? What will serials processing consist of? How will the jobs of serials support staff and serial managers change with the increase in electronic materials? Will the World Wide Web replace paper publishing? How will serials managers account for their staff resources in continued tight economic times? How much serials cataloging will be done on-site and how much will be outsourced to vendors like OCLC? These are all questions that cannot be answered in full today, but that must be considered as serials librarians prepare for managing serials processing and serials staff in the next century. One can posit that serials in paper will not disappear completely, but that much, much more serials information will be electronic, whether it be entire journals or just the ready availability of selected articles. Serials managers need to plan for these changes and to be contemplating what their expanded or different roles will be in the years ahead, and how to move their staff forward so that they are prepared for the graphical world of Windows and the rapid developments in electronic publishing that will impact on their job duties.

REFERENCES

American Federation of State, County and Municipal Employees. Local Union No. 590. 1994. "Collective Bargaining Agreement between Local Union No. 590, affiliated with the AFSCME, AFL-CIO, and its District Council Number 47 and the Trustees of the University of Pennsylvania for Designated Library and Archives Support Staff Classifications, July 1, 1994 to July 1, 1997."

Gable, J. Harris. 1935. "The New Serials Department." *Library Journal* 60 (November 15): 869–887.

Gorman, Michael. 1985. "Dealing with Serials: A Sketch of Contextual/Organizational Response." *Serials Librarian* 10, nos. 1/2: 13–18.

Hammer, Michael. 1993. *Reengineering the Corporation*. New York: HarperBusiness.

Harrington, Sue Anne. 1985. "Serials Organization: A Time for Reappraisal." *Serials Librarian* 10, nos. 1/2 (Fall/Winter): 19–28.

Horny, Karen L. 1987. "Fifteen Years of Automation: Evolution of Technical Services Staffing." *Library Resources and Technical Services* 31, no. 1: 69–76.

McCue, Janet. 1994. "Technical Services and the Electronic Library: Defining Our Roles and Divining the Partnership." *Library Hi-Tech* 12, no. 3: 63–70.

Potter, William Gray. 1981. "Form or Function: An Analysis of the Serials Department in the Modern Academic Library." *Serials Librarian* 6, no. 3: 85–94.

Stanford University Libraries. 1995. *Redesigning the Acquisitions-to-Access Process; Final Report of the Stanford University Libraries Redesign Team*. January. Unpublished report.

Weber, Hans. 1979. "Serials Administration." *Serials Librarian* 4, no. 4: 43–65.

3

Management of Serials Information in a Changing Environment

INTRODUCTION

The Journal as a Medium of Communication

Nearly all disciplines of study make use of serials, particularly the scholarly journal, as a primary means of communicating new research results, new theories, and new critical approaches. This is especially true in scientific and technical fields where journals (rather than monographs) dominate the printed literature. In many of these scientific fields, speed is of the utmost importance, and consequently, preprints of journal articles shared with colleagues represented the first time the results were put into print and shared with colleagues prior to formal publication. Physics is an example of a field where preprint activity was common in the print world, and since 1991 has been the norm for some specialties through electronic archives. "These archives serve over 35,000 users worldwide from over 70 countries, and process more than 70,000 electronic transactions per day. In some fields of physics, they have already supplanted traditional research journals as conveyers of both topical and archival research information" (Ginsparg 1996). With all of this activity on the Internet, there is the added advantage that the readers are able to have virtually instantaneous e-mail dialogue with the authors. Most of these prepublication documents do eventually find their way into print in a journal, in part because the academic review and tenure process in the United States has not yet come to terms with electronic publication as a substitute for publication in a peer-reviewed print journal. This may well be changing, however, as the more prestigious scientific and engineering societies, and the major commercial STM publishers begin to experiment with offering their stable of titles on the World Wide Web (WWW). For now at least, the concept of a journal issue still persists, but this, too, is blurring around the edges as the possibilities for single article publication anytime by anyone expand and the ability to continually update, edit, and refine the text only becomes easier. In a recent article, the term "hermaphrodites" was borrowed to describe a new type of electronic publication that seems to have elements of both monographs and serials and be updatable and changeable: "another category needs to be defined for those publications that incorporate the features of both serials and monographs. These materials are complete in one part (like monographs) but have the potential to continue (like serials)" (Graham and Ringler 1996, 73). The key distinction is that serials are intended to continue forever, while hermaphrodites have the potential to do so, but not the intent.

Historically, the literature of some fields has been heavily journals-based and, not surprisingly, 75 to 85 percent of the acquisitions in these disciplines (chemistry, physics, engineering, for example) has been spent on serials materials. The journal as a form of publication has existed for several hundred years; for nearly all of this period, the journal and its contents have existed on paper and individuals and libraries purchased subscriptions for print copies. For at least 50 years, libraries have also been able to purchase back volumes of selected journal or newspaper titles in microfiche or microfilm, but paper has generally remained the medium of choice for the individual reader. Today, several of the large technical societies (the IEEE [Institute of Electrical and Electronics Engineers], for example) and a number of publishers (Johns Hopkins University Press, Academic Press) are actively pursuing electronic publication of their titles and perhaps even preparing for the demise of their journals in paper form.

Use of the Journal Literature

Not so very long ago, using the journal literature meant that the individual researcher had to make a trip into the library to locate the specific issue or bound volume containing the article or articles desired. With the advent of online document delivery services in the 1980s, the same researcher was given the option, generally for a fee, of searching for and locating an article from his or her office or dormitory room, and then requesting that a copy of it be mailed, faxed, or perhaps even e-mailed to that site. In less than three years, the widespread availability of Mosaic and Netscape, software tools for browsing the World Wide Web over the Internet, has dramatically changed the look of serials publishing, and the potential of the World Wide Web promises more drastic changes in some disciplines. Much more information and more full texts are accessible from the individual researcher's desktop, and a number of experts are predicting a true revolution in the future existence of the print journal (Okerson and O'Donnell 1995).

As one pair stated it, "it is now necessary to begin the collective migration to a more streamlined post-modern 'collection of collections' mediated by new electronic networking technology that connects scholars across space and time" (Harloe and Budd 1994, 85). At the same time that information is being presented in new and exciting ways, scholars and librarians expect the new format to fulfill some of the same purposes as the traditional print journal. "Even though they [electronic journals] must fulfill the same roles as printed journals, they will do so with second-order effects that are quite different from those of print. More precisely, electronic journals, like their print counterparts, are expected to act as communication tools, to allow for archival functions and to provide a degree of legitimacy and authority to authors" (Guedon 1995, 67). This electronic capability is transforming and has already begun to reshape the way academic libraries are used, and how they are structured and organized; in so doing, this new technology will alter how libraries carry out their primary mission: the delivery of information to the academic community. Serials staff who check in paper journals today are likely to see these print title subscriptions replaced by subscriptions to online journals that are rich with graphs, tables, and photos and that include embedded hypertext links to allow for the quick retrieval of related material.

While the technology offers a great deal already in terms of providing serials information, acquiring the relevant articles often comes at a cost, and for some time, there will continue to be undergraduates, graduate students, and faculty who will want or need to come to the library to use materials. More of them will arrive in the library already having done much of their searching, however, and they will spend less time overall on-site. It will be instructive for libraries to try to measure any decline in their so-called foot traffic (building entrances and exits) by type of patron over the next several years, as this could be an early indicator of the changing use of the library's collections in favor of online or remote materials, and to begin to get out the message that librarians are information experts who possess some valuable skills. "Information . . . remains the basic commodity of the educational institutions. Libraries and librarians are best placed to organize and promote the flow of this information, a fact that librarians have almost overlooked in their insistence on the fact of 'the library,' even though the building and its contents are now only one factor in the whole range of information services" (Martin 1992, 8).

With this in mind, the focus of this chapter will be on how to manage serials information as it exists today, with special attention paid to: the current arrangements of serials materials, who the users of serials are and how their needs are being met, and what the functional relationships are between serials staff and other departments. Lastly, there will be a brief exploration of how serials publishing is evolving and the future role of the library in providing serials information.

USERS OF SERIALS

Knowing who the library's primary users are is essential information for providing good service. In many large research libraries, the most intensive users of the collection are the graduate students, followed next by the undergraduates, and then the faculty. In smaller academic libraries, especially those that are four-year institutions, the undergraduates are the core users and their needs are different than research students—usually more oriented toward general materials.

Undergraduates

Undergraduates typically use the library both as social space and study space, and often, primarily as a source of assigned reserve materials for specific courses. Many regularly frequent the current periodicals collections for the latest issues of their favorite news magazines or for the most recent copies of their hometown newspapers. When term papers are assigned in their courses, undergraduates are often faced with the task of locating appropriate journal articles, and this means that they must master searching of indexes and abstracts for relevant citations and then track down the actual articles themselves. This used to be a strictly manual task that involved several distinct steps: (1) searching through one or more print indexes for relevant citations, (2) checking the card catalog to determine if the library owned the journal and if so, noting the location and call number, and finally, (3) pulling the relevant issue or bound volume from the shelf. With the advent of online catalogs, the second step, determining if the title was held locally and where, could be done at a computer terminal. In the past five years, many academic libraries have purchased or made available online files of some of the most heavily used indexes and abstracts; this means that in some instances, even the first step of the research process, searching the *Humanities Index*, for example, can now be done online. This progression of providing more and more online access has continued, and today the provision of full texts of periodicals and other materials online is in its infancy, but fast approaching adolescence. Lexis/Nexis, for example, is a powerful, albeit complex, search tool, that enables the user to access full-length articles from a number of significant newspapers and magazines. Many college and university libraries subscribe to this database for their patrons, and even though it can be cumbersome and definitely not intuitive to use, it is very popular with students just for the simple reason that it does provide the full text of the citation right then and there. In addition to the online databases, the number of electronic journals on the WWW is proliferating at a very rapid rate, and while the total number represents only the smallest fraction of the total universe of journals, the journals that are being presented on the Web are some of the most popular and heavily used, and increasingly, some of the most scholarly journals as well. So, why does the student need to come to the library at all? The main reason is that while all of this online access is being provided, it is not comprehensive nor complete; limited back runs of electronic journals are online; many, many titles are just not yet available in this format; and only a handful of index services are probably available online at any given academic library. It is fair to say, however, that an undergraduate could go a long way toward doing much of the research and searching for a paper before ever having to come to the library.

Graduate Students and Faculty

Library use by graduate students and faculty is more likely to involve a historical component, at least in the social sciences and humanities, and therefore it is more likely that there will be a need for older materials that exist in print, not electronic, format. Also, the more narrowly focused serials and periodicals are generally not the ones that are being digitized. With a greater emphasis on undergraduate education and the particulars of the undergraduate curriculum across the country, some faculty are strongly urging that there ought to be a formal research component to the undergraduate experience. The addition of such a research requirement has implications for the collections and the type of access provided by the library. The faculty at any given college or university may or may not visit the library regularly, preferring instead to access the online catalog or indexes from their offices or to send their graduate students to retrieve relevant articles and books for them. This certainly varies somewhat by discipline and by individual faculty member, with some faculty making greater use of the library to browse current issues of the journals in their particular fields, for example, than others. One could even speculate that the use of library serials collections, especially periodicals, may actually increase as more libraries provide access online to the journal article databases such as *Current Contents* and *Reader's Guide to Periodical Literature*, thereby alerting library patrons more easily to relevant materials in their fields. It is not unrealistic to posit a transitional period of increased in-library use of journals due to greater availability of journal indexes online, which will be followed by a decline in the in-house use of journals as the number of full-text options continues to grow and to become affordable through one of a number of online sources. What is clear is that all library patrons are desirous of having as much full text online as possible, and, therefore, some undergraduates in particular will need to be reminded that for many journal articles, they may be able only to get the citation online, and that then they must actually go to the stacks, find the volume, and then read or copy the pertinent article. Informal comments from some faculty users suggest that the number of trips to the library is already decreasing as these users take advantage of all of the online searching they can do from their homes and offices. By the time they visit the library, they have already done more searching and preparation than in the past, and may need only to go to the shelves to locate the desired material.

Library Space and the New Librarian

Libraries planning their serials budgets will want to consider the impact of the availability of electronic materials and probably allocate a greater percentage of the budget for electronic formats and electronic access (making electronic journals accessible from the local campus via links to the library's Web server or gopher). Providing this access, however, may require the cancellation of these titles in print form or a reassessment of whether certain titles available online are more useful than some other titles in print form. Likewise, as academic libraries evaluate how they allocate their physical space, they may want to re-think the space allocated for reading current periodicals and provide for work-stations in this area. On many campuses, the library functions also as social center and central meeting place as well as a venue for quiet studying, functions that are exclusive of the materials and collections housed in the building. Most librarians and administrators expect the library to continue to play this study space/social center role for the foreseeable future. In five years' time, less space may be needed for just reading periodical issues, but the same amount of space will be required to meet the study and other needs of the campus community.

The format of academic course materials is also changing, and some of the materials that traditionally were put on reserve in the library, such as course syllabi, supplemental reading lists, and exams and problem sets, are also, or sometimes only, being posted to class listservs. As an alternative, these course materials can be scanned and mounted on a server; library cataloging staff are then providing brief bibliographic records in the OPAC for them, and the records are hypertext-linked to the actual documents. This gives the individual student access to all of these materials anytime, from the privacy of his or her computer in the dormitory room, and again can affect the real traffic into and out of the library. This impacts directly on how the academic library is used and means that librarians ought to be considering their information roles in the campus community and how best to promote the unique services they can offer—or-ganizing and providing logical access and pointers to the information that exists, and teaching others how to access it. There is so much material on the Internet and the number of new URLs is growing so rapidly that, even as the Internet search tools (e.g., Lycos, InfoSeek, Alta Vista) become more sophisticated, the unguided user can get lost in a plethora or mire of available information. The librarian as tour guide, as scout, or as information guru are roles that may be worth investigating and cultivating. For serials librarians in particular, this means creating meaningful roles outside of the technical services area and in the wider arena of the campus. Examples include: (1) assisting with bibliographic instruc-tion for electronic journals and other materials, (2) acting as a liaison to an academic department, if not as the primary subject specialist, then perhaps as an electronic tour guide, and (3) working to present or prepare resources that enable the library user to make the best use of all aspects of the library's serials collections. For the print collection, this might be special bibliographies; for the online collection, it may be creating the bibliographic records in the library's OPAC as pointers to what is available on the library's Web server. A serials librarian position that is too narrowly focused on paper journal processing and claims runs the risk of becoming "old hat" very quickly, and the incumbent might find him or herself marginalized and left out of all of the very exciting developments of the next five years. Today, the amount of time spent on matters relating to electronic journals and the WWW may represent only 5 to 10 percent of the activity of the serials department, if indeed it is that much. Yet, the Web has become such an attractive, visible, and exciting medium for the presentation of information that once the commercial publishers finally figure out how they can be on the Web, rather than on paper, and still generate revenue, it will become even more potent and all-encompassing.

USE AND LOCATION OF PERIODICALS COLLECTIONS

Use of current periodicals collections is both casual and more serious; at one end of the spectrum there are the browsers, those who come in daily to read their favorite local newspapers or to see the latest issues of *Time* or *Newsweek*; at the other end are the researchers who need the latest issue of a particular quarterly for a course paper or other research. The library's goal should be to facilitate the use of unbound issues of periodicals by both groups of patrons. The current periodicals reading area can and ought to be an attractive, inviting place for anyone who has a few spare minutes to relax and catch up on the latest publications. In the present-day academic library, the physical location of the current periodicals collections is often relegated to where the responsibility for managing the collection sits on the organization chart. If the current periodicals collection is a part of the serials department and if there is a service desk with it, then there are compelling reasons to locate this area near the serials processing unit. Even in the best of libraries, however, this is not always possible, and one may find a current periodicals service desk on the second floor and the serials processing staff on the first floor in a different wing of the building. This is not desirable and requires extra effort on the supervisor's part to maintain good communication with this staff outpost, but it can be made to work.

Ideally, one would like to have the current periodicals collection near everything else—the reference desk, microforms, the main entrance, and so on. When library patrons used to have to rely exclusively on print indexes and abstracts to find relevant citations to the journal literature, it was extremely useful to have the reference collection, or at least these index tools, located near the periodicals collection. It was a logical progression for a patron to use the index or abstract, make notes about the desired citations, then move on to the actual journal issues. With many more index tools available online and often searchable from the same terminal or workstation that contains the online catalog, there is less need for the journals to be next to the reference collection. Many libraries locally load and provide access to journal index files such as the Wilson indexes, PsycInfo, ABI Inform, or MEDLINE; they may also provide remote access through Dialog or other commercial services via the Internet to these databases or others including Lexis/Nexis, MLA, and others. These indexes may be linked to the library's holdings so that in the same search the patron is able to not only see the citation, but also know immediately if that is a journal that the home library owns. Even though the index tools are online, however, it may be still be advantageous to locate the periodicals collection near reference staff. Since many reference desks are staffed solely or primarily by librarians, and the serials or periodicals service desk is more apt to be support staff, then having professional staff readily at hand to answer more complicated questions could be beneficial to patrons. If there is no staff at all assigned to the periodicals collection, then locating the collection near reference would enable the reference staff to assist with any problems that may arise in locating journals.

WORKING RELATIONSHIPS WITH OTHER UNITS

In general, a close working relationship between serials staff and reference staff is mutually beneficial. The serials staff process the material and are aware of what has been received and whether or not it needs to be claimed, and can provide useful guidance to reference librarians in dealing with patron inquiries. Reference staff interact directly with the library users and often are the first ones to be told about problems, issues that have not been received, bibliographic records that need correcting, and title changes or cessations that may have been missed. Also, many of the non-periodical serial titles that an academic library receives are housed in the reference collection, and therefore the reference staff are the direct recipients of some significant material handled by the serials staff.

There is also a logical alliance between periodicals and microforms. Depending on how the library shelves its bound periodical volumes, there can be service advantages to locating periodicals and microforms adjacent to each other and even perhaps creating a shared service desk. If the periodical collection includes any significant number of current newspapers, then having the microfilm copy of that same paper close by will save steps and time for the users. If the library has invested heavily in microfilm or microfiche in place of binding its periodicals, then having these two collections near each other can facilitate the use of both parts of the collection. For those libraries that do not now staff their current periodicals areas, creating a service desk that serves both periodicals and microforms may reduce user frustration and lead to a greater use of both formats. Most librarians would agree that it is difficult to have a successful microforms area without providing staff assistance. Figuring out how to use a microfilm reader or printer for the first time is not always intuitive, and there may well be charges for printing and a need to provide security for the lenses for these machines. Putting staff together to provide help in finding periodicals and using microforms can result in the added advantage of staff who are cross-trained and can together or separately provide a richer, more complete service to the patrons.

CURRENT PERIODICALS COLLECTIONS

Shelving of Unbound Issues

No matter how few or how great the number of current journals an academic library receives, it must still decide on where and how to shelve them. Several studies of a general nature (Wright 1977; Segesta and Hyslop 1991) and one detailing a specific library's approach to the question of periodicals arrangement (Pontius 1989), plus discussions on the SERIALST listserv, highlight some of the key questions. How should the periodicals be arranged—alphabetically or by call number? If alphabetically, should it be by title or strictly by cataloging main entry? Where will the back issues be shelved, those that are unbound and those that are already bound? What about current newspapers and newspapers on microfilm? What about other microform holdings of periodical titles? In their study, Segesta and Hyslop found little agreement on what constituted the best arrangement:

The three formats—bound, unbound, and microform, may be interfiled with one another so that all the holdings of a particular title are together regardless of format, or they may be kept in three separate collections. Each format may be arranged alphabetically by title or classified. If classified, one or, rarely, two or all three formats may be interfiled with the monographs, or all the periodicals may be kept separate from all the books. . . . Considering all the possible variations it is imaginable that few college or university libraries in America treat periodicals in exactly the same way. (Segesta and Hyslop 1991, 22)

From the standpoint of the user, one can make a compelling argument that arranging unbound periodicals alphabetically makes them easier to find and therefore, easier to use. Knowing which title he or she wants, the user can go directly to the shelf without having to look up a call number first. Some libraries display just the most current issues on titled, easily browsable shelves, while the other loose issues are located somewhere else. Again, having all of the unbound issues together on the shelf, either stacked or on display shelving with the latest on top and the other issues under a shelf that can be lifted up, facilitates the use of this material.

If the unbound issues are shelved by call number, it is more likely that they will be shelved along with the bound volumes all in one sequence. This arrangement has its advantages, since the user may not always know ahead of time whether the material that is needed is already bound or not. Having both bound and unbound issues together means that all of the issues for that title are in one place. The user must still deal with the hurdle of having the call number before going to the shelf, and this author, having worked with several different arrangements, remains adamant that this (the requirement to look up a call number first) is indeed an impediment to the use of the most current material.

In very large collections, the current issues may be physically separated from the bound collection by one or more floors and therefore, the fact that the two pieces of the collection are shelved differently matters less. Having all bound periodicals shelved together and arranged by call number apart from the monographic portion of the collection may seem unnecessary, but for the patron who knows that he or she wishes to use just periodicals, this can be more efficient than having to traverse the entire length of the stacks for periodical volumes. This arrangement, however, may stress the library's space planning to a greater degree, since growth space needs to be figured for all of the current titles, and it also may be a less efficient use of overall library stack space. Although the literature cited provided little in the way of consensus on arrangement of periodicals, it is true that the more subscriptions a library receives and also the higher the degrees it grants, the more likely it is that the bound periodical volumes will have numbers, usually the classification numbers, on them (Segesta and Hyslop 23).

Arrangement of Bound Periodicals

The SERIALST discussion cited earlier also looked at the shelving of bound periodical titles and found that there was a small preference for call number arrangement over alphabetic. Again, though, the differences in the number of libraries choosing one arrangement over the other were very small. A further question, and a relevant issue for serials librarians and others charged with making shelving recommendations, was whether or not the bound volumes were shelved with the monograph collection or shelved separately. In this case, there were more libraries that shelved their bound volumes separately, regardless of whether or not they had call numbers. Probably the chief advantage of shelving bound volumes by call number is the ability to keep all the variations of title together over the life of the journal. Even if the title changes and the numbering restarts with volume one, many libraries keep the same basic class number and just vary the cutter number slightly. Having the periodicals shelved completely separately from the monograph collection has the advantage, in a large collection, of cutting down on the distances one must cover in the stacks to find six different periodicals. On the other hand, it can be argued that this isolates the periodicals as somehow different or even perhaps less important materials. In smaller branch or subject libraries, there is probably greater precedent for separating out the bound periodical volumes from the rest of the collection. Isolating periodical volumes, but near copy equipment and microform formats, however, can be desirable if it promotes patrons to take care of the material and reduces the amount of mutilation.

Nevertheless, shelving periodicals intermixed with monographs by call number does have the advantage for the subject browser of putting all the print material on a given topic in the same area in the stacks. This frees the user from having to know ahead of time if the material to be located is a periodical or a book or something else, and perhaps promotes more browsing of the entire collection for other items and increases the chance of serendipitous discoveries. Shelving all material in one sequence may also be more straightforward for the stack staff and for those in the library charged with planning for the most efficient use of a finite amount of stack space. One disadvantage is that in very large collections, the user may have to cover the length of several floors and more than one floor to find all of the needed periodical volumes.

What is clear from this and the other studies is that there is merit in a number of the approaches to the arrangement of periodical and other serials material; each library will have to decide for itself which mix of factors carries the most weight in determining how and where in the collection to shelve bound periodicals.

NEW FORMS OF SERIALS INFORMATION

Electronic Journals

In the past year, the number of free electronic journals has mushroomed, and there is now a listserv, NEWJOUR-L, devoted just to announcements of new online titles. Until very recently, many of these titles were online versions of existing print journals, and the vast majority of them were free. Early on, an individual or a library might choose to subscribe and then would receive the journal issue in his or her personal e-mail account or in an institutional account. With the widespread availability of Netscape and its rapid acceptance as the browser of choice, most new electronic journals are available on the World Wide Web and offer a combination of text, color, and graphics. To make one of these titles available on one's own campus, it is merely a case of linking from the home computer to the URL (Uniform Resource Locator) of the journal's Web site, and voilá, the patron in this library can be reading a journal housed on a computer across the country or around the world. Continuing to make this title available does require some minimal maintenance in the form of a manual or automated check that the URL is still the correct one and that the link is still active. As an example, the University of Pennsylvania library home page (http://www.library.upenn.edu), as of this writing, includes more than 700 electronic journals and newspapers; the journals are arranged by subject area and also in one alphabetic sequence. The newspapers are subdivided by language and by country of publication. Until very recently, all of these were free publications, "free for the linking."

Electronic Subscriptions

There is now a great deal of activity on the part of commercial publishers and societies to make their titles accessible on the Web, usually for a fee. The first paid subscriptions online were the medical titles distributed by OCLC as part of its Electronic Journal Online product, namely, the *Online Journal of Current Clinical Trials*, and later, the *Journal of Immunology* and others. OCLC's titles required the use of a special software interface called Guidon, and the hours of availability were limited. Guidon from the beginning had the capability to support graphics, formulas, tables, and links from one part of the text to another. In the past three years, Netscape has clearly emerged as the browser of choice; as a pioneer in electronic distribution, OCLC continues to be a leader and is currently developing a Web interface called WebZ which will work with Netscape and Mosaic to access OCLC databases and journals.

As more and more publishers take the leap into cyberspace, they must decide how much control they wish to exert over how and by whom their journals are accessed. Clearly, the baseline issue for them is the cost of providing Web products and the need to maintain an incoming stream of revenue. Charging policies vary; this is an area where no one way has yet become the standard, and perhaps there will never be just one approach. Some publishers are charging the usual subscription rate for the print journal with a somewhat higher cost if online access is desired as well; others are pricing the WWW version separately without any reference to the print subscription or any requirement to subscribe to the print as a quid pro quo for being able to access the online title. Still other publishers (Association for Computing Machinery [ACM], for example) have boldly stated their intention of phasing out their paper journals in favor of the electronic publications. If there is a license or subscription fee for accessing the title, then there are usually some restrictions on who may access the title. For institutional library subscriptions, this is often limited to anyone from the home college or university; a more restrictive approach is to limit the number of passwords or simultaneous users who can be viewing the title at one time from a particular campus. Limiting the use of a title to individuals with a particular IP (Internet Protocol) address (all of the users from one university campus, for example) can be a relatively easy way for a publisher to enforce and monitor use, but may necessitate some systems work for the library. This more restricted access is a change from the relatively universal ''open door'' policy that many academic libraries have followed for access to their online catalogs, for example.

Electronic Players

Other players in the movement to put journals online include the Mellon Foundation, Elsevier Science Publishers, and Johns Hopkins University Press. The Mellon Foundation, as part of its support for the development of a digital library for arts and sciences, is currently working with the University of Michigan as the Web site for its JSTOR or Journal Storage Project. The aim is to put ten titles in economics and history online (http://www.jstor.org/) or about 750,000 pages. The University Licensing Project or TULIP, an initiative of Elsevier Science Publishing, recently completed a five-year project to distribute bit-mapped images of approximately 40 materials science titles to nine universities, including Michigan, University of California, Carnegie Mellon, Cornell, Georgia Institute of Technology, MIT, University of Tennessee, Virginia Polytechnic Institute and State University, and the University of Washington. Individuals outside the participating institutions are able to access a demo interface which includes a small subset of the journals. The goals of TULIP were to study the technical aspects of networked distribution of journal text to multiple institutions, to arrive at an understanding of what kind of costing, subscription, and marketing models might be viable (or economically acceptable) for this new format, and to study user behavior and how the delivery and retrieval tools might be improved (See http://www.usc.edu/library.tulip/tulip.html for one institution's implementation). In early 1995, Elsevier and OCLC announced a partnership for providing fully electronic subscriptions to all of Elsevier's journal titles (http://www.oclc.org/oclc/promo/els9254/9254.htm). Through EES (Elsevier Electronic Subscriptions), OCLC will provide its SiteSearch system and also Guidon, its graphical user interface. One of the components of SiteSearch is WebZ, a server that allows users using Netscape or Mosaic to access on OCLC SiteSearch servers or other Z39.50-compliant servers. The service was expected to be widely available in 1996.

Perhaps one of the most exciting projects, from the librarian's standpoint, is Project Muse, a joint effort of Johns Hopkins University Press, the Johns Hopkins University Library, and the university computing center. (Cochenour 1995). By the end of 1997, Project Muse will mount the full contents of the 42 journals published by the press. Access will be on a subscription basis for an entire institution and limited to IP addresses from the institution. Response thus far to the initial twelve titles has been very positive.

These are only a few of the vendors and publishers whose new publishing ventures are changing the face of the serial literature in bold and exciting ways. While publishers grapple with how best to publish electronically (no longer whether to or not) and still make a profit, while vendors and agents test out new roles as distributors of electronic information, serials librarians must begin to forge a new definition of service and carve out new relationships within, but especially outside, the library.

REFERENCES

Cochenour, Donnice. 1995. "Project Muse: A Partnership of Interest." *Serials Review* 21, no. 3: 75–81.

Ginsparg, P. 1996. "Winners and Losers in the Global Research Village." *Joint ICSU Press/UNESCO Expert Conference on Electronic Publishing in Science.* http://www.grainger.uiuc.edu/icsu/ginsparg.htm (September 1, 1996).

Goodyear, Mary Lou, and Jane Dodd. 1994. "From the Library of Record to the Library as Gateway: An Analysis of Three Electronic Table-of-Contents Services." *Library Acquisitions: Practice and Theory* 18: 253–264.

Graham, Crystal, and Rebecca Ringler. 1996. "Hermaphrodites & Herrings." *Serials Review* 22, no.1: 73–77.

Guedon, Jean-Claude. 1995. "Electronic Journals, Libraries and University Presses." In *Filling the Pipeline and Paying the Piper: Proceedings of the Fourth Symposium*, 67–75. Washington, DC: Office of Scientific and Academic Publishing, Association of Research Libraries.

Harloe, Bart, and John M. Budd. 1994. "Collection Development and Scholarly Communication in the Era of Electronic Access." *Journal of Academic Librarianship* 20: 83–87.

Harrington, Sue Ann. 1989. "The Central Periodicals/Microforms Room: One Way to Ease User Frustration." *Serials Librarian* 16 (Fall/Winter): 1–15.

Hawks, Carol Pitts. 1994. "Building and Managing an Acquisitions Program." *Library Acquisitions: Practice and Theory* 18, no. 3: 297–308.

Lanier, Don, and Norman Vogt. 1985. "The Serials Department, 1975–1985." *Serials Librarian* 10, nos. 3/4: 5–11.

Martin, Murray S. 1992. "The Invasion of the Library Materials Budget by Technology Serials and Databases: Buying More with Less?" *Serials Review* 18, no. 3: 7–17.

Okerson, Ann, and James J. O'Donnell, eds. 1995. *Scholarly Journals at the Crossroads: A Subversive Proposal for Electronic Publishing, An Internet Discussion about Scientific and Scholarly Journals and Their Future*. Washington, DC: Office of Scientific and Academic Publishing, Association of Research Libraries.

Pontius, Jack E. 1989. "The Current Periodicals Room Reconsidered." *Serials Review* 15: 49–54.

Segesta, Jim, and Gary Hyslop. 1991. "The Arrangement of Periodicals in American Academic Libraries." *Serials Review* 17: 21–28, 40.

Wright, Geraldine Murphy. 1977. "Current Trends in Periodicals Collections." *College and Research Libraries* 38: 234–40.

4

Measuring Journal Use: Why, How, and for What Purpose?

Scholarly journals are obsolete as the primary vehicle for scholarly communication. The recent furor over "cold fusion," for example, developed entirely outside the scholarly journal process.

Rogers and Hurt (1989)

What is the future of the scholarly journal and do libraries still have a need to own journals? Rogers and Hurt's extreme statement was uttered even before the explosion in the use of e-mail and before it became relatively easy to obtain online the full text of a journal article not held at one's own library. The exponential growth in the number of WWW sites (2 million new URLs added per month) (Wiggins 1995) and the dramatic increase in the availability of full-text journals online (e-journals) are reshaping how libraries build their serials collections and how they provide access. These developments, coupled with mandated serials cancellation projects to meet declining or steady-state serials budgets, are changing the library landscape. Nevertheless, libraries are still purchasing many journal titles in paper and probably will do so for some years to come. Therefore, evaluating the use of individual journal titles and their value to the library collection remains a matter of interest. Bibliometrics, or the statistics and study of the use of books and other printed material, has been of concern to librarians as long as budgets have been finite and decisions have had to be made about which materials to acquire and which to retain. This chapter will focus on some of the reasons for designing a journal-use study and some of the more common methods for determining use.

In addition to the budgetary reasons already cited, there are a number of other reasons why serials librarians may find it desirable and useful to conduct a journal-use study. These include: (1) needing use data in order to most effectively weed a collection because of space constraints, (2) wanting to identify low-use, currently received titles for possible cancellation, and (3) desiring to better shape the collection in the context of supporting the curriculum of the institution and the research interests of the faculty. In recent years, the significant rise in journal costs has put added pressure on serials librarians and collection development staff to hone their collections, to contain the percentage of the budget spent on serials, and to winnow out unnecessary titles in order to generate funds for the purchase of new titles as new disciplines and subdisciplines emerge and splinter off into still other new research areas. Not so very long ago, when a library cancelled a paper journal subscription, it and its patrons had to rely on requesting needed articles through interlibrary loan. With the advances in technology, it is now possible to provide access to a large number of journal articles through commercial sources such as UnCover, or EBSCOHost, for example. Both allow the user to search for citations online and then to request the articles. In some cases, the full text may already be present online; if not, it can be delivered via fax, e-mail, or U.S. mail. The number of journals available online that contain the full text plus graphics, tables, and other illustrative material is increasing, and in addition, more and more society and commercial publishers have committed to mounting their journal offerings in the near future, and as of late 1996, some of the major publishers have already done so.

TYPES OF USE STUDIES

General Guidelines

In order to have a successful use study, it is important that the library administration clearly define in advance the objective of the study; it may be to identify low-use titles for cancellation, or the purpose may be to enrich the collection by providing more depth in a particular field. In the latter case, the use of citation data could facilitate identifying the other major titles in the field that could be added. Surveying patrons, both faculty and students who use the collection, is another way to find out what titles they feel would be worthwhile additions. With so many software packages available, it makes sense to investigate whether there is an appropriate one for manipulating the raw data from the study and assisting with the analysis. Likewise, if the library has an integrated online management system with a sophisticated report-writer function (one that makes use of SQL, Standard Query Language, for example), it should be possible to take advantage of it for producing reports. This would be especially true if the library were taking advantage of the circulation or inventory features of the system for collecting data.

If there is a public face to the use study, if the data collection is going to be apparent to library patrons, then it is essential that the library staff carefully put forth the rationale for the study and give some indication of the means of data collection and the use to which it will be put. If faculty and student opinion or preferences are being sought, their involvement must be carefully coordinated; letters or other publicity should be distributed (Dole and Chang 1996, 35–38). A clear statement also needs to be put forth that it is the library management's responsibility to make the final collection decisions and that the recommendations and responses of faculty and students are advisory to the whole process. After having stated that, it behooves the library to have internal procedures that allow for the review of the results and for the possible reinstatement of titles that may be cancelled or the return to the former location of titles that have been relocated or removed to storage or more remote areas of the building or the collection. If the high cost of materials is the reason for the collection review or use study, then sharing as much information as possible on how the costs locally have risen and what the impact is on this particular library's budget will help place the study in an acceptable context. Many academic libraries have faculty library committees or departmental library committees; informing these individuals of the need for the review and making them allies in the process should also help gain acceptance for unpopular results.

Tips and Caveats

In addition to publicizing the use study and explaining the rationale behind it, it is wise for the library to try to put the problem (rising costs, lack of shelf space) into a regional or national context as well as a local one. Being able to cite peer institutions and libraries with similar constraints often makes this bitter medicine easier to swallow. Having concrete statistics (both local and perhaps national) that are clear and not open to multiple or ambiguous interpretation can bolster the library's case.

The savvy serials librarian will also take into account both faculty and semester schedules as well as publisher and vendor deadlines in setting up a time frame for the use study that is reasonable and realistic. Asking for faculty input in May, during exams, or the first week in September, at the beginning of classes, generally means that faculty input will be minimal to non-existent. On the other hand, if identifying titles to be cancelled is the goal, then the serials librarian needs to have the list of affected titles in hand by the end of the summer to get to the vendors by early September. If standing order titles are part of any review, timing is less of a factor, since these orders can be stopped at any point in time. Lastly, often the most painless way to cut titles is to first eliminate duplicate paper subscriptions and then look at any subscriptions in alternate formats. More and more, as periodicals are available on the World Wide Web, libraries will be evaluating whether or not they need to continue their print subscriptions.

Reshelving Studies

Historically, librarians have attempted to quantify in-library use of their own serials, especially periodical titles, in order to justify current subscriptions or to determine low-use titles for cancellation. There are several approaches, all of which have been detailed in the literature, and two of which have been used for many years. The various types are: using reshelving data, soliciting faculty and librarian evaluations of individual titles, and conducting citation analysis studies. Measuring in-house use is critical for academic libraries, since many of them do not allow current journal issues to be charged out of the library. This is usually done in one of two ways. In the "sweep" method, patrons are requested not to reshelve any material, and then the staff whose job it is to reshelve material each day note the titles and record one use for each piece or volume to a master tally sheet or database. The other method is to ask the patrons to make a hatch mark or cross off a number on a label on the front of the journal issue or volume each time it is used. In both cases, the library staff are relying on library patrons to be compliant with specific instructions and then to refrain from reshelving the material or to note their usage of an issue themselves. Decisions need to be made about whether or not to include bound volumes or to focus exclusively on unbound current issues. This will depend to some extent on the length of the study, its purpose, and the mechanics involved. Several studies employing one or both of these methods were conducted at SUNY Buffalo (Naylor 1990, 1993) and the State Library of New South Wales (Ventress 1991). At SUNY Buffalo, the sweep method was used and then in the subsequent study, the patron record method was employed; there was a significant difference in the use of the same set of journals in the second study as opposed to the first.

The 43 percent lower use demonstrated by the user check-off method over the reshelving or sweep method could be accounted for by a switch in reader preferences for other titles, or by a general marked decrease in current science periodical use. Unless there are significant variables other than the ones examined that affect the use of these titles, the conclusion follows that the difference lies in the methodology. Patrons are not as diligent as paid shelvers . . . in recording their use of library materials. (Naylor 1993, 62)

Another method is to take advantage of the technology of automated systems and to barcode individual periodicals issues (whether or not they circulate) and then scan in the label for all issues that have been used within the library. Many systems allow for a count of "browses" (or in-house use) in addition to counting true check-outs to patrons. This allows the library to take advantage of the existing automation. There is some debate about the usefulness of this data compared to the extra time it adds on in the reshelving process. One study found little correlation between the usage of serials as measured by reshelving data as compared to citation analysis and no correlation between citation data and faculty or librarian's evaluation of the titles. The explanation may be "that citation counting, subjective evaluations of titles, and reshelving counting measure different aspects of journal use. [Also] reshelving counts may reflect use by students or others who do not write for publication. And citation counting may describe the use of a journal for research while not counting its importance for instruction (Swigger and Wilkes 1991, 52).

Cost Analysis

Other approaches to reviewing the use and/or desirability of specific titles in a collection are: computing the use of a title and comparing it to the cost of the title and then reviewing lists of titles by discipline. Staff at the Memorial University of Newfoundland combined measuring use of a title by patrons' tagging a label on the issues covers with relating the level of use to the cost of the subscription (Milne and Tiffany 1991). Their goal was to determine the cost per use of each title by taking the yearly subscription cost and dividing it by the total number of uses that journal could be expected to receive over that year. The cost per use was then compared to the cost of an interlibrary loan transaction; if the cost was greater than the interlibrary loan cost, then the title became a candidate for cancellation. The results of their study were intriguing and show clearly the need for careful judgment by library staff: "results showed no correlation between the opinions expressed by faculty members about the value of particular serials to their work and the cost-effectiveness of the library's subscriptions. Similarly, we found that serials generally thought to be 'core' or to have high prestige were not necessarily cost-effective. Indeed, we found quite a few mainstream journals that could not be cancelled" (Milne and Tiffany 1991, 143). These results also pointed up the fact that if the library could replace some of the cost-ineffective journals with reliable fax or electronic delivery of articles, then canceling them would become an acceptable alternative.

Faculty Evaluation

At the University of Arizona, library staff and faculty embarked on a three-year review of serials in all disciplines in order to meet mandated reductions in the size of the serials budget (Tallman and Leach 1989). Theirs was an intensive process that involved a serials review committee who determined the criteria for deselection, then compiled lists of titles by discipline which were then sent to faculty for their opinions on which titles should be cancelled in order to meet the mandated savings. Although faculty and administrative involvement in the review process was substantive, there was still unhappiness with some of the cancellation decisions reached; consequently, detailed procedures were developed to evaluate the inevitable requests for reinstatement of cancelled titles.

At Loughborough University, a study to determine how academics actually used journals, when they read them, and how many they personally subscribed to clearly demonstrated the desirability of electronic transmission of text (Simpson 1988).

Besides the obvious use of use studies to identify titles for cancellation, another reason for doing collection analysis is to determine if the library owns the core material in a discipline. Taking advantage of the various citation reports or doing an internal citation analysis may help the library evaluate the strength of its collection in a given area and formulate a plan for either building up a particular area or weeding another. A comparative review of data gathered from two studies of the use of biology journals, one a circulation study and the other based on citations and faculty perceptions of the key journals in the field, did not reveal significant differences in the results (Schmidt et al. 1994). This study did, however, underscore the importance of local use studies to accurately reflect both the expectations and the actual use patterns at a particular library on a specific campus. The particular area within a discipline that faculty at a campus specialize in or focus on will affect the journal use within that discipline and also what specific titles are purchased in addition to the basic or core titles within the field. Also impacting on the results of any study of journal use is the type of academic institution and the kinds of degrees it offers; a research university or one that teaches master's and doctoral level courses as well as undergraduate would expect to have different use patterns which would, in part, reflect a more focused, in-depth collection.

CITATION ANALYSIS

In order to carry out a successful bibliometric study that will yield meaningful results, there are a number of factors to be considered. The first is to determine what exactly is to be studied, whether it be overall use of all of the current journals in a particular library or collection by the library's own patrons, or if it is to evaluate local use of some portion of the collection compared to standard lists of the core journals in a field, the faculty's list of the key journals, or against citation data. Several articles in the literature deal with the logistics of analyzing citation data (Greene 1993), the creation of core journal lists and overlapping groups across disciplines (McCain 1991), as well as with the problems inherent in this kind of approach (MacRoberts and MacRoberts 1989).

Citation analysis may involve determining which journals the college or university's faculty (and perhaps graduate students) cite in the research they publish. This kind of analysis can be labor-intensive and time-consuming, and a library would probably only use it to evaluate the journals in a specific discipline. Nonetheless, it is possible to do some of the data collection using the online versions of Science Citation Index called SCI SEARCH along with a Rank command provided by Dialog (Schmidt et al. 1994, 47). Another form of citation analysis is the Impact Factor developed by the Institute for Scientific

Information (ISI). The Impact Factor is an indication of a journal's importance for a field based on the number of times articles in it are cited divided by the number of the articles in the journal in a specific period of time; these can be found in ISI's *Journal Citation Reports*. Results of studies comparing a library's reshelving data with citation data for those same journals can be less than conclusive. In one such study, "fifty percent of the titles on the 'most heavily used' list [developed as a result of a reshelving study] were on the list of cited journals, indicating a substantial degree of correspondence between the results of reshelving and the results of citation counting for the heavily used. However, the majority of the cited journals are not heavily used in [this] library, according to the reshelving study" (Swigger and Wilkes 1991, 46).

Other Approaches

Besides these methods of determining and evaluating local use of all or portions of the library's journal collection, some libraries have chosen to arrange to get statistics from their patrons' use of tools such as EBSCO's Magazine Articles database. Although a library user may search for and then print or download a particular citation for any given article, it does not necessarily follow that the patron will then go and actually read the journal article itself. Other libraries have occasionally asked faculty in certain departments to rank lists of journals from the major abstracting services in terms of importance; the results are compared against the library's holdings and can be illuminating or in such discrepancy with the collection as to not be of much value. It is worth bearing in mind that the outside rankings of journal titles and citation data may not be reflective of either the type of periodicals collection in the library or the particular focus it has, or of even in what kind of milieu it finds itself. A smaller academic library in an area rich with other academic resources may be able to get by with a more narrowly focused set of journal titles than a similar institution in a more isolated area that has to try to be all things to all patrons. This is another way of saying that local needs are often unique, and that local use patterns are local and can be influenced themselves by which courses are being taught in a given semester or what journals a visiting professor is using. A library's journals collection should have as its primary justification meeting the curricular and research needs of its students and faculty. Beyond that, aspiring to be a research-level collection is a bonus.

THE FUTURE

With all of the emphasis on new technologies and new forms of information, one may well ask if there will continue to be a need for local use studies and surveys. But to back up a step, one should first consider if and how technology has changed the data-gathering process. Certainly, hand-held scanners (light pens and wands) are more sophisticated and can now not only read but store and manipulate a certain amount of data—this alone making it easier to do title-level counts of in-house use of a collection. New statistical software packages make it easier to analyze data that may be already collected on how many searches are being done on which abstract and index databases; whether or not this can easily be analyzed at the individual journal title level is a another question. It is probably fair to say that computer technology allows for more detailed and precise analysis of certain kinds of data (citation data, journal costs, for example), but that other methods will persist for reshelving studies and others.

One could be brazen and ask the unaskable: if all of the core journal titles are available on the World Wide Web in five years' time, will there be a need for use studies at all? Perhaps the need to measure use of physical journal issues and volumes will diminish, but at that point, serials librarians will probably be looking for creative ways to obtain data on their patrons' access of online resources in order to justify the dollars being spent to provide this access. In the ideal world, these kinds of use statistics will be provided by the publisher or distributor of the journal as part of the total online access package.

REFERENCES

Dole, Wanda V., and Sherry S. Chang. 1996. "Survey and Analysis of Demand for Journals at the State University of New York at Stony Brook." *Library Acquisitions: Practice and Theory* 20, no. 1: 23–38.

Greene, Robert J. 1993. "Computer Analysis of Local Citation Information in Collection Management." *Collection Management* 17, no. 4: 11–22.

MacRoberts, Michael H., and Barbara R. MacRoberts. 1989. "Problems of Citation Analysis: A Critical Review." *Journal of the American Society for Information Science* 40, no. 5: 342–349.

McCain, Katherine W. 1991. "Core Journal Networks and Cocitation Maps: New Bibliometric Tools for Serials Research and Management." *Library Quarterly* 61, no. 3: 311–336.

Milne, Dorothy, and Bill Tiffany. 1991. "A Survey of the Cost-Effectiveness of Serials: A Cost-Per-Use Method and Its Results." *Serials Librarian* 19, nos. 3/4: 137–149.

Naylor, Maiken. 1990. "Assessing Current Periodical Use at a Science and Engineering Library: A dBASEIII + Application." *Serials Review* 16, no. 4: 7–19.

Naylor, Maiken. 1993. "A Comparison of Two Methodologies for Counting Current Periodical Use." *Serials Review* 19, no. 1: 27–34, 62.

Rogers, Sharon J., and Charlene S. Hurt. 1989. "How Scholarly Communication Should Work in the 21st Century." *Chronicle of Higher Education* (October 18): A56.

Schmidt, Diane, Elisabeth B. Davis, and Ruby Jahr. 1994. "Biology Journal Use at an Academic Library: A Comparison of Use Studies." *Serials Review* 20, no. 2: 45–64.

Simpson, Annette. 1988. "Academic Journal Usage." *British Journal of Academic Librarianship* 3, no. 1: 25–35.

Swigger, Keith, and Adeline Wilkes. 1991. "The Use of Citation Data to Evaluate Serials Subscriptions in an Academic Library." *Serials Review* 17, no. 2: 41–46, 52.

Tallman, Karen Dalziel, and J. Travis Leach. 1989. "Serials Review and the Three-Year Cancellation Project at the University of Arizona Library." *Serials Review* 15, no. 3: 51–60.

Ventress, Alan. 1991. "Use Surveys and Collection Analyses: A Prelude to Serials Rationalization." *Library Acquisitions: Practice & Theory* 15: 109–118.

Wiggins, Richard. 1995. Presentation on the Use of the World Wide Web. American Library Association Annual Conference, Chicago.

5

Collection Development or Collection Access: Serials Ownership in the Millennium

INTRODUCTION

For many years, one of the hallmarks of the prestigious research library has been the size of its collections; that is, the total number of volumes held (monographs, serials, microforms, and other materials), the number of new volumes cataloged and added annually, the number of active serials subscriptions, and other such measures of holdings. To be large and to have more was understood to be better. To a great extent this is still the case today, and academic libraries continue to be concerned about where they stand in the rankings appropriate to their type of library (Association of Research Libraries statistics, for example). However, new forms of publishing, greater concerns about costs, and ever easier access to an increasing diversity of materials through rapid document delivery options or on the World Wide Web are propelling librarians to rethink old assumptions about what materials need to be held locally and to reexamine past purchasing practices, often in favor of new interlending relationships, consortial partnerships, and document delivery packages from commercial sources. The World Wide Web has also had a great impact on the concept and emerging development of the "library without walls" or the virtual collection—available anywhere, anytime, wherever the user is. The business of the college or university is education, and by extension, the academic library's stock in trade is as the institution's primary information provider and broker. Increasingly, the library patron can locate this information while he or she is off-site and perhaps even relaxing in the comfort and convenience of his own study or bedroom. Libraries, therefore, must be sensitive to the increasing ubiquity of information as they strive to reshape and redefine their roles and their places in the university of the twenty-first century. "Libraries and librarians are best placed to organize and promote the flow of information, a fact that librarians have almost overlooked in their insistence on the fact of 'the library,' even though the building and its contents are now only one factor in the whole range of information services" (Martin 1995, 8). What then does this new technological environment hold for serialists?

Universities and colleges are actively engaged in reshaping their own agendas and identities, and many are planning for, if not already distributing, their faculty's wares (lectures, presentations) on cassette tape or over the Internet. This increased emphasis on "distance learning" holds out the possibility that an individual may be able to become certified in midwifery electronically, without ever attending a class in person; may analyze Greek poetry with interested students from around the world; or even track down esoteric citations to medieval law at 3:00 A.M., without ever leaving the bedroom. The university of ten years hence will be a far more interactive and mission-driven enterprise than the academic institution of 1995. Librarians, too, must heed the clarion call to be proactive and visionary, and to become leaders in these new endeavors as the campus administrators around them rethink and retool their own approaches to the delivery of education.

In the past fifteen years, serials collection development policy and practice have been greatly impacted by the several, or one might say, ongoing crises in serials journal prices (Houbeck 1987). Although serials prices had ebbed and flowed previously, it was not until the late 1970s and early 1980s that the combination of large serials collections, a weak dollar, and differential pricing came together to make serials librarians angry, wary, and eventually combative. Contributing to the severity of at least one recent crisis, in 1991, was the overall state of the U. S. economy. Recession-like conditions made state and local governments closely examine their budgets and many state-supported academic institutions had their budgets slashed. The cuts in college and university budgets necessitated by less income were often passed on, in part, to libraries who then had to decide which areas of their budgets to reduce. Since salaries are difficult to trim without putting individuals out of work, the acquisitions budget was an easily identifiable large item within the library budget that could be trimmed. During the decade of the 1980s, almost by accident, many academic libraries found that the percentage of acquisitions monies that was being expended for serials titles (especially journals) each year had been inching upward, and that the number of titles and amount of money spent on monograph titles was dwindling, sometimes to the point where libraries were not able to maintain reasonable levels of collecting in current literature and recent scholarly research. During the period from 1976 to 1988, the average amount expended for serials for members of the Association of Research Libraries (ARL) increased from

40.4 percent to 56.2 percent of the material budget (Okerson 1990). In 1988, for example, the average cost of a journal for one library was approximately $129; in 1993 it was $233, or an increase of 82 percent. In 1988, this same library subscribed to 3,313 journals for a cost of $426,000; in 1993, the library received 2,983 current journals and paid almost $700,000, again an increase of 82 percent (Walch 1993). Many libraries found themselves with materials expenditures so skewed toward serials that they eventually realized they could no longer continue to support the serials budgets at these levels at the expense of the monograph collections. Consequently, a wave of journal cancellation projects swept through academic libraries; cancellation projects of two and three hundred thousand dollars' magnitude were the norm at some institutions. Cancellations of this magnitude have repercussions in the publishing world and for other libraries; some titles die, some small publishers are forced out of business, other titles will need to be priced even higher to accommodate the reduced size of the subscription pool, and some publishers will explore, if they have not already, alternate means of publication.

Academic librarians responded to the serials pricing crisis in a variety of ways, but two initiatives stand out. One was the cooperation between member libraries and the Association of Research Libraries which functioned as mediator, communicator, communications funnel and clearinghouse to assist libraries in their desire to act as a group in indicating their displeasure to the publishers and to provide the heft of its hundred plus membership. The second initiative was the Aqueduct Action Agenda, a manifesto of first principles related to serials acquisitions and scholarly publishing which grew out of a meeting of librarians in Chapel Hill in 1992. The items in the agenda ranged from the most broad, "examine carefully all of the implications and ramifications of the access versus ownership debate," to the very specific, "analyze subscription invoices carefully and verify the accuracy of vendor service charges," and included the directive that librarians "engage library users in a continuing dialog about the issues associated with serials pricing" and thereby seek their assistance in identifying and then cancelling very costly titles ("Aqueduct Action Agenda" 1992).

This chapter will focus on the trends in serials collection building and particularly on the following: allocating money for serials, publishers' journal pricing policies, the emergence of new formats for serials and how they fit into the collection, and finally, on the impact of Internet resources on library access and ownership issues.

ALLOCATING MONEY FOR SERIALS

General Considerations

There are a variety of approaches an academic library may choose in allocating its materials budget and determining how much money will be spent on serials (Bustion et al. 1991, 75–89). Many academic libraries adopt the programmatic approach and allocate the materials budget in terms of broad areas within the curriculum (humanities, social sciences, engineering and physical sciences, health sciences, etc.). Other libraries may prefer a divisional approach which follows the school or departmental structure of the college or university—school of arts and sciences, business school, medical school, or chemistry, history, and philosophy departments—or some combination of these two. A more unusual method and one which perhaps better incorporates into the initial stages of the allocation the diversity of materials libraries collect (print, microform, electronic) is to allocate based on the users' needs for information; are the users in a particular discipline or school ''leisurely or in a hurry, focused or unfocused, prepared or unprepared, or knowledgeable or ignorant?'' (Martin 1995, 9). Asking these questions for each program or discipline enables the serials and selection staff to assess what types of resources will best meet their users' needs and what mix of print or more traditional formats and document delivery or online access meets their time and research needs. The particular approach taken will undoubtedly be a reflection of the size and focus of the library and the total size of its acquisitions or materials budget, as well as on the place of serials within the organization and who is responsible for serials selection. Regardless of which approach the library decides upon, there will still be constituencies that are sure they deserve or could spend more money than is being allocated.

The Allocation Process

The arrival at an annual budget for serials expenditures most likely will be a multistep process. In most colleges or universities, the director of libraries is required to submit a budget request for the entire library as part of the institution's overall budget planning process. This may be requested and submitted as much as six months ahead of the start of the next fiscal year. The chief bibliographer or head of collection development is often the individual charged with making a recommendation to the library director on how much monographs and serials prices are likely to increase in the coming year, and therefore how much greater the next year's acquisitions budget needs to be to maintain the status quo. This individual will probably find it useful to consult with his or her colleagues in serials and monograph acquisitions. The serials librarian or manager may then be asked to provide some early indication of the trends in serials prices and what a likely price increase might be in the next subscription year. Since publishers typically do not set their prices for the following calendar year until July or August of the previous year, obtaining accurate information in November or December of one year for the subscription year that begins in January more than a year hence is a little like taking a stab in the dark. Furthermore, most subscription agents do not provide even their earliest projections for the following year until about March, and even then these are just projections based on trends in the economy and the strength of the dollar against key foreign currencies. A determined serials manager might find it worthwhile to make a few selected calls to the library's primary serials agents to try to get an early reading on the probable increases. Other than the exchange rate for foreign publications, other factors that impinge on journal prices include increases in U.S. or foreign postal rates, increases in the cost of paper or shortages in the available paper supply, and, of course, increases in the number of pages or the number of issues included in a given title for the year.

Once the director or his or her designate has determined the total amount available for the next year's materials budget, then the process of allocating for specific funds or areas can be undertaken. This drawing up of budgets for individual departments (serials, acquisitions) and individual selectors or bibliographers can be handled by the collection development head or perhaps a broader-based group consisting of the collection development officer plus the head of technical services, the heads of serials and acquisitions, the budget officer, and others, as appropriate. For a library divvying up its budget for the first time or working to establish new categories for allocation, there will be a fair amount of guesswork as well as reliance on whatever figures are available on expenditures in previous years, even if these figures were not broken out or categorized in the same way in the new budget. Consideration should be given to the differing costs of materials by discipline; therefore, it is not unreasonable to allocate more money and/or a greater percentage increase to the science and technical areas than to the humanities and social sciences. The March 15 issue of *Library Journal* each year includes an analysis of periodical price increases overall, as well as separated out by discipline; it is a useful tool for determining the average cost of a title in a particular subject.

In order to allocate the monies fairly, setting general guidelines that address (1) the usual increase for all disciplines; (2) areas that need special allowances or an increased emphasis due to curriculum changes; and (3) whether or not some funds will be held aside in a reserve fund for special purchases, unforeseen increases in periodical prices, and the like will inform the process and more likely make the resulting budget more acceptable to all concerned. Decisions need to be reached about whether to maintain the status quo in purchasing power across all areas of the budget, whether there are programmatic areas that need to be reduced in allocation or expanded to reflect changes in curricula and programs, and whether or not there are new courses of study that need some additional seed money for buying older materials. If the library has particular strengths in a given area, such as German history, or wishes to develop a new area, thought needs to be given to how best to accomplish that and whether new money needs to be allocated for serials in that field. If the library participates in any book approval plans, how much, if any, monographic series material or other serial titles will be received through these plans? Or are serials specifically excluded from them? It is also possible to devise a formula for doing subject-based budgeting that takes into account a range of internal factors such as the number of faculty, the number of programs and student credit hours offered in each discipline, as well as external variables such as the cost of monographs and serials in the specific subject area and an indicator of the use of both by the relevant department (Rein et al. 1993). In order to use this kind of approach, however, there may need to be a significant investment of time in collecting the data to put into the formula the first time, and some ongoing maintenance of the figures so that the underlying assumptions are correct each year that the formula is in use.

Another, perhaps more important, question is which part of the budget is allocated first: monographs or serials? In recent years, many libraries have had a policy of estimating what their serials would cost (particularly the periodicals portion), allocating that amount for serials, and then leaving the rest for monographs. In this way, the serials were protected, but they also began to devour an increasing percentage of the budget, from 40 percent to 50 percent to 60 percent, and even as high as 70 percent for some libraries. At the same time, the purchase of current monographs fell off, and since many of these titles go out of print very quickly, the opportunity to add these monograph titles was lost. Due to the increased serials costs, libraries began to reexamine their budgeting practices and to realize that they could no longer allow the monograph collections to be undermined in this way. Out of this dilemma came the first cancellation projects. Today, some libraries have instituted an add one, cancel one policy. For every new serial title to be ordered, another title or titles of equal cost must be canceled first. Furthermore, libraries that have traditionally subscribed to multiple copies of heavily used titles, whether popular or scholarly, have begun to scrutinize more carefully whether these duplicate and triplicate subscriptions are really justifiable. In some cases, where branch libraries are scattered on a campus, there may still be a demonstrated need for a second or third copy of heavily used titles such as *Nature, Journal of Chemical Physics, Scientific American*, and others. The most difficult choices are often those decisions affecting interdisciplinary titles that will be used by the clientele of several different libraries. Consequently, almost every library and its serials selectors have become more cautious about how many and which new serials titles they add to the library's collection. It is also fair to say that in the years ahead, libraries will continue to be engaged in this kind of close scrutiny as part of the overall trend toward leaner budgets for academe and the need to pay more attention to costs in general.

A third consideration for apportioning money within the serials budget is the concept of an ideal balance in expenditures between serials and monographs; that is, should the split be 50–50 or is 60–40, books to serials, more desirable. Likewise, some would argue that there are desirable or maximum percentages of serials for each subject area. For example, if 95 percent of the physics budget is devoted to serials expenditures and only 5 percent to monographs, is this healthy? Is a better balance 85 percent for serials and 15 percent for books? Obviously, the publishing pattern of the particular discipline enters into determining the optimal percentages of differing types of material; many scientific and technical fields tend to be more journal oriented than fields such as English and philosophy. A library can set its own optimum percentages for its various subject areas, and then work to bring the allocation process in line with this over several years. There is probably not a single answer to this, and it will depend to some extent on the particular strengths or biases of the library's collection.

Impact of Electronic Publishing

Complicating the picture are the recent, fast-paced developments in electronic publishing. Academic libraries today more often have a choice among multiple formats for the same journal or index title, and must decide whether two formats are better than one or none and whether or when a virtual or online format is an appropriate or even preferable substitute for paper. This raises the issue of who pays for a physics title if it is mounted on a local library server or accessed on the Web. If it is a paper title, few would quibble with charging the physics serials fund; if it is an electronic journal devoted to physics, then again perhaps the cost should be taken from the subject fund. But if the paper journal title is currently being received at several different library branches on campus, and it is now also being made available on the Internet, then who pays for the electronic version? Which library (or do all) cancels its paper subscription and which library reaps the benefit of the savings, the likely difference in cost between the expensive paper subscription and the more reasonable charge for online access? The sheer fact that electronic journals are available outside the walls or boundaries of one library to all of the library community argues for some consideration of centralized payment for these titles out of some general electronic journal or electronic access fund.

With the proliferation of online journals, online databases, and other remote resources, chances are that the typical academic library is spending more on access to these electronic resources than five years ago, when many of them did not exist. This expenditure for online access or use will increase and the percentage spent on straight serials will probably decrease. As an example, the Duke University Library formerly spent 58–60 percent of its material budget for serials. In FY95/96, it spent 11 percent for access (for electronic materials of all sorts), and it predicts that this will converge with serials costs, and in a few years the materials budget expenditures will be split between 30 percent for access, 30 percent for serials, and a steady 40 percent for monographs (McCarthy 1995, 11).

SERIALS PRICES

Currency and Exchange Rates

With all of the attention paid to the effect on serials budgets of a fluctuating dollar in the past several years, publishers have been reexamining and sometimes modifying their pricing policies. More publishers are choosing a standard currency in which to price their journals, such as the U.S. dollar or the German Deutschemark. This one price is then in effect for the entire world. Also, partly as a direct result of pressure from the library community, many of the large journal publishers are committed to setting the next year's subscription price by August 15 of the previous year for the calendar subscriptions that begin in January of the next year. This enables libraries to have a clearer idea of exactly how much they will be spending for subscriptions in the following year, and it facilitates the budget planning process. Some foreign vendors who price in their own currency and service journals for libraries in the United States set a conversion rate in August of one year which is in effect for billing throughout the entire year. Regardless of whether the dollar rises or falls, the library has the advantage or disadvantage of the rate that was set the previous August. While this may temporarily cause a greater increase for some libraries, it should make for fairer pricing over the long term.

New Journals

For any new paper journal, there is generally a start-up time of from at least three to five to seven years, until the title is making a profit for the publisher. This is attributable to the high production costs associated with traditional journal publishing: labor costs, paper and printing, and postage have all increased significantly in recent years. If a journal in the scientific, technical, or medical arena is successful, then the publisher often feels an obligation to increase the size and/or frequency of the journal due to the amount of material waiting to be published. There are more scientists and engineers alive and working today than ever before in history, and this translates to a monumental research effort worldwide which then translates to many, many papers for publication. If a publisher increases the frequency of a title (monthly to bimonthly, for example) or the number of volumes per year (six volumes instead of four each with four issues), then that increase is generally passed along to the library in terms of a higher subscription price. This often happens with the journal titles that are already at the high end and priced at five or six hundred dollars per year or more. From the publisher's perspective, there is more material out there to be published (research in the United States has probably doubled in the last fifteen years), but libraries and individuals have insufficient funds to buy the additional research papers even if they were published (Cameron 1993, 23). In the past, nearly all of a publisher's revenue came from subscriptions (with 5 to 10 percent being realized from the sale of back issues). The reduction in library budgets has resulted in subscription cancellations which translates directly to a decline in publishers' revenues. "One major STM journal publisher [talked of a] 5% decline in subscription revenue annually for the foreseeable future" (Cameron 1993, 23). With economics like this, publishers are being forced to look at other forms of income such as document delivery services that include both paper copies and fax or electronic delivery.

Pricing Information Sources for Libraries

For collection specialists and serials librarians who are responsible for monitoring the current year's serials budget and planning for the probable increase in costs for the following year, keeping up with the serials price projections can be a dizzying and often confusing proposition. It sometimes seems that conflicting or, at best, varying information is being put forth by the various players in the pricing arena. In the past few years, the major subscription agents have all devoted more time and more press releases, and certainly more internal resources, to providing planning projections to their customers. Some vendors have also offered pricing seminars at the American Library Association midwinter and annual conferences. As one works with the vendors, one can begin to get a sense of how reliable a particular vendor's predictions are likely to be and whether or not the range of increases they predict is conservative or optimistic. It is worth bearing in mind that a particular library's mix of titles is usually not the same mix as the vendor's total portfolio and so the percentage increase will vary somewhat for that reason alone. Of course, there is a marketing element to all of this, since the vendor would prefer not to have libraries unhappy that they did not allow enough money for the increases for that year. Likewise, the vendor that is too conservative may have the benefit of a larger than needed prepayment from a library; this is money that the vendor can use rather than the library. As with most situations that result from a fluctuating economy and other factors beyond any individual corporation's control, planning the serials budget for the next fiscal year is at least one part gazing into the crystal ball.

All of the attention focused on serials prices has spawned at least one publication devoted solely to this topic. The *Newsletter on Serials Pricing Issues* is published electronically on a frequent, but not regular, basis and is available over the Internet by individual subscription. For the latest on currency trends, individual publishers' pricing practices, what individual libraries are doing to cope with increased costs, and the peculiarities of an individual journal's frequency and pricing policies, this newsletter is an invaluable source. Contributions from serials librarians and others are welcome and can be sent to the editor. ACQNET, an electronic network newsletter devoted to library acquisitions (primarily monographic acquisitions) also includes items of interest to serials practitioners. Another source of regular information on the pricing scene is the regular column in *Serials Review* entitled simply "Serials Prices." With the widespread use of electronic mail and easy access to the Internet, the latest developments now appear first in the online listservs and newsletters. In addition, most of the major periodicals vendors have instituted regular newsletter-type print publications which are mailed to their customers. Examples are: *At*

Your Service (EBSCO), *The Faxon Report,* and *BHB Review* (B.H. Blackwell). These announce new personnel, tout new products, and provide updates on periodical prices.

FORMAT CONSIDERATIONS

CD-ROMs

Ten years ago, the issue of format generally referred to paper versus microform and a library could decide to subscribe to paper and then purchase and retain a permanent copy in microfilm or microfiche. In recent years, several new formats have been introduced; of these new formats, the chief one that is tangible and not virtual or solely online is the CD-ROM (Compact Disc—Read Only Memory). CD-ROMs can store massive amounts of text and graphics, as well as sound, on what is a very small disk. The CD-ROM medium has become a popular and some might even say, preferred, format for index and abstract titles, and also for census data and maps. The ability to do complex searches across multiple years of a title using keyword and Boolean techniques, with the added benefit of being able to sort results according to user-determined parameters, makes this format appealing to the library user, while its small size is an advantage to libraries facing shelving constraints. Although CD-ROMs initially were limited in use to a single workstation, there are a variety of LAN (Local Area Network) packages available that allow a library to link CDs and make them searchable by multiple users simultaneously, and a number of libraries have experimented with this approach as a way to link their CD-ROMs. Doing this enables users in multiple locations to access the same CD-ROM title and therefore expands the use of a given CD-ROM title beyond an individual workstation and may, even with the increased cost of the network, make the per-use cost of the title less. Examples of CD-ROM titles run the gamut from *Reader's Guide to Periodical Literature* to *The Foreign-Born Population in the United States* (summary tape file data from the 1990 Census), to the *Toxic Release Inventory.* Most CDs contain the necessary software to search and access the data on the disk, but occasionally the library must provide this software.

With the proliferation of titles available on CD, the serials librarian and collection development staff may well confront the issue of duplication. Many libraries acquired indexes and abstracts on CD as supplements to the print titles and maintained subscriptions to both versions. As serials budgets have been squeezed by rising prices, librarians have been forced to face the duplication question. If the counterpart of *Psychological Abstracts,* the CD-ROM title, PsycLit, is in the library's collection, does the library need to continue receiving the paper title? Are there differences in coverage between the print and the electronic versions? Can the library justify the cost of both of these products? These are difficult questions and the response of libraries has ranged from the conservative (keep both) to the pragmatic (only one format is justified in the current budget environment). A recent article in *Serials Review* details some of the cost considerations for various titles offered on CD-ROM (Getz 1992).

In the late 1990s, however, the CD-ROM may well represent a format that increased in popularity and use, had its heyday, and now is being pushed aside by more online access through the Internet, specifically on the World Wide Web. This is not to say that new titles are not being offered on CD-ROM; they are, but some titles that might once have been issued on CD are bypassing that format and being mounted on the WWW, or are being published simultaneously in a CD-ROM version and on the Web. One example of a heavily used title that is being distributed in multiple formats is the *Monthly Catalog of United States Government Publications*. In 1996, the coverage in the paper title was reduced significantly, but simultaneously, the title is being offered on the Web. In addition, there are at least two commercial CD-ROM versions of the title: *GPO Monthly Catalog* (from OCLC) and *GPO on SilverPlatter*. A fuller discussion of the utility of the CD-ROM as a collection medium can be found in a later chapter.

Floppy Disks

The computer floppy disk is also being used selectively for both journal publishing as well as for some U.S. government-issued periodical titles. Examples are: *Current Contents*, a commercial publication from ISI which is sold in both IBM and Macintosh versions, and the U.S. Geological Survey *Professional Papers*, a series available on depository, of which selected issues are being provided on floppy disks. In general, however, the floppy has not gained wide acceptance as the medium of choice for publication of journals.

Also of concern in the format debate is the issue of permanency, that is, the life span of a CD-ROM disk or a floppy disk and the possibility that this technology will inevitably be replaced by some newer format. Will libraries with CD-ROM files be left with a format that becomes outdated and unusable and hence with information that is inaccessible? Will the current floppy disks be replaced by a different kind of disk? Little has been written about this issue, but certainly there is a heightened awareness of the need for technical standards for CD-ROMs just as there are standards for the various kinds of microforms. Currently, there are several technical standards for CD-ROMs, and one only hopes that these will persist as long as the medium is actively in use.

Computer Tape Files

In lieu of databases on CD-ROM, many libraries have opted to load entire journal article database files locally. Examples are the Wilson indexes (*Reader's Guide, Humanities Index*, etc.) and ABI Inform (a business database). The library places a tape subscription with the publisher or distributor, and each month receives the latest indexing to mount on its own machine. The advantages of locally loaded databases are twofold: (1) multiple users can access the database simultaneously from many different locations, either in the library or from their homes or offices; and (2) there is often a link between the journals indexed and the home library's holdings, which enables the user to know immediately if the library owns the particular journal from which the article is being indexed. Like CD-ROM files, computer tape databases offer a range of searching options and the ability to print and download result files to one's own disk. Given the expense of both leasing and loading computer tape files, a library's decision to purchase such a file is a often a distributed responsibility with a special committee or group making recommendations on which files should be purchased. Database files are usually treated like subscriptions and in addition to an initial fee for load programs or special software, there is one annual cost and then the library receives regular updates. If present, the link to the local library's serials holdings gives these databases real added value. The best holdings link is a straightforward link between the ISSN in the database citation and the ISSN in the bibliographic record in the local library's OPAC. This results in the holdings portion of the library's bibliographic record displaying in its entirety, which lets the patron see the particular volumes the library holds, not just the title itself. Other ways of providing holdings information as part of a citation database search require that the library enter some holdings notation into the database record for each title covered that it owns. This gives the patron the advantage of knowing that the title is held locally, but does not usually provide the full holdings statement as in the other, more direct link to the bibliographic record.

Format and Budget Considerations

As has been noted earlier, there are some libraries that have decided to divide their budget among serials, monographs, and access or electronic resources. The issues involved in deciding how best to allocate for and track the expenditures for electronic and other formats are several. When the material (books, journals, microforms) ordered by one branch library is to be housed and used in that site, it seems reasonable that it be paid for solely out of funds assigned to that location; when the format of the title (tape file, electronic journal, or electronic access) means that it will be used by students or faculty from several different schools or departments and its location is only online where it is accessible by anyone affiliated with the institution, then either centralized funding or a division of the charges based on the probable percentage of users from different areas or branch libraries seems advisable. Some examples are *Current Contents*, available on floppy disk or as a tape-loaded file in the library's own online database, and full-text journals or reference titles (the *Oxford English Dictionary*, for one) available electronically. It is both a serious consideration for the library and an exciting one to decide how to budget for electronic formats. If they are not CD-ROM titles housed in one location, but computer tapes available through the online catalog, who pays for them? Should the money for computer tapes be part of the materials budget at all or should there be some separate electronic budget? If they are not paid out of the materials budget, then who is doing the selection? It would seem that they indeed are materials, and that having them in the acquisitions budgeting process helps ensure that the selection, probably done by a group rather than an individual, is overseen by bibliographers and that provision is made for whatever equipment is required to use or view the material. Given the fact that many integrated systems are now making it possible to access computer databases as options from a full selection menu screen that also includes the online catalog, there may be a resurgence of interest in this database format and some lessening of interest in networking of CD-ROM titles. Some systems vendors have developed software whereby this multiple database access allows for a link to the library's own holdings by matching on the ISSN field. This makes for a powerful search tool with results that can be found in the user's home library.

With the widespread use of the World Wide Web and the library's ability locally to point or link to files and text elsewhere, the library needs to consider even further which electronic resources it needs to purchase and maintain locally, which ones it is sufficient just to point to, and which ones it can safely ignore, since they are not within the scope of the library's collection development policy. To date, the vast majority of electronic journals are free, free to the local library for the work of setting up and maintaining the link on the URL (Uniform Resource Locator). In the past year, there has been a geometric increase in the number of paid electronic journals, and consequently, academic libraries have had to weigh more carefully what to add, what the additional cost of the electronic version is, what kind of online backfile exists for an electronic title, and whether or not to cancel a corresponding paper subscription. Previously, it was a simple matter to recommend a new electronic journal to the appropriate subject bibliographer, have that recommendation be accepted, and then link the title to the library's home page. The University of Pennsylvania Library, for example (http://www.library.upenn.edu/resources/ej/xej-index.html), has an extensive list of links to more than 1,000 journals and newspapers, arranged both alphabetically and by subject. Only a small percentage of these are purchased titles for which the library pays a fee to gain access or is given access by virtue of having already paid for a print subscription. In these cases, use of the electronic title is generally limited to individuals associated with the university, and the access is provided based on looking at the IP (Internet Protocol) address to see if the user's address is part of the university's domain. This area too is evolving rapidly as more players enter the e-journal arena; in addition to publishers and consortia, subscription vendors, too, are looking to carve out a role for themselves. B.H. Blackwell, for example, hopes to entice libraries to let it be the intermediary with e-journal publishers and will act as the distributor for about 300 such journals beginning in January 1997. Blackwell will assume responsibility for all of the local access issues (IP address checking, special logons if required) as well as sending payment to the publishers. Other subscription agents are sure to follow.

RESOURCE SHARING

RLG Conspectus

Collection development librarians and directors have made a lot of noise about shared collection development and shared resources over the years, but there have not always been tangible results to show for the concern. Libraries within the Research Libraries Group (RLG) have been involved over the years with a number of conspectus projects to determine individual member libraries' holdings in key subject areas. Disciplines surveyed include German-language materials and chemistry titles. Libraries participating assigned a rank to the strength of their holdings (monographic and serial) within various areas of the discipline and, for certain serials titles, agreed that they would retain those titles for a set period of time. If a library decided to withdraw or not receive any of these titles, it agreed to notify RLG. Shared collection development is a sound idea in theory, but many libraries pay only lip service to it, feeling that in a crunch, even though the library 30 miles away owns the title and it could be borrowed on interlibrary loan, their patrons really need to have it on-site at all times. Thus, the concept of "ownership" versus "access" has held sway. Concurrently, the annual statistics reported and published by the Association of Research Libraries highlight which libraries own the greatest numbers of volumes. Colleges and universities have emphasized their own libraries' positions in the rankings, and consequently, "ownership," having the title or the volume, is a primary concern. There have been no prizes awarded for the library doing the greatest amount of borrowing on interlibrary loan. Times are changing, however, and the ongoing concern about periodicals prices and how much of a budget a library can allow them to consume (combined with the increased sophistication of transmission technology, and also the development of the RLG Ariel workstation for interlibrary loan for transmitting ILL documents via the Internet more quickly than with conventional fax machines), may together be the key ingredients for a shift in perception and behavior. Some individuals have even gone so far as to suggest that the ARL size of collection rankings should be abolished if the emphasis continues to be on access rather than ownership.

Document Delivery and Full Text

In addition to advances in transmission technology, document delivery a la the Web and its counterpart, the provision of full text in general, have emerged as the new frontiers, the latest way to supply readers with the periodical articles they need, in a timely fashion. The pioneer in this effort was the CARL System based in Denver. For several years now, members and subscribers to CARL (now UnCover) have had access to a database of articles that has increased in size to over two million citations from more than 10,500 journal titles. By searching UnCover, users have the ability to identify articles of interest for their research; now, users will be able to order copies of particular articles to be faxed to them within 24 hours or less. Access to UnCover2, as the new service is called, is possible from library terminals or home computers and the cost can be charged to a personal Mastercard or Visa, or to a library account or a deposit account. The price of getting the article includes payment to the copyright holder. In addition, some articles, which are so noted, are available for one-hour turnaround. The timeliness with which this information can be made available will have a significant impact on a library's interlibrary loan activity and may well reenergize the debate over which titles need to be held locally and which can be accessed remotely. There are those skeptics, however, who maintain that the research process benefits from the serendipity in searching the stacks and that the size and scope of a library's journal collection is still a valid measure of its richness and value. It may well be that rich collections will continue to grow richer, but that smaller collections will become more dependent upon store-houses of periodical literature held elsewhere and acquired and printed upon demand. In a further step, several institutions outside Colorado have been experimenting with accessing UnCover from their own libraries, and in one case, the UnCover gateway provides ownership and location information for all titles already held in the home library.

Other vendors, especially the periodical subscription vendors who have seen some shrinkage in their business, are also becoming players in the document arena. EBSCO has recently begun marketing its own EBSCODoc service, a commercial document delivery service that will attempt to obtain any kind of material (serials, monographs, gray literature, conference proceedings) from anywhere for a price. The library that chooses to use this service can set limits on how much it is willing to spend for a document and how long it wishes it to search. EBSCO has an in-house database of articles, links with some particular libraries across the country, and other special sources upon which to draw. Furthermore, document requests can be initiated on the Web by individuals who wish to set up an account and pay themselves and through libraries who decide to subscribe to the service. Likewise, the Faxon Company has a current awareness service called Finder FlashTOC through which individuals may receive tables of contents from any of more than 11,500 journal titles weekly by e-mail or fax. In addition to these offerings, EBSCO, the Information Access Company (IAC), and UMI all have other full-text search and retrieval services that are still in their infancy. These products typically include a mix of titles, all of which are indexed and have abstracts online, but only some of which are full text. Increasing the number of full-text titles of interest to the greatest number of clients is the key as each vendor seeks to position its product as the most desirable. Other differences include whether or not the graphic materials (charts and graphs) are indexed. Two of these vendors have Web versions of their products today while the other's Web site will debut in several months.

THE YEAR 2000 AND BEYOND

How rapidly will the transformation from paper to electronic publication occur and where will libraries be five years from now? What about electronic journals, for example? Will their proliferation change the work and the role of serialists? How will all of this impact on collection development? In what formats will we be acquiring? What will be optimal and what will be the hardware and software costs to libraries? Will libraries really be able to own less provided they can provide access? Presently, the Association of Research Libraries (ARL) statistics still place the emphasis on what a library *has* in terms of volumes added, current serials subscriptions, and so on, and not on what the lending or sharing activity has been. Do librarians need to become cybrarians—a term the author of a recent newspaper article on computing and libraries used to identify her profession? What must librarians do to continue to be perceived as valued players in the university's enterprise? Why should administrators look to librarians to gather, point to, and index this information when it becomes ever easier to locate more of it on one's own without the librarian as intercessor and intermediary? Answering these and other questions regarding the role of academic librarians and serials specialists, in particular, is the critical challenge we all face in the next five years.

REFERENCES

"Aqueduct Action Agenda." 1992. *Newsletter on Serials Pricing Issues*, NS24.2.

Bustion, Marifran, Tanya Wiggins, Jeanne Harrell, and Suzanne D. Gyeszly. 1991. "Methods of Serials Funding: Formula or Tradition?" *Serials Review* 17, no. 1: 75–89.

Cameron, Jamie. 1993. "The Changing Scene in Journal Publishing." *Publishers Weekly* 240, no. 22: 23–24.

Getz, Malcolm. 1992. "Electronic Publishing: An Economic View." *Serials Review* 18, nos. 1/2: 25–30.

Houbeck, Robert L., Jr. 1987. "If Present Trends Continue: Responding to Journal Price Increases." *Journal of Academic Librarianship* 13, no. 4: 214–220.

Ivins, October. 1990. "Do Serials Vendors' Policies Affect Serials Pricing?" *Serials Review* 16, no. 2: 7–27.

Lenzini, Rebecca. 1990. "Serials Prices: What's Happening and Why." *Collection Management* 12, nos. 1/2: 21–29.

Martin, Murray S. 1995. *Collection Development and Finance: A Guide to Strategic Library-Materials Budgeting*. Chicago and London: American Library Association.

Martin, Murray S. 1992. "The Invasion of the Library Materials Budget by Technology

Serials and Databases: Buying More with Less?'' *Serials Review* 18, no. 3: 7–17.

McCarthy, Connie Kearns. 1995. ''In the Face of Change.'' *Insitute of Physics Publishing Library Newsletter* (August): 10–11.

Moline, Sandra R. 1989. ''The Influence of Subject, Publisher, Type and Quantity Published on Journal Prices.'' *Journal of Academic Librarianship* 15, no. 1: 12–18.

Okerson, Ann. 1990. ''Report on the ARL Serials Project.'' *Serials Librarian* 17, nos. 3/4: 111–119.

Ratzan, Lee. 1995. ''The Internet Cafe: What a Tangled Web We Weave When First We Practice to Perceive.'' *Wilson Library Bulletin* 69, no. 5: 66–67, 125.

Rein, Laura O. et al. 1993. ''Formula-Based Subject Allocation: A Practical Approach.'' *Collection Management* 17, no. 4: 25–48.

Thompson, James C. 1989. ''Confronting the Serials Cost Problem.'' *Serials Review* 15, no. 1: 41–47.

Walch, David B. 1993. ''Inflation, Budget Cuts, and Faculty Needs.'' *College and Research Libraries News* 54, no. 3: 125.

6

Acquiring Serials in Paper: Making the Most of the Options

INTRODUCTION

The chief function of the serials department or serials ordering unit, wherever it may be placed organizationally in the library, is to obtain those serials the library decides to add to its collection. This requires knowing the likely sources for this material, choosing the most reliable supplier for the best price, and then negotiating through the thicket of service charges, discounts, shipping costs, and subscription terms that publishers and vendors offer. In the late 1990s, the vast majority of serials still are received in paper; with the growth in electronic publishing, however, the number of new titles added in paper to a given library's collection may begin to decline. This chapter, therefore, deals exclusively with serial material acquired in paper, the format that has dominated and continues to dominate the processing stream of serials operations at the present time; serials in other formats are discussed in another chapter.

Although smaller academic libraries may entrust the responsibility for ordering all materials to one central acquisitions department, larger libraries traditionally have been likely to separate out the serials acquisitions responsibility; this practice of separating ordering by material type, however, is being critically reevaluated in many academic libraries as part of overall reengineering and restructuring projects. In some libraries, the serials acquisitions function, formerly grouped with serials receipt and cataloging, has been recombined with monograph acquisitions to create a mega- or super-acquisitions and receiving operation. Most technical services operations in libraries of any size are under increasing pressure from library and campus administrators to reexamine all of the tasks they perform, to eliminate unnecessary steps, and ultimately in some significant ways, to simplify and streamline the work flow, and simultaneously reduce costs. These kinds of discussions and any changes resulting from them will have an impact on the library's serials processing operations.

WHAT IS A SERIAL?

Although libraries may evolve their own local interpretations of what constitutes a serial, the AACR2 definition remains a solid base from which to proceed. It states that a serial is:

A publication in any medium issued in successive parts bearing numeric or chronological designations and intended to be continued indefinitely. Serials include periodicals; newspapers; annuals (reports, yearbooks, the journals, memoirs, proceedings, transactions, etc., of societies); and numbered monographic series. (AACR2 1988, 622)

This is an all-encompassing definition, and, in fact, a given library may choose to alter this definition somewhat in order to meet local operational needs. In an article dealing with choosing a vendor, McKinley offers the following test as one way of determining what is received in a serials unit: "serials staffs should be able to record receipt of incoming material in some *ordinal* [italics supplied] manner—by number, date, season, or even sign of the zodiac. Unfortunately, there will be unavoidable exceptions. An example is unnumbered extra material received on memberships or as supplements. Still, serials librarians should try to accept orders for numbered or dated material only" (McKinley 1990, 51). Internal library distinctions among types of serials may determine which library unit is responsible for acquiring specific types of serials and from what source. Nonetheless, the key element for deciding what is treated as a serial is that it have a number or a volume or a year; most serials departments do not handle unnumbered monographic series for this reason. Recording receipt of an unnumbered item that has not been ordered by its own title or author requires that the staff member doing the receipt note at least a brief title; this is not a particularly sophisticated or precise method for showing receipt to anyone but staff. Unnumbered titles on standing order are also difficult to track and maintain since the order of volumes published is not always apparent.

In many libraries, periodicals are handled separately, and what constitutes a periodical is determined by the local library. A widely accepted definition of a periodical is a title which is a collection of individual articles and which is published at least twice a year. In other libraries, the monographic series titles are separated out from other serials and, along with monographic sets (collections of an author's works or encyclopedias), may be handled by the monograph acquisitions unit or department. When distinctions are made among the subcategories of serials, it is usually because the method of payment and the common practices governing their receipt are different, as shall be discussed further. It is usual practice for the serials ordering unit to order all serial titles regardless of format: paper, microform, CD-ROM, floppy disk, and other electronic formats.

TOOLS FOR SERIALS ACQUISITIONS

For a general discussion of serials acquisitions policies and procedures, see the relevant sections of *Acquisitions Management and Collection Development in Libraries* (Magill and Corbin 1989). There is also a brief ALA guide on acquiring serials and periodicals (ALCTS 1992). The journal *Library Acquisitions and Practice* and the listservs SERIALST and ACQNET are also useful resources for staying current with the latest trends and issues in the acquisitions area. For information on specific serials vendors, more and more companies are posting descriptions of their services on the World Wide Web; Faxon, EBSCO, and Readmore, for example, have home pages that present in capsule form who they are, what they do, and also point to a variety of other helpful guides and publishers' catalogs. Faxon has a wealth of information on standards related to serials as part of its offerings, while Readmore provides links to several listservs as well as to related journals about serials publishing, such as *Against the Grain.* EBSCO's site details its subscriptions services and also includes descriptions of its document delivery and publishing services.

Librarians find out about new serials in a variety of ways, some of the most common of which are publishers' brochures, sample issues, reviews in library professional journals and scholarly publications, and recommendations from faculty. New serials are reviewed in scholarly journals in specific disciplines, and in library-related journals, such as *Choice, Publishers Weekly*, and *Library Journal.* Many serials departments subscribe to second copies of one or all of these titles to be used as selection tools; others route the main copy to the appropriate individuals before the issue goes to the public shelves. Libraries are also deluged with print circulars, publishers' catalogs, and sample issues, all of which serve to highlight the existence of new titles; most often, the serials department is the primary beneficiary of this influx of mail. Since the selection process or culling to decide which new titles to add is usually the responsibility of bibliographers or subject selectors or others outside serials, the serials staff handle the task of sorting and routing this material to the appropriate individuals. The selectors may route a flyer back to the serials department and request that a sample issue be acquired for review. Given the amount of money that goes into serials subscriptions and the fact that serials are usually purchased with the intent of continuing to receive them indefinitely, reviewing a sample issue can be a cost-effective way to evaluate likely candidates for inclusion in the collections as well as titles that are borderline for consideration. Most reputable publishers will send a sample issue free of charge; occasionally, a publisher will ask for the cost of the issue in advance or will send the issue with an invoice. If the library receives a sample copy with an invoice and did not previously request or agree to pay for this sample, then the library has no obligation to pay for the issue or to return it (the returning of an unsolicited sample copy is a courtesy beyond the call of duty).

Some libraries rely almost exclusively on faculty recommendations for new titles; others use a combination of recommendations from faculty and decisions made by bibliographers or collection development staff. Even if collection development staff are the primary selectors, faculty recommendations are closely scrutinized and usually rejected only for very compelling reasons.

CHOOSING A VENDOR

Domestic or Foreign

In selecting a vendor for periodicals and other serials, the serials librarian will want to consider whether to use a domestic vendor that also handles titles from abroad or to choose a vendor in the country of origin of the publication. Most U.S. vendors state that they can service publications from all over the world; this has been true of both EBSCO and Faxon, for example, and these companies have had regional offices in parts of Europe and Asia for many years. The sale of Faxon's foreign offices to Swets in summer 1994, and the subsequent sale of the rest of the Faxon Company to Dawson should not affect the range of titles a library is able to order through the Faxon Company. For a library with a smaller collection, it may make excellent sense to consolidate all of its periodical orders with one vendor based in the United States. This means fewer account representatives with whom to deal, more meaningful and more comprehensive management reports, and fewer invoices to process. If the foreign titles to which this library subscribes are fairly mainstream and not esoteric ones, they can probably be well serviced by a domestic vendor. Also, by selecting a single vendor for all its periodicals or even all of its serials, the library has the possibility of more favorable terms for service charges and discounts as well as the advantage of building a relationship with one account representative and one customer service individual.

Larger libraries have the choice, as do smaller ones, of dealing with one primary vendor or with many vendors. Even though the domestic agents state their willingness and ability to handle orders from anywhere in the world, the large library may still wish to deal with a vendor based in the country of publication, the reason being that such a vendor knows better the language of the country, has a greater familiarity with the publishing milieu of that region, and may have built up valuable contacts within the publishing industry over many years. Since it is desirable to be able to contact and talk with someone in the vendor office, a library choosing to use country of origin vendors will want to find out whether the vendor has a representative or office in the United States.

If not, the next best thing is an e-mail address for someone who will correspond in English. In the past couple of years, the number of vendors and agents with electronic mail addresses on the Internet has increased dramatically, and this is changing how librarians deal with their vendors both abroad and here in the United States. Previously, foreign vendors were more apt to make heavy use of faxing letters if rapid communication was required. E-mail, however, enables library staff to communicate more quickly with any vendor, but especially foreign ones, and can greatly reduce the communication time for claims. If a foreign vendor does not have someone who can conduct effective correspondence with American libraries, however, then many of the advantages of dealing with a country of origin vendor may be negated. Other options for communicating with foreign vendors, besides the postal service, include telephone and facsimile. B.H. Blackwell, for example, with its headquarters in Oxford, England, has a toll-free number to its Help Desk in New Jersey. A librarian can relay his or her concern to staff at this number who then call or fax the offices in England. Likewise, the Harrassowitz company has two customer service individuals based on the East Coast who can deal with some problems while relaying others to Germany. Other vendors make frequent use of the fax machine to resolve customers' questions and problems quickly.

Selecting a Particular Vendor

A good resource for locating vendors who handle material from specific countries is the most recent edition of *International Subscription Agents* (Wilkas 1994); this handbook is arranged by country and includes detailed information on the services offered and the particular countries or regions served. Asking a serials librarian at another institution about the service he or she has experienced with a vendor can be a valuable piece of the information-gathering process. For more detailed information on the specifics of purchasing serials and working with subscription agencies, another resource is *Buying Serials: A How-To-Do-It Manual for Librarians* (Basch and McQueen 1990).

Service and Discounts

The best recommendation, by far, for any vendor is that the company provides superb service—orders placed promptly, claims handled expeditiously, invoices accurately prepared—and employs knowledgeable, courteous staff. The best way to assess a vendor's track record is to talk with several current customers. Most reputable vendors are delighted to supply the names of several customers in the prospective client's region. In a very large company with a highly dispersed sales staff, it is always possible that the company's reputation may be colored by one librarian's experience with a particular company representative; multiple references may mitigate the effect of one negative comment. It is useful to explore not only who the library's particular sales representative would be, but to meet him or her to discuss the details of the service the vendor would provide. One option is to give the vendor a list of titles to quote for service. In the case of periodicals, this could be the entire subscription list or a portion relative to that vendor's area of coverage. The vendor should then be able to give the library a quotation on what the service charge would be for this title list and to outline any other terms of the service, including what reports would be provided (claim reports, price histories, etc.) and how often. For standing orders, the library might provide a representative list of the types of titles it would expect to order from this vendor or a list of the specific titles that might be ordered new or transferred from an existing vendor. In this case, the library can expect that the standing order vendor or dealer will be prepared to discuss standard discounts on materials (if there is one), who pays for the shipping costs (the library or the vendor or is it split between the two parties), how returns are to be dealt with, and whether or not there are any per-item handling charges. Again, the serials librarian will want to know what kinds of reports the vendor supplies and how often. How is the library informed of delays in publication and what is the procedure for dealing with standing order claims? Finally, does the standing order dealer provide a summary of volumes shipped or the total amount billed on some predetermined frequency or are these reports that can be requested on an as-needed basis?

In any evaluation of vendors, it is important to find out from the beginning what the standard discounts are for serials, how service charges for periodicals are determined, and what some standard percentages are, as well as how postage, shipping costs, and other charges may be apportioned. Generally, there is a direct correlation between the amount of the business the library does, and the size of discount or service charge. Having this information from the outset can eliminate possible misunderstandings later on.

PERIODICAL SUBSCRIPTIONS

Ordering

Periodicals are usually the most straightforward serials to order. The library pays in advance for a subscription period of one year or several years, and the issues arrive unbound according to a predetermined, regular frequency. Having said this, it is important to acknowledge that there are many exceptions to the assumed regularity of a periodical title. Sometimes periodicals become irregular in frequency, sometimes the format or the title changes, sometimes an issue goes astray in the mail or in the internal delivery within the library, and occasionally, the issue in hand does not clearly indicate how many pieces are published each year. Nonetheless, perhaps 85 percent of a library's periodical publications will follow a predictable pattern.

In acquiring periodicals, the library again has the option of subscribing directly with the publisher or placing the order with a subscription vendor. Most libraries opt to use a vendor for the vast majority of their periodical titles for several reasons. The vendor will place the order and it will: (1) continue forever, or (2) continue until the publication ceases, or (3) continue until the library cancels the title, whichever of the three possibilities occurs first. Second, the vendor will provide an annual renewal list for review and an annual renewal invoice; this saves the library staff the trouble and work of receiving and processing individual invoices from the publisher, invoices which might not clearly indicate what time period is being billed. Also, the vendor will deal directly with the publisher on claims for missing or damaged issues; this not only should save the library the work of multiple phone calls and letters, but allows the library to take advantage of the vendor's greater leverage with the publishers. Finally, a good vendor will supply management reports on the library's subscriptions. Examples of these reports include: three-year price histories showing yearly or cumulative increases, breakdowns of the library's titles by price (most expensive to least) or by country of publication, library fund code, or other criteria. An informed vendor will also alert the library to forthcoming title changes (if the publisher has passed that information along), and will keep its library clients aware of pricing and currency exchange developments. With all of the fluctuations in the world currency markets and the vacillating and often weakening dollar, subscription agents have devoted more attention to providing early, timely, and frequently updated predictions on price increases and foreign exchange rates for the next year. This has been greatly facilitated by the existence of listservs available through e-mail, since the most current information can be distributed out to a wide audience very quickly. This is not to say that most vendors don't still send a printed letter to their clients detailing these predictions; it just arrives so much faster electronically!

Developing a close working relationship with a vendor and the vendor's account representative can make processing periodicals smoother and more efficient for the library. Using a vendor for periodical titles also, indirectly, increases the library's clout in dealing with publishers, since the vendor may handle hundreds of subscriptions for a given title. Periodical vendors usually set up the orders so that the publisher mails the issues directly to the library, but some vendors, especially foreign ones, will receive the periodicals from the publishers first, check for missing issues, and then send the issues on to the library once a week or more frequently. Vendors who gather the material before sending it usually include a delivery list of what titles and issues have been sent.

In placing a subscription for a new title, the library needs to specify with which volume and year the subscription is to begin. There is a significant amount of lead time or delay from when the library places a subscription order with the vendor to when it is received, processed, and sent to the publisher, and when the first issue is actually received in the library. It is advisable to start an order with the first issue of the next volume to be published or with the beginning of the calendar year, taking into account the frequency and publication schedule of the title. For frequently published titles, such as weeklies, requesting that an order begin with the next available issue is also an option. This means that the library is willing to take "potluck" in terms of which issue the subscription starts with, but it usually also means that the issues begin to be received that much sooner. Some subscription agents are more receptive than others to trying to get back issues for the library. Therefore, it is better to start the new order with issues published within the previous year only and not go back in time. If other back issues are desired or a backfile order is to be placed to get volumes one through five (if the current volume is number six, for example), then this is best done as a separate order either to the vendor (if it handles this sort of request) or directly to the publisher.

Service Charges

A subscription agent makes its profit on the difference between the subscription price the library pays and the discounted price the publisher charges the agent, and on the fees it charges the library to provide service on the titles. Usually, the library pays a certain percent of the total cost of all of the titles it receives to the vendor to cover the handling of these titles. The service charge depends upon the size of the library's account with the vendor as well as on the particular mix of titles. The vendor may get a significant discount on the price it pays from some of the scientific, technical, and medical publishers, and if there are a lot of these titles in the library's list, this helps to reduce the overall service charge. Although humanities titles, for example, are inexpensive compared to scientific titles, they are usually not discounted to the vendor, often require more service from the vendor than scientific titles, and hence, have a service charge associated with them. Service from the vendor may be required because the publication pattern is irregular, the publication is slow or delayed, or the place of publication may move with the editor every several years. The percentage of titles for which the vendor receives a discount, compared to the titles that have no discount and are harder to service, contribute to making up the library's service charge. If a library is choosing a subscription vendor for the first time or looking to make a change from one vendor to another, it is prudent to have several vendors review the library's title list and provide a quotation for the list including what percent service charge will be levied. Sometimes a vendor will guarantee a low service charge for several years in the interest of getting the library's business. One effect of the sluggishness of the U.S. economy over the past few years and the significant cancellation activity by academic libraries is that many publishers have had to reduce the size of their discounts to subscription vendors, and consequently, the vendor's cost of doing business has increased, resulting in higher service charges to individual libraries.

The issue of service charges can be a sensitive one, and recent discussions have centered on what exactly constitutes a service charge. There is a certain mystique associated with service charges, and, some serials librarians have become quite assertive in working to dispel this perceived haziness and in trying to pinpoint all the variables a vendor uses in arriving at the service charge. It has been suggested that the vendor should unbundle service charges and allow libraries to negotiate and pay for only the specific services they actually use. Using this approach, if a library wishes to receive a three-year price history report once a year, but is not interested in receiving any other vendor reports, the library would pay for that one report and not for all of the others. A thorough discussion of this concept of unbundling can be found in the article "Unbundling Serials Vendors' Service Charges: Are We Ready?" (Barker 1990). Whether or not a library feels it is necessary to have all of its service charges separated out and priced individually or shown billed on a title-by-title basis (which is generally an option on the renewal invoice), it is to the library's advantage to have the serials librarian closely monitoring what is paid for service and questioning any sudden increases or decreases from one year to another.

Billing Options for Periodicals

Subscription vendors offer different billing plans depending on, for example, whether or not the library wishes to receive one annual invoice only or will deal with what are called added charges or supplemental invoices. In the latter situation, the library receives additional invoices if the title increases in price between the time of the initial billing and the start of the subscription period. If the library would like to receive just one renewal invoice and to, in effect, lock in the price, the library generally agrees to pay an extra percentage of the subscription price which is built into the subscription price when it is billed. This is like paying insurance so that no other invoices will be sent for those titles. If the library does not elect this "one bill only" payment option, then it is wise to have the annual invoice come as late in the fall (if the standard subscription period is January through December) or as close to the end of the subscription period as possible in order to have it include as many of the next year's prices as have been set. Most of the major publishers review and set their subscription rates in mid- to late summer for the following calendar year. It can, therefore, be a definite advantage to have the library's subscription year follow the calendar year, even if the fiscal year is something else. In this case, then, an early November billing is ideal; if this is too late for the vendor's purposes, then October is desirable.

As a result of serials librarians' concerns over the high cost of periodicals and the need to budget more accurately, many vendors have worked to encourage publishers to set their next year's subscription rates as early as possible and to get them to the subscription vendors earlier than before. In 1993, close to 85 percent of publishers had set their rates for 1994 by mid-August. This meant that the invoices libraries received in the early fall had definite or firm prices for the next year, and there would be no added-charge invoicing associated with most titles. Most vendors now clearly indicate on the renewal invoices those titles for which the publishers have already supplied the firm price. This new information enables serials librarians to better predict serials costs for the remainder of the fiscal year. There is now general agreement among the major periodicals publishers (with a high degree of compliance) that they will set their following year's prices by mid-August as a matter of policy.

Another option for billing is to request that the vendor place multiyear (two- or three-year) renewals for all titles or only when the multiyear rate represents a reduction in the subscription price. The advantage of multiyear subscriptions is that the library is able to pay in advance for a title and does not have to pay for increases in the subscription cost each year or bear the brunt of devaluation of the dollar against foreign currencies. Typically, multiyear renewals tend to be available for the more popular, mass market titles. A disadvantage of this approach, however, is that it means the library is generally not able to cancel that title for several years. With the rapid increase in serials prices and the weak dollar of the past few years, many libraries have had to cancel titles. A one-year renewal allows the library the greatest flexibility in being able to cancel peripheral or expensive titles. One-year renewals also allow for better tracking of overall serials expenditures in different subject areas, since approximately the same group of titles is being renewed and billed each year. In the multiyear approach, there is usually a pattern of peaks and valleys in the expenditures or, at least, something other than a straight line. This makes it hard to calculate how much the library's titles really cost in any given year and exactly how much they increased in price over the previous year.

Prepayments

Many of the larger subscription vendors, both domestic and foreign, offer some enticement for prepaying periodical subscriptions. If the library does a sizable amount of business with a particular vendor, making a prepayment can be worthwhile and cost-effective. The enticements may take one of the following forms: (1) a credit that is a percentage of the invoice total with the amount of the credit decreasing from a set maximum down to zero, depending on how far in advance of the next year the prepayment is received; (2) a fixed, reduced service charge for the upcoming year; or (3) a fixed value of the dollar against the foreign currency the vendor normally bills in, based on the point in time when the renewal invoice amount was calculated. The first option of a percentage credit is commonly used by some of the U.S. vendors; the other two options have been part of the packages for some foreign vendors. Not only does the library realize some savings in making prepayments, but the serials librarian also is able to plan the serials budget for the year, knowing that a certain portion of the money is already spent and that what is left can be used for other invoices and possibly new titles. It is true that in making these large prepayments, the library, or more likely, the college or university, usually loses whatever interest it would accrue for itself by having the money in its own account until later in the fiscal year, unless some special arrangements are made with the vendor. It could be useful to calculate what the trade-off in savings is between the credit or discount offered by the vendor and the amount of interest the library would earn if the money were in its own account several months longer before being paid out. Before the library makes any kind of prepayment, the astute serials librarian will do the necessary checking in order to be confident that the vendor to whom the library is prepaying is on stable financial footing. If it is not, then the library runs a greater risk of losing some or all of its prepayment or not receiving issues, if the vendor should experience serious cash flow problems. In less clear-cut cases, it is possible for the library to request that any prepayment monies be held separately in an escrow account and not be added to the vendor's operating funds nor be disbursed until they are used to pay the publishers for the next year's subscriptions.

For libraries that track their fund allocations and payments in an online system, it is possible to log and keep track of prepayments online also. Many prepayment invoices take the form of a one-line invoice for the total amount of money estimated to cover the next year's periodicals. It may take some creative working of the particular system involved, but it is possible to create a prepayment fund for each vendor to whom the library prepays. The total cost of the prepayment to the vendor can be charged online to the prepayment fund. If the titles covered by the prepayment are to be charged to individual subject funds later, rather than to the vendor's prepayment account, the library can allow for an overexpenditure on the vendor account of an amount equal to the prepayment, and then charge the prepayment account the amount of the prepayment. This results in a negative expenditure balance in the prepayment account. When invoices to be applied to this prepayment account are processed, the titles on the invoice are charged to the appropriate subject fund and then the total amount due on the invoice is posted as a credit line to the prepayment fund. This has the effect of making the amount due on the invoice zero (since the money has already been sent to the vendor in the form of the prepayment) and of showing the negative balance in the prepayment fund as decreased by the amount of the invoice. In other words, there is no money owed on the detailed (title-by-title) invoice, and there is less money left (a declining balance) of the prepayment amount to put toward future invoices. While this seems like a somewhat complicated procedure and involves some tinkering, the money spent for the prepayment is not deducted from the real funds from which serials are paid until the itemized invoice is received; in an accounting sense, the money gets spent and the individual charges for the periodical titles are also reflected. The library is able to both make its prepayment and then track its actual expenditure against detailed title-line invoices, and to simultaneously monitor the actual dollars spent in each subject area such as engineering or English literature. Some libraries prepay at the end of one fiscal year for the material to be received the next fiscal year. This may allow the library to get the largest credit for early payment, but it can create accounting complexities, especially in an automated system, if the librarian needs to determine exactly how much money was spent on serials for a given year. Mixing payments in one fiscal year for receipts in the next can also make keeping statistics troublesome.

Invoices on Computer Tape or by FTP

For libraries that are using automated systems for serials receipt and billing and that have large numbers of subscriptions with a few vendors, getting the periodical renewal invoice on computer tape can be an efficient proposition. The great advantage of this approach is the savings in serials staff time in not having to key in subscription period, price, and fund information. Another advantage is that there are generally reports associated with the system vendor's invoice load programs that will identify titles that meet certain conditions: for example, titles for which there have not been any recent receipts, titles that have increased more than a certain percentage (set by the library), and titles where the fund code in the vendor's file does not match that in the library's record.

Getting ready to load a vendor's invoice on tape or from a file will normally require that the library do some preparation of its order records, such as including a vendor's title or subscription number in the order record for each title and then sending a tape or file of all of the library's orders to the vendor. Some vendors are able to supply their title numbers in a barcode form that can be scanned, rather than keyed, into the order record. The vendor will use the extract tape generated by the library to add the library's unique order number to its files in order to have a match point when the payment data is added online. Going through the preparation process can be tedious, but most likely it will be helpful in identifying dead or cancelled titles and other problems with orders that may have been ignored or unknown in past years. Since every vendor's in-house software is somewhat different, loading tapes from different vendors may not be straightforward the very first time. The library should be prepared for bugs or glitches the first time it loads any vendor's tape or file, and preferably, should load it first in a test area of the system; or if that is not possible, the library should be sure that the order file against which it is run is backed up or closed while the initial run is being done. It is critical to check and see that multiple copy subscriptions are correctly posted. Although the invoice is being loaded on tape, the library will want and need a paper copy of the renewal invoice as well. Generally, the tape load program generates paper reports and lists of titles whose payments did not post for some particular reason. These payments need to be processed manually and keyed, and the online invoice record approved. The most compelling argument for having a really "clean" order file is that it will reduce the number of items that do not post, and hence reduce the amount of manual keying of payment information that needs to be done.

It is also possible now to take advantage of FTP (File Transfer Protocol) and move invoice files over the Internet instead of on computer tape. The mechanics of preparation are the same and the end product is the same, but without the physical steps of having to mount and run a magnetic tape. Once any initial bugs have been worked out, this method can be a further time-saver for both the library and the vendor. EBSCO, Faxon, B.H. Blackwell, Harrasowitz, and other vendors are already using or exploring this method of invoice data transfer. In the future, both of these methods may be replaced by the use of EDI, Electronic Data Interchange, or a direct, computer-to-computer transfer of data. Some vendors are currently making use of the X12 standard for claiming, while others are actively exploring the use of UNEDIFACT, the European EDI standard, for the transmission of invoice data and eventually orders, claims, and claim responses.

NON-PERIODICAL SERIALS

Definition of a Standing Order

In ordering serials other than periodicals, the library may also find it advantageous to use an agent or vendor for most titles. For this material, a standing order, or what is also called an open order or a continuation order, is placed. The library indicates the volume or year with which the order should start, and in return, it expects to receive all volumes that are published until the library instructs the agent otherwise. Standing order material is generally billed at the time of receipt rather than being prepaid like a periodical subscription. The invoice often is sent with the items, but may be mailed ahead of the package and even occasionally after receipt. One reason for billing at the time of receipt is that this kind of serial material (annuals, monographic series, reference titles) is usually not tied into as tight a publication schedule and the number of volumes published in a given year may not be determined ahead of time. Likewise, the price of a given volume may not be known until closer to publication. The library pays the cost of each item, sometimes less a certain percentage discount, and will usually be expected to pay a charge for shipping and handling. Some vendors with whom the library is doing a substantial amount of business may be willing to negotiate who pays the cost of the shipping; sometimes it is split in half between the library and the vendor, or the vendor might assume the entire cost of shipping on a sizable account.

Many periodical subscription vendors can also handle standing orders for annual titles, but it is the experience of this author that, at least for a library with a large collection, service is better on standing order titles from a vendor that specializes in this type of serial material. Using a subscription vendor rather than a standing order dealer for these annuals generally means that the library is invoiced ahead of publication and there may be a long delay between payment and actual receipt of the volume.

Standing Order Vendors

A good standing order dealer will be bibliographically current with the series titles it provides and will inform the library when the title is changing or, if the series has acquired a subseries, will poll the library about whether it wishes to receive excessively expensive volumes in the series before shipping them, and will alert the library when the series ceases publication. It is also desirable that any foreign standing order vendor bill in U.S. dollars, and many of the larger vendors do. This saves work for the library staff, and also means that the vendor knows ahead of time how much money will be received for that invoice. This can eliminate discussion about the exchange rate in effect at the time when the invoice was paid, particularly if a vendor who billed in the native currency feels that the library's payment was too little.

It is worth noting that orders priced in and invoices received in foreign currencies will be less work for library staff as more online systems begin to provide online currency conversion, a feature that some system vendors have already added to their serials and acquisitions modules. A possible drawback of the online currency conversion is that in some systems, the order record retains only the amount in the foreign currency, not both the foreign amount and the U.S. dollar conversion. This means that the librarian loses the ability to eyeball an order record and easily see how much a title has increased in cost from one year to the next. In this situation, there may be a need for sophisticated SAS, SQL, or other report-writing programs to pull out comparative pricing histories of titles in a given discipline.

One of the most troublesome aspects of dealing with some standing order vendors is the fact that they do not ship the invoice and the material together. Some vendors do this because they are sending the invoice first class mail, and shipping the material some other way. Many serials operations have a policy of not receiving any paid item until the actual invoice is in hand; this way, staff can clearly verify that the item received and the item billed are one and the same, and that the item is coming from the correct source. Libraries that hold materials until the receipt of the invoice occasionally must resort to correspondence soliciting the invoice from the vendor in order to be able to receive the volume or volumes. In this instance, access to a fax machine is a boon, since it reduces the time for getting an invoice request to the vendor from days or weeks to just minutes.

Memberships and Blanket Orders

Other types of orders for material published in paper that may be placed through the serials department include memberships and blanket orders. If the library has a membership in a particular association or society, it will usually receive all the publications of that body. Sometimes, becoming a member is the only way the library has of obtaining the primary journal of the organization.

The disadvantage of a membership is that it may also include ephemeral material such as newsletters and annual reports that the library does not wish to retain. Determining what is included in an organizational membership is the first step before placing this type of order. Then the serials ordering unit will need to decide which titles or pieces will be kept, which will be cataloged, which discarded, and so on. Recording this kind of information, preferably in the online system, will save time later when what appear to be unsolicited publications arrive in the library. It is possible to place memberships with the regular subscription vendor as long as the library and the vendor are clear that it is a membership and what titles exactly are included. If the subscription vendor does not include that organization's membership in its catalog or title listing or if the society or group is very small, it may be more expedient to place the membership directly. There is always a risk, however, that the organization, particularly if it is small and publications are mailed out by a treasurer or secretary whose term of office is only a few years, may not invoice the library promptly for future years and the material will stop coming.

A blanket order is a general standing order for all of the publications of a certain type from an organization. For example, a library might place a blanket order for all Unesco publications, or all publications of the American Library Association of interest to academic libraries, or all of the IEEE (Institute of Electrical and Electronics Engineers) conference publications in a certain area of electrical engineering. The advantage of a blanket order is that it is intended to be global or all-encompassing and ensures that the library receives all of the publications of a certain type without having to order them individually as monographs or separate serials volumes. One disadvantage is that it is harder to plan for what such an order will cost each year; also, the library may receive an occasional volume that is not appropriate to its collection. Generally, blanket orders cover monographic-type material, rather than true serials. One exception, however, is the IEEE periodical plan, a blanket order for the Institute's 90-plus periodical titles. In 1996, a library paid not quite $14,000 to receive all the currently published IEEE periodicals as well as any new titles or new sections of titles added during the year. Each year, the library receives notification of what the cost will be and what new titles are to be added to the plan for the next year.

Direct Orders

There was a time when it was quite common for serials librarians to order most serials titles directly from the publisher. Today, the majority of serials librarians use subscription vendors or standing order dealers for all but the most esoteric or unusual publications. Determining when it is appropriate to order something "direct" instead of with an agent can be tricky and requires making some judgments about the serials publication in question. Some serials librarians are of the opinion that it makes more sense to order foreign newspapers directly, for example. Newspaper publishers, in general, allow very little lead time for payment before the subscription expires and are very unforgiving about untimely receipt of payment. If the payment has not been made, then the paper is not sent. A library has to be alert to be sure to catch upcoming newspaper expiration dates and anticipate them, since sometimes the publisher does not send an invoice for renewal.

Some publishers make it a policy not to accept any standing orders or subscriptions except those that are placed directly. In this case, the library has no choice if it wishes to receive those publications. If a serials librarian is curious about whether or not a vendor can handle a certain title, then that vendor's catalog is a good source of information. The fact that a title is in the catalog generally means that the vendor has placed a certain minimum number of orders for that title. It is worth remembering, however, that if a title is not in the catalog, that does not preclude its being handled by the vendor. Most vendors will gladly research and order any title not in their catalogs, provided that the library supplies as much bibliographical information as possible to the vendor. If the information that the library has is sketchy, it may be appropriate to go direct, assuming that the publisher will be able to identify its own titles. Sometimes the publication to be acquired is esoteric or part of a very small print run, and ordering it directly from the source seems to offer a greater likelihood of receipt; examples are unusual conference proceedings that may have been produced from someone's house or garage, or statistical guides for Third World countries.

BACKFILE AND REPLACEMENT ORDERS

From time to time, there will be a need for a one-time order for a replacement periodical issue needed for binding or for a back volume of a periodical or a serial. Whether or not these one-time orders (not subscriptions or standing orders) are handled by the serials department will depend on the individual library, but in many libraries they are, since the item being received is still a serial publication.

Acquiring a replacement issue of a periodical can be an expensive and time-consuming process, and libraries often maintain ongoing ''want'' lists of periodical issues that are needed. If the issue required is fairly recent (published within the past two years), a library may have the best chance of success in getting it by going directly to the publisher. This will cost more money, but if the issue is part of the publisher's back stock, it can be acquired relatively quickly. Most orders of this type require prepayment, so if the library does not know how much the issue will cost, it must wait for the publisher's response, put through the necessary paperwork for payment, and then wait until payment has been received before the issue is sent. Some colleges and universities provide staff who have purchasing responsibilities with the use of a procurement credit card. This special charge card enables the individual to charge certain types of merchandise up to certain, specified dollar amounts. A procurement card can be especially useful in making prepayments for single issue or backfile orders, since it the gives the publisher the money immediately and eliminates the delays of waiting for a check to be cut and mailed before the material can be sent to the library. If an entire volume of a journal is needed, there are a host of back issue and back volume dealers who specialize in acquiring these and reselling them to libraries. Examples are: Jaeger, Jerry Alper, and Kraus, the latter dealing mainly in reprint editions. If the library does not want to spend as much money in this process, it is possible to get some missing issues through USBE, which charges a flat fee for any issues it has in stock; EBSCO's Missing Copy Bank service (an online service which is part of EBSCONET and which has popular magazines and a concentration in health science titles); or exchange lists received from other libraries. If a library joins the Duplicate Exchange Union, a condition of membership is producing one list a year of one's own offerings in exchange for receiving lists regularly from the other member libraries. Often, other regional organizations also informally or formally offer and exchange unwanted issues and volumes.

Other one-time serial orders may be for runs of titles on microform or in hard copy or for a single volume of a reference serial where no standing order is desired. Back runs of older titles are often available in microform or in reprint editions from publishers that specialize in producing quality reprintings of significant titles. The most recent few years of a title may be part of the publisher's stock and therefore, can be ordered direct. For individual volumes of serials (the latest published or a specific volume or year), the most expedient means of acquiring the piece is usually a direct order to the publisher. It is worth noting, however, that many publishers will require prepayment for these single orders and this can add to the time between placement of the original order and the actual receipt of the volume or issues.

CANCELLATIONS

Sometimes it is necessary to cancel an order for a current title. If it is a periodical, then it usually cannot be cancelled until the end of the subscription period. This means that the library has to allow enough lead time to the subscription vendor so that the title is not automatically renewed with the publisher for the next year. Most vendors must have periodical cancellations in hand by September 1 or October 1 at the latest, for titles that have a subscription period beginning with January of the following year. It is preferable to notify the vendor as soon as the decision is made, and the ideal would be sometime in the late spring or early summer. For the sake of accuracy and documentation, all cancellations should be put in writing to the vendor, even if they are initially given to an account representative over the phone. This ensures that the library has the paperwork or online documentation to prove that a title was cancelled if there are problems later on; if, for example, the library is billed for the next year, or the publisher is supposed to credit part of a multiyear renewal and does not. The library should also request confirmation of the cancellation. This indicates that the vendor indeed received and processed the cancellation letter. If the library does not get confirmation of the cancellation, it should, nevertheless, proceed assuming the title is indeed cancelled.

Canceling standing orders is simpler than canceling periodicals in one respect, and that is that the vendor or publisher can be instructed to make the last volume received by the library the last volume and not to supply any future volumes. Problems may arise if the next volume in the series or the serial is already in process and it crosses in the mail with the cancellation letter. In this case, the library is generally obligated to receive the extra volume, since the vendor would not have been able to act on the cancellation notice. If subsequent volumes are received after allowing time for the cancellation to be processed, the library should feel free to return them with a note indicating the effective date of the cancellation. This is permissible only if the library has not marked or stamped the volume in any way. The vendor needs to receive a clean volume back in order to be able to sell it to another library or return it to the publisher.

For any number of reasons, such as dissatisfaction with a vendor's service, the desire to consolidate all orders with another vendor, or the vendor's decision to cease doing business, the library may decide to transfer all of the orders it has with one vendor to another vendor. The usual procedure is to compile a list of all the orders with the first vendor (either from the library's own files or by requesting it from the vendor who presently has the orders), determine the last volume or year received, and then to send a cancellation letter to the first vendor indicating when the order is to end. Orders for these titles can then be sent to the new vendor. It is helpful to indicate to both vendors in question that the title is being transferred to another vendor or was formerly with the other vendor. The new vendor may offer to assist the library in this endeavor by providing some staff assistance or helping with the paperwork. It is the opinion of this author that a vendor's offers of assistance with a transfer project need to be very carefully considered before being accepted. Determine exactly what is being offered and how it will work. The time it would take to explain the library's internal procedures to the vendor before it can really be of assistance may negate the advantage of this offer. On rare occasions, a vendor may negotiate some special financial package as part of the transfer process or in lieu of providing clerical assistance. When a library is moving a sizable amount of business to a new vendor, it makes sense to raise the issue of service charges (periodicals) or postage and handling charges (serial standing orders) in order to negotiate the most favorable terms for the library. If the library already has an account with the vendor gaining the new business, this increase may be enough to warrant additional reductions in service charges and the like. If transfers are being carried out in an online system, careful attention to setting action dates for the new orders can simplify tracking the receipt of the new titles in a timely fashion.

TRACKING RECEIPT OR THE CLAIMING PROCESS

It may seem superfluous to be concerned about claims when the newly ordered paper titles have not even begun to be received, but as any veteran serials
librarian knows, claims are a large part of the serials processing. All reputable
vendors realize that claims are a fact of life and that not all publications or
periodical issues will either be published on schedule or be received in the
library when expected. The prevailing view several years ago was that with the
introduction of online systems in libraries, and the resulting ease with which
claim letters could be produced, serials staffs went overboard in generating
claims; consequently, the vendors were flooded with too many claims too soon,
and there was a perception among serials librarians that some vendors were
ignoring all first claims from automated systems. Whether or not this was actually true is beside the point; the fact is that automation does make claiming
easier, and one can hope and realistically expect that serials librarians and their
staffs are now setting reasonable claim intervals and not claiming needlessly.
Most of the claims being generated, even out of automated systems, are still in
paper, although a number of individual libraries have carried out small experi-
ments with particular vendor partners to transmit claims electronically in a variety of ways. For claiming problems that need immediate attention, there is
always the telephone call to one's service representative, and for less urgent,
but still pressing matters, an e-mail message that the vendor representative can
receive right then and deal with as time permits can be an efficient use of both
parties' time.

The library needs to set its own internal parameters for how many times it
claims a particular item before a decision is made to forget it or try to obtain it
from some other source. The number of claims may be different for periodicals
than for standing orders. In addition, many periodical publishers have instituted
strict claiming policies, and the window of time in which they will even respond
to a claim may be as short as 30 or 60 days; awareness of these policies may
influence the serials staff to annotate the order records with these restrictions to
ensure prompt claiming. For some publications, there is little chance of getting
a claimed issue if it is not received right away just because the print runs are
so small, and there are not extra copies available; this is often the case with
some Russian and East European titles and some mass market general audience
magazines. For some titles that are not kept permanently, such as newspaper
issues and popular magazines, the library may wish to set a policy of ''no
claims.'' The time involved to place the claim and actually receive the issue
may be so great that, by the time the missing issue is received, the need for it
is gone. Or, in the case of popular titles that are actually handled by one of the
big distribution centers, it may be almost impossible to get a missing issue;
more likely, the publisher will offer to extend the library's subscription by one
issue to make up for the lacking issue. In this case, if the issue is of importance

to the library's patrons, it may be simpler just to purchase a copy from the local newsstand.

For those libraries that are depository sites for United States, United Nations, or European Union documents, there are very specific procedures for claiming missing material. UN documents, for example, must be claimed on a particular form from the particular office in the area of the world responsible for the distribution of that material, and generally, the library is required to do a certain amount of checking beforehand to document that indeed the missing piece was actually published. Likewise, U.S. depository publications must be claimed within 60 days from receipt of the shipping list and even then, there are often shortages in the print run that make obtaining a copy unlikely; if one is sent, it may be in microfiche even though the original distribution was in paper. For most depository items, careful checking of any shipping lists for distribution lists is required before a claim can be placed. Doing this sort of claiming is especially time-consuming, both because these organizations do not usually accept the standard, system-generated claim letters and because of the extra verification required.

The best hope for the future of claiming is that, in the next three to five years, enough vendors will develop truly functional EDI capabilities which will enable libraries to transmit the claim information and then to receive the claim replies back—all electronically from the library computer to the vendor or supplier's computer and back again.

THE FUTURE

Although the number of electronic journals and full-text online services continues to increase, libraries will probably continue to receive the majority of their periodicals and serials in paper for the foreseeable future. Nevertheless, the mainstream periodical and serial vendors are exploring ways they might exploit the library world's growing interest in obtaining access to electronic journals; B.H. Blackwell recently announced a prototype e-journal service and would like to be the intermediary between the library and the journal's producer to handle technical issues and the like. Developing good working relationships with one's periodical and standing order vendors is a key to being able to provide paper journals and, eventually, other materials in a timely fashion. It is important that serials librarians apply standards of fairness and what is reasonable in their dealings with both vendors and publishers, and recognize that libraries, vendors, and publishers all depend on one another for their mutual success in providing information to the user community.

REFERENCES

Anglo-American Cataloguing Rules. 2d ed. (AACR2). 1988. Chicago: American Library Association; London: Library Association Publishing; Ottawa: Canadian Library Association, 622.

American Library Association (ALA). Bookdealer-Library Relations Committee. 1992. *Guidelines for Handling Library Orders for Serials and Periodicals.* Rev. ed. Chicago: ALA.

Barker, Joseph W. 1990. "Unbundlng Serials Vendors' Service Charges: Are We Ready?" *Serials Review* 16, no. 2: 33–43.

Basch, N. Bernard, and Judy McQueen. 1990. *Buying Serials: A How-to-Do-It Manual for Librarians.* New York and London: Neal Schuman.

Magill, Rose Mary, and John Corbin. 1989. *Acquisitions Management and Collection Development in Libraries.* 2d ed. Chicago and London: American Library Association, 195–215.

McKinley, Margaret. 1990. "Vendor Selection: Strategic Choices." *Serials Review* 16, no. 2: 49–64.

Schmidt, Karen A., ed. 1990. *Understanding the Business of Library Acquisitions.* Chicago and London: American Library Association.

Wilkas, Lenore Rae. 1994. *International Subscription Agents.* 6th ed. Chicago and London: American Library Association.

Woodward, Hazel, and Stella Pilling. 1993. The International Serials Industry. Aldershot, U.K., and Brookfield, VT: Gower Publishing.

7

Serials in Many Forms: Newspapers, Depository Publications, and Computer Files

INTRODUCTION

For many, many years, serials existed almost exclusively as text on the printed page. With the development of high resolution camera technology, the presentation of text on film became possible, and new possibilities emerged for archiving fragile materials and for offering space-saving, permanent copies of popular journals and newspapers on either microfilm or microfiche. Microfilm and microfiche took up much less shelf space than paperbound volumes and held out the promise of little deterioration in the quality of the image over time, if the proper storage conditions were maintained. Before 1988, when serials librarians referred to alternative formats for serials titles, they generally meant microfiche or microfilm. In the past five years, however, several new formats have been introduced; these new formats offer many advantages, but they are also challenging serials librarians to think about information delivery in new ways. What are these new formats? And how are they changing the serials landscape? Two examples are CD-ROM, computer files on the same size disk as is used for music audio CDs; and electronic journals, online text and graphics on the Internet. This is text distributed online, often by subscription, over the Internet, and is also referred to as e-journals.

While periodicals are often the focus of many discussions about serials processing, there are other types of serials that in practice can be more problematic to handle and therefore need some special accommodation apart from the usual journal issues. These include newspapers and government depository publications. This chapter will address how best to acquire, receive, and handle these types of serials as well as the serials in microform and on CD-ROM. Electronic journals are discussed in a later chapter.

MICROFORMS

Overview

With the rise in popularity of the CD-ROM, microfilm and microfiche have become somewhat overshadowed and some individuals have raised questions about their continuing place in library collections and whether or not their usefulness as a preservation medium will be surpassed by the CD-ROM. Although microfilm and microfiche lack the "pizazz" factor associated with electronic media like the CD-ROM, they remain a useful and popular alternative to binding paper issues of periodicals. Microfilm and microfiche take up less space than do bound volumes, and the library is guaranteed of having complete volumes and runs without the staff time (which can be quite significant) and expense of searching for, ordering, acquiring, and processing replacement issues. For some publications in certain languages or from particular types of publishers, there are no additional copies of issues to be had to replace copies lost or never received. For heavily used periodical titles, it may also be desirable to own and bind a paper copy as well as purchase the microfilm or fiche copy.

For newspaper titles, microfilm continues to be the most widely available and the least expensive way to retain them permanently in a collection. Most mainstream newspapers and periodicals are available through one of the large microform vendors, such as University Microfilms or Research Publications. For some foreign language material and more esoteric titles, it may be necessary to consult the *Guide to Microforms in Print* for the name of the distributor, or one of the large microform vendor's catalogs, such as UMI's *Serials in Microform*. The dealer Norman Ross also specializes in foreign microforms from France, Japan, China, and almost anywhere else in the world. Occasionally, foreign periodicals or other serials are only available through the country's national library or a university library. To acquire these titles, it is wise to write for a price quotation for the particular run of volumes and years the library wishes to acquire. This will avoid surprises about the price later on and aid in budgeting. Titles made available from research or national libraries are most often filmed on demand and the price will be quoted at the time of filming and be valid for a specified period of time.

It is important when ordering microforms to be sure to specify whether fiche or film is being ordered, and then to indicate what size film or fiche is desired. Microfilm generally is available in three sizes: 8mm, 16mm, and 35mm. For the library market, the choice most often is 16mm or 35mm reels, with most libraries preferring the larger 35mm format. Fiche comes in sheets that are either 3" × 5" or 4" × 6" with the 4" × 6" size more commonly used now than it was in the past. It should also be possible to indicate the film polarity (positive or negative), although if there is not an option, it is more likely to be positive film. The chief advantage to ordering negative film or fiche is that when paper copies of an article are made, they have positive rather than negative images (black letters on white, instead of white on black) which can be easier to read. Sometimes, particularly with newspaper titles from commercial vendors, the library has the option of specifying the type of film on which the material is being photographed: diazo, vesicular, or silver halide. For preservation purposes, silver halide is preferred, since it has been demonstrated to have a longer shelf life than either diazo or vesicular and is less subject to certain kinds of deterioration over time. Silver halide is more expensive than the other types of film, but most research libraries believe it is worth the extra investment for the materials they are adding. Most microforms are added to library collections with the expectation that they are permanent and that the title will be retained forever; therefore, the extra cost can be justified. Some vendors offer newspaper titles only on silver film.

Film versus Fiche

When a choice between microfilm and microfiche for a given title is offered, the type of material being ordered should be considered. Microfilm is generally preferred for long documents or titles in which the page size is larger than the standard 8 1/2" × 11"; hence, it is customary to offer newspaper titles on microfilm only. One issue of a daily paper will not fit comfortably on a single fiche sheet. Some periodical titles may be offered on film or fiche. Fiche has the advantage of being somewhat easier for the patron to use, since there is no threading required at the reader. It is also somewhat easier to find a given issue or page using the eye-legible header information on the individual fiche. Refiling fiche, however, can be more tedious for staff than refiling film boxes, but fiche are more easily lost or misplaced than film reels. A given library may make a conscious decision that it will try to acquire all of its periodicals on fiche and limit its acquisition of film to newspapers. This may be easier for a smaller library to accomplish than a larger one, given that the larger library may be acquiring a greater diversity of material and more of it foreign with fewer options for fiche rather than film. There are also the security considerations; it is easier for a patron to either mistakenly or deliberately walk off with a single fiche sheet than with a microfilm reel. Microfilm reels in a drawer are easier to browse, since the title labels on the sides of the boxes can be easily read, while to browse microfiche requires thumbing through a drawer and looking more closely to see the title on the header. Refiling of film boxes is a faster process than refiling fiche.

Checking upon Receipt

Most libraries will want to check in microform materials in the same way that other serial material is logged in. In addition, for these materials, it is recommended that library staff not only verify that the film or fiche received is the correct volume or year, but also remove the material from its box or envelope and visually inspect it and then look at it on a reader. This extra check on the quality of the reproduction may not be necessary for subscription titles received on a regular basis from a known vendor or supplier, but it is a step that probably should be considered essential for large and expensive runs or backfiles and for the first titles received from small or unknown sources. This quality check enables the serials staff to pay for the material knowing that it is what it should be and saves the serials staff and the public services staff from possible embarrassment later on. If a patron discovers irregularities or poor quality after the title has been paid for, it is probably too late to return it and harder to complain to the supplier. Staff should also look closely and determine that the film boxes are clearly and correctly labeled with the actual contents of the reels. If labeling problems or questions about the actual quality of the reproduction arise, contact the source before payment is made and before the material is marked in any way.

It is worth noting that a few periodical publishers require that the library have a current subscription to the paper copy in order to be able to purchase microform for the latest year. Some publishers also require that the library have a current paper subscription in order to purchase any volumes (current or backfile) in microform. These publishers are by far the exception.

Shelving and Cataloging

Microforms may also present a shelving challenge for the library, not so much for how to shelve them, but where. The issue is how best to handle them and what are the relative advantages and disadvantages of shelving microforms of periodicals in a separate area or interspersed with the bound volumes of the periodicals. The answers to these questions depend to a large degree on the size of the collection, the nature of the clientele, and the amount of equipment available to support reading and copying microforms (Farrington 1981). Having microforms in a separate area, if the collection is large, argues for having staff available to assist with questions and using the readers and printers. Putting microforms in the stacks with bound volumes may increase their visibility and possibly their use, provided the reading equipment is fairly close by.

If microforms are cataloged, and there are strong arguments in favor of doing so in order to provide access in an online catalog, then some interesting questions will be raised if and when the concept of multiple versions (all forms of the same item on one bibliographic record) is adopted. One might ask if it is inherently more confusing for a library patron to have a paper copy, microfilm copy, and a CD-ROM copy all on the same record or to continue to have three separate bibliographic records, one each for each of the formats. The gathering of all holdings in one record would seem to be a major benefit despite the format differences, and there are libraries that have locally made the decision to include at least microform holdings on the same bibliographic record with the hard copy. This is discussed more fully elsewhere, but potentially has the greatest impact on microform collections, since microfilm and microfiche titles often exist in the library already in paper form. Another consideration in cataloging micro-forms is whether or not to classify them and, if so, whether it is desirable that they have Library of Congress or Dewey call numbers like the library's circulating collection. This is probably most desirable if these titles are being shelved with or near the paper volumes. Some libraries choose to create their own internal, sequential numbering scheme, instead of a formal classification number, with a format designator as part of the call number. An example is: "Microfiche 22" for a periodical or serial on fiche, or "Film news 365" for a newspaper. Whatever type of call number is decided upon, it should be one that is easy to interpret and makes sense within the shelving constraints of the library's collections.

NEWSPAPERS

The decision to add a newspaper title to the library's collection requires careful consideration and selectivity; newspapers are more expensive than most paper titles (outside the scientific and technical areas) with the cost of a yearly subscription easily running into the hundreds or thousands of dollars, particularly if it is published daily and it is being sent airmail from abroad. The cost of one newspaper, therefore, rivals the cost of some scientific and technical journals. When the newspaper subscription is placed, the library must decide whether or not to pay to have it sent airmail and how long to retain the issues. The retention question raises the issue of whether or not the newspaper should be permanently retained in the collection on microfilm. If the paper will not be acquired in microfilm also, then a retention period of three months for a daily newspaper or six months for a weekly is usually sufficient and may be all that the news-paper shelving will tolerate. Whether or not the library chooses to add a film subscription in addition to the paper copy depends in large part on the type of use the newspaper title will receive (casual reading by students wishing to keep up with the local city newspaper or with the newspaper from their home country or city, structured use by students as an adjunct to foreign language study, or research use for a variety of disciplines) and whether or not the title is indexed in some source the library owns or in one of the online databases like *Newspaper Index* or *Lexis/Nexis*. Trying to measure the usefulness, particularly of foreign newspaper titles, is a worthy endeavor given the high costs associated with each individual newspaper title.

Although they may be overlooked in the serials literature, newspapers tend to be a very heavily used component of the current periodicals collection. Consequently, their timely receipt or lack thereof is closely noted by library users. It is critical, therefore, that the serials staff monitor newspaper subscriptions, both the receipt of current issues as well as the renewal for the next year. There are two ways to acquire newspapers: subscriptions by mail or local delivery or pick-up. For a city or region's local newspapers, many libraries contract with a local distributor for delivery to the library or make arrangements with a corner store or newsstand to hold papers for pick-up on a daily basis. These latter arrangements can be very complicated and dependent on an individual staff member's attendance at work, but they do work and they may be the only way to have the newspapers in-hand when the library opens to patrons each day. Local distributors, the alternative, will usually bill on a monthly or quarterly basis for the papers and will accommodate delivery of multiple copies of the newspapers in question. If many copies of local newspapers are being received each day, then this kind of daily delivery can result in more reliable service.

The serials manager must then decide if it is essential to log receipt of these newspapers in the manual or online file or whether it is acceptable to rely on the staff who put the newspapers out for patrons to check each day and see that the requisite number of copies have been delivered or purchased. Certainly, receiving individual newspaper issues online requires more staff time, but it has the advantage of providing patrons who are accessing the online catalog remotely with information about which issues are actually there. When newspapers are received through the mail, they will come into the serials department along with the other periodical and serial material. This should make receiving them either manually or online relatively easy to do. There may have been a tendency in some libraries in the past to skip noting receipt of individual newspaper issues. In today's online environment, however, where patrons have ready access to current receipts, it seems shortsighted not to give them this information about such heavily used, popular titles. As public services staff will be only to willing to attest, not having that day's local newspaper or that day's *New York Times* makes for nothing but unhappy patrons all day long.

Subscriptions to newspapers are extremely time-sensitive and require close monitoring. It is possible to place subscription orders through vendors or to order the newspaper directly with the publisher. Using a vendor should mean that the renewal is handled in a timely fashion and that there will be no lapse in service. Newspapers, unlike other periodical publications, usually do not allow for any grace period. If the money is not received prior to the start of the new subscription period, then the newspaper stops coming immediately. If the newspaper has been ordered direct, there are sometimes no renewal notices or reminders, and even getting an invoice from the publisher can be difficult, particularly if the newspaper is a foreign title. Processing an invoice for payment can take up to eight weeks in some large libraries, which means that there is that much more delay until the newspaper issues begin coming again. Foreign newspaper publishers seem to be more casual about sending renewal invoices.

Nonetheless, one advantage to placing a newspaper order directly with the publisher is that the time for a claim and claim response to be exchanged is probably less than working through a vendor. This is definitely the case if the library chooses to fax its claims for missing newspapers.

Shelving of newspapers can also be a challenge. Given their size and flimsy paper, newspapers can quickly become messy on the shelves. The only effective way to combat this tendency is through constant vigilance on the part of the periodicals and newspaper public services staff if the newspapers are in an open stack area, or keeping the newspapers in a restricted shelving area that is only accessed by library staff. Some libraries use ranges of large flat shelves for the papers with the latest issues of the most heavily read titles in display racks on bamboo poles. Other libraries put out only the most recent issues for the public and then page the older issues from a non-public area. This reduces the potential for public clutter, but may require more staff or student help if the number of titles is large. Another option is to purchase special bookcases with metal rods which will hold large hanging folders. Newspapers in this type of arrangement are visually less cluttered-looking, but it is also easier for patrons or staff to refile the papers back in the wrong folder, making them virtually unfindable. Therefore, regular maintenance of newspaper shelving, whether public or restricted, is necessary to keep these titles in good order.

GOVERNMENT PUBLICATIONS

While it is customary in many libraries to staff and support a separate government documents unit, there are libraries in which the responsibility for receiving and claiming government publications falls to the serials staff. This may be the case when the library is a depository site for certain government publications, or the serials department may simply be the unit responsible for ordering and receiving only the paid government serials the library acquires. One reasonable argument for maintaining depository receipt records in the serials department is that many of these titles are serials and hence are cataloged and treated like serials even though they are depository items. Dealing with government serials on a subscription basis is fairly routine. There are vendors who specialize in handling government publications, either domestic or foreign. For example, Bernan is a good source of U.S. documents, while Manhattan Publishing Company and Unipub are distributors for Council of Europe and UN documents, respectively.

U.S. Documents

If a library wishes to become a depository site for U.S. government publications, it must go through a formal application and review process before being so designated. In all, there are approximately 1,200 depository libraries in the country. There is at least one full depository or regional library in every state and there are one or more libraries within a given congressional district that are selective depository libraries. In the latter case, the vast majority of depository libraries, the individual library chooses which item numbers (representing one Superintendent of Documents [SUDOC] classification number or several SUDOC numbers) it wishes to receive for its collection. Most depository agreements, and the U.S. program is no exception, have some requirements or understandings regarding the receipt, retention, and availability of material received on deposit. Probably the most detailed guidelines and instructions are those for the U.S. government depository libraries. The *Instructions to Depository Libraries* along with *Administrative Notes* and *Administrative Notes Technical Supplement* (newsletters each published once or twice a month) provide basic information and ongoing guidance about what is expected of depository libraries ranging from how to receive materials, to how to claim them, to what the requirements are for weeding and retention. In the past, most U.S. depository libraries received their government publications and checked them in the Kardex or some other sort of manual file. The Kardex, if it was located in a separate government documents unit, was probably arranged in SUDOC number order, since the U.S. government shipping lists include this number and most libraries shelve their documents collections separately by this number. It is an alphanumeric classification system which assigns codes based on the government issuing agency. The basic class stem for the Department of State, for example, is S 1. Serials departments that handle U.S. documents may also have had a Kardex arranged in this order or may have chosen the usual arrangement of alphabetic by title or by issuing body. For libraries that shelve by SUDOC number, receiving material this way can be quite efficient, since the SUDOC number has to be added to the piece for shelving and it can be taken from the shipping list as it is being checked against it. In the online environment, retrieving records by SUDOC number might be more difficult and being able to do this will depend to a large extent on the sophistication of the system's indexing capabilities. The item number, which is another number assigned to one title or to a group of titles from the same agency, is not necessarily unique to any one title, but can more easily be set up as an access point in the online environment.

The depository library program also assigns each SUDOC number or several SUDOC numbers an item number, for example, 508-E. Depository libraries actually select by item number, not by SUDOC, and libraries are required to maintain a file of item numbers selected, either online or in a card file. It is possible to purchase a file of GPO MARC records based on item numbers selected and load these records on a regular basis. This file contains bibliographic records for all the pieces the library will be receiving on a regular basis, and the file is timed to arrive before or at about the same time as the material itself. Subscribing to this kind of automated record service can greatly reduce the amount of in-house cataloging and greatly simplify the receipt process. Several companies including MARCIVE and Autographics offer this service. Although not necessarily unique for a given title, the item number can usually be made searchable in most online systems.

Whether the documents are received on a depository basis or as paid titles, the library, in this case the serials staff, will need to receive and process them. In separate documents units, it was usually customary to check in U.S. government publications in a Kardex that was arranged in Superintendent of Documents number (SUDOC number) order rather than in alphabetical order. The shipping lists received from the U.S. government for depository items include both the item selection number and the SUDOC number. Arranging the Kardex in SUDOC number order can make for more efficient and faster processing of the materials than trying to determine what the issuing agency is for something received on an item number that is for "general publications" or "handbooks, manuals, guides," and then finding that entry in an alphabetical Kardex. The SUDOC arrangement, of course, makes sense for libraries that shelve their U.S. documents by this number. Also, SUDOC numbers are perhaps more constant than issuing agency names that change form. In the online environment, the ideal situation is to have these internal document control numbers indexed so they can be used as the point of access for retrieving the receipt record.

Even with good indexing of both GPO item numbers and the SUDOC number, depository publications are one of the greatest challenges to online serials control. Not only are there serial and periodical publications that are issued fairly regularly, but there are also a myriad of pamphlets, brochures, and monographic titles (those in numbered series and those that are just separates) that need to be logged in somehow and routed in an appropriate way. One would expect that whatever system is used for serials and documents receipt would allow for searching by SUDOC number or item number or both. Creating mock bibliographic records with the issuing agency as the corporate author and the umbrella title as the title field will enable the staff member to search by these elements as well. In the example that follows (Figure 7.1), it is possible to search the corporate author, the title, and the item number (074 field).

United Nations and European Union

United Nations (UN) and European Union (EU) publications may also be handled by the serials staff, and they can also be acquired on a paid basis or on depository. The importance of keeping accurate records of what has been received cannot be overemphasized. Most depository agreements are made with the stipulation that the material be made available to patrons either indefinitely or for a fairly lengthy period of time (five years' minimum for U.S. publications, for example). For this reason, it is essential that the library know what it has

Figure 7.1
Brief Bibliographic Record for GPO Collective Item Number

NOTIS CATALOGING

UP- EAD3978 FMT S RT a BL s DT 01/18/91 R/DT 02/25/94 STAT cc E/L   DCF a D/S S
SRC d PLACE dcu LANG eng MOD   OA a REPRO   S/STAT c DT/1 19uu DT/2 9999
CONT S/T m FREQ u REG u MED   GOVT f TPA u IA u CIA u ISDS 1 CONF 0 SLE 0

074/1: : |a 1063-K-05
086/1:0 : |a Y 3.P 31:8/
110:20: |a United States Institute of Peace.
245:10: |a [Handbooks, manuals, guides]
260:00: |a [Washington, D.C.] : |b The Institute,

received from the particular government or multinational body and where that material is to be found once it has been processed. With the advent of the single market economy in Europe in 1992, European Union publications have been in great demand and much more heavily used than several years ago. Likewise, the increasingly important role played by the United Nations in the Persian Gulf War and international affairs elsewhere has made the deliberations of the UN Security Council and its other records and publications a focus of interest.

The number of European Union depository collections in the United States is very small (approximately 50 libraries as compared to more than a thousand U.S. depository libraries), and therefore, it is more likely that most libraries interested in particular publications will purchase those that are offered for sale. To locate other EU publications that may not be offered for sale, the Delegation to the European Union Office of Inquiries in Washington, DC will readily direct librarians and patrons to those EU depository libraries that are located closest to them.

The depository programs for UN publications are not free; rather, the library contracts on a yearly basis to receive a large and fairly comprehensive body of material or else a smaller, but also fairly sizable, range of publications from most of the UN agencies. In each case, the library pays an annual fee and then is sent the appropriate publications. This is different from the U.S. depository program where, periodically throughout the year, new item numbers and new publications are either offered to the library for selection or rejection ahead of time or, more commonly, the new publication is shipped and cited on the shipping list as new and being sent to libraries that have selected a related item number. The library then has the option of deselecting that new item number. Like publications from other depository programs, the UN publications are generally classed according to which body within the organization (General Assembly, Security Council, etc.) issued the piece. Some publications that are more commercial in appeal, called sales publications, are published with a sales number, but no class number. Both the UN and the EU are putting more resources into making certain types of materials available on CD or online, but much more of their material is still in paper compared to the U.S. depository program.

Claims

Claiming of government depository items often is more complicated than claiming other serial material and does not always lend itself to the online environment. Most depository programs require that the library use a specific form and that the item number or class number information be included on the form. This is the case for U.S., UN, and EU publications. For UN publications, the office from which the missing publications are claimed varies, depending on the agency involved and where it is located. This generally means that libraries tend to hold back before claiming depository publications and then do the investigative work that is necessary in order to submit a complete claim. In 1993, the U.S. government depository drastically changed its claiming policy and identified a core list of publications that could be claimed if not received. All other government publications were no longer able to be claimed by the depository libraries. This concept of the ''core list'' focused government resources on trying to fill claims for key titles rather than sending rainchecks for lots of unavailable publications. Feedback was solicited from the depository library community on the core list, titles were added to it, but then GPO decided to return to the former practice of allowing libraries to claim all but titles for which no rainchecks were to be issued. As a result, GPO has made a concerted effort to fill claims for all titles missed and with a perceived higher success rate. GPO will also now accept faxed claims as long as they include the required information; this can be a real time-saver.

The time involved in claiming these publications coupled with the problem of short print runs can result in a significant number of unsuccessful or unresolved claims. The U.S. program often issues rainchecks indicating that not enough copies were printed and that the library will get a copy eventually. Sometimes there are just no more copies available, period. This argues for claiming U.S. publications that are not received on the shipping lists as soon as possible and well before the 60-day limit has expired. Even doing this, however, does not guarantee that the claim will be fulfilled. In the past year, however, GPO has been making many more publications available online on the World Wide Web; for many libraries this eliminates or at least reduces the need to have a paper copy of a particular publication. Also, there are several places on the Web where libraries can easily obtain copies of missing shipping lists in order to determine what they need to claim. This is in addition to the Fax Watch service which has greatly facilitated getting recently issued shipping lists by fax.

In the case of UN and EU publications, it is sometimes difficult to tell if something has indeed been distributed on depository. The UN does not provide shipping lists and those that the EU office sends do not arrive with the material and often come many weeks after the items; as a result, library staff need to be both astute and determined to track down missing items. If a library is only interested in a relatively small number of publications from these organizations, then this can be avoided by just deciding to subscribe to the desired titles through a vendor. This means the vendor has accountability and the library can more easily claim any publications that do not come on an invoice. In fact, some depository libraries enter a paid subscription for heavily used depository titles if they need to have the title in the most timely fashion and they want to be sure that they receive all of the issues or pieces. This extra expenditure for selected items can save time and patron frustration over the long term. However, not all of the material that is distributed through the depository programs is available for sale, and a library that really has need of the wide range of material will find that becoming a depository library for any of these programs is worthwhile, despite the commitment of staff time.

Small Press Publications

There are some periodicals and serials that are published by such small, esoteric publishers or by individuals that the best way to ensure getting them is to subscribe directly. It may be possible to order them through a vendor, but the likelihood of success is greater by dealing directly and following up as needed with phone calls, e-mail, or faxes. Examples of types of publications that could fall into this category are: small literary journals or poetry reviews, conference proceedings, and other titles that appear to be published by very small companies or individuals. The potential disadvantage of using a vendor for some of these titles is that the library may end up paying several years in advance of when the issues are published. Low-budget presses with limited staff often fall behind in their publication schedules or combine issues. As long as the title is still active (not declared "dead"), a vendor will occasionally continue to bill the library even though no issues have been received in the past year. Eventually, the vendor will, most likely, make the title a "bill later" item and suspend billing the customer until the publication schedule catches up with the previous billings. Going direct with the publisher may help prevent any billing in advance, but does mean that the library has to deal with an individual or the press. Renewal reminders from the "shoestring" publisher may be fine, but occasionally are tardy or missing.

There are also examples of publishers who make it a policy not to deal with the vendors and agents and who will only supply their material directly to libraries. Some will not even take standing orders at all, either through a vendor or direct. Annual publications from associations are sometimes the sort of publications that cannot be obtained on standing order; the publisher simply does not accept them. For these publishers or associations who do not deal in standing orders, but who publish titles on a regular basis, the library will need to set up some sort of reminder system to prompt ordering of the title each year or whenever. In the days before automation, many serials librarians had their own personal "tickler" files in their calendars to remind them at such-and-such a date to order a particular title. This can be made simpler in the online environment. Most systems will allow for the creation of an order record that is solely for internal use; this order can be noted "standing order not accepted." An action date is added with a notation that the next year or volume should be ordered each November or whatever. The action date, in most online systems, will appear on some sort of report that will then alert the serials staff that something needs to be done. This kind of tracking is one of the boons of automated systems and can greatly improve the serials department's efficiency in this area.

CD-ROMs

CD-ROMs have now been available long enough that they are commonplace in most academic libraries, yet some would argue that their use as the medium of choice is on the wane. Their widespread distribution and their acceptance by library patrons has meant that many serials and collection development librarians grappling with tight budgets have nerved themselves to discontinue their paper subscriptions in favor of the same title on CD. CD-ROMS are compact in size, have enormous storage capacity, and offer the user the ability to easily search across a mass of material using sophisticated keyword and Boolean techniques; this makes the medium attractive and cost-effective for large text databases such as indexes and abstracts as well as for statistical material. Consequently, commercial publishers and the U.S. government agencies have made extensive use of CDs for distributing indexes, tables, and statistical material of all types. This pervasiveness of the CD format is borne out by the figures; the number of titles available increased from a few hundred in 1988 ("CD-ROM Update" 1990, 63) to more than 3,000 in 1992 (Nicholls and Sutherland 1993, 60). The kind of material published on CD has also evolved and newer CDs include source or reference material; at the same time, the median price dropped to a low of $453 in 1992, and a greater percentage of titles, about 25 percent, were available for the Macintosh (Nicholls and Sutherland 1993, 61).

Titles on CD-ROM consist of digitized information on plastic disks that are similar in appearance to audio compact disks. Text CDs are generally marketed for an IBM or IBM-compatible workstation that consists of a PC with an additional compact disk drive. Generally, the retrieval software is provided with commercial disks (here the emphasis is on commercial), but occasionally, it must be separately acquired. In addition to commercially produced titles, there has been an explosion in the number of CD-ROM titles and databases being produced by agencies of the U.S. government. This trend toward CDs produced by the U.S. government can only be expected to accelerate, as outlined in a recent report on government information. "Overall, less information will be printed. While some information will remain exclusively in print because of its unique characteristics or user needs, electronic formats will be the only requirement for other information products and services. This will be particularly true for statistical, bibliographic, scientific, and technical information, for which electronic technologies are especially well suited. . . . Because information will be created electronically, increasingly it will be available first in electronic formats'' (*GPO 2001* . . . 1991, 6). Many of these are offered through the library depository program, and initially, a significant number were distributed without sophisticated retrieval software or no software. With government agencies actively producing in this format, there has been an increase in the availability of statistical files on CD (the 1990 census files, for example), some of which are being produced only on CD or magnetic tape. In 1996, the U.S. Government Publications Office took a bold next step and proclaimed its intention to move to a totally electronic distribution of material by 1998; after a period of general comment and further study, the final recommendation was for a more gradual, five- to seven-year transition running through FY 2001 (*Study* . . . 1996, iii). For depository libraries, in particular, but also for other libraries acquiring material from the government, this will mean a probable increase in the number of CDs being received, and, more significant, growth in the number of electronic files stored remotely that are accessed over the Internet or by other means.

For any library contemplating adding CD titles to its collection, there will be start-up costs for the appropriate hardware and possibly, the need to invest in a retrieval software. Initially, index and abstract titles such as *Reader's Guide to Periodical Literature* and *Psychological Abstracts* were the most common type of CD. Increasingly, however, the U.S. government has issued text and data files from a wide variety of agencies, such as the Bureau of the Census, the Internal Revenue Service, and OSHA, on CD. Also, other voluminous titles, such as the *Beilstein Handbook of Organic Chemistry*, are being reformatted and issued on CD. Springer Verlag's CD-ROM version of the handbook, entitled *Beilstein Current Facts*, was announced with an initial annual subscription price in excess of $30,000; while steep, this is less than the price of the print version each year and will offer all of the expanded searching capability that makes CD-ROM a desirable format and one that is attractive to patrons. The relatively high cost of any given CD-ROM title, however, of necessity means that a decision to purchase is a very deliberate one. As one writer succinctly stated, ''CD-ROMs have risen to an important serials issue because of budget considerations, impact on overall development of the collection, maintenance requirements for both software and hardware, additional skills and education for staff, cataloging challenges and decisions about cancellation of duplicate paper products or online services'' (Nissley 1989, 20). Consequently, serials librarians have responded with new ways to handle this format and have integrated it into their work flow.

Acquiring CD Titles

Once the decision has been made to place a subscription for a CD-ROM title, the serials librarian must decide from whom to acquire it. Most of the traditional subscription vendors will handle library subscriptions for CD titles, and some of them will even arrange for the library to try out a sample disk. Examples are EBSCO, Faxon, and B.H. Blackwell. There are also firms that specialize in supplying only CD-ROM titles, and they can provide detailed information on each title, such as software required, number of disks per year, coverage, original source of the data, and licensing requirements. Since they have many of the databases in-house, they can also make arrangements for libraries to test and evaluate specific titles. Currently, the dominant producers and vendors for CD titles of interest to libraries are: SilverPlatter, Wilson, and DIALOG. In each case and for each title, whether it is *PsycLit* or *Reader's Guide* or *NTIS*, the serials staff needs to know at the time of ordering whether the subscription involves outright purchase of the disks or if the disks are being licensed for use. In the first instance, the library owns the disks and generally receives a series of update disks over the course of the subscription; these disks can be retained permanently by the library. Even if the library ultimately cancels the CD subscription, it owns the disks. H.W. Wilson markets its titles in this manner. If the publisher only licenses the library to use the title, the more common approach, then the library leases the disks and retains them only for the duration of the subscription. The licensing agreement is a contract that covers the type of use and contains specific language about any restrictions on the use of the disks. Warro discusses the actual limitations on what a library can and cannot expect in a typical contract (Warro 1994, 173–177). There is also an ALA guide to CD-ROMS (Bosch, Promis, and Sugnet 1994). Generally, use of the disks is limited to the patrons or clientele of that particular library. In an academic library setting where users of other area libraries and local citizens are often allowed building access, but not borrowing privileges, restricting the use of the CD-ROM title to only one's own users can sometimes be problematic. Meeting the terms of the agreement may require close monitoring of CD-ROM workstations and special sign-up procedures.

For titles that are licensed, each disk in a given year is usually cumulative and supersedes the previous disk, and the previous disk must be returned. Cumulative or archival disks that span several years, 1990–1994, for example, may be issued as well, and these become part of the library's collection as long as the library maintains an active subscription. In 1989, the average cost of a year's subscription to a serial title on CD-ROM was a little more than a thousand dollars. Today, although CDs can still be among the more expensive subscripitons for humanities and social sciences titles, their prices have not increased as dramatically as periodicals in general and in a few cases, the price of selected titles has even gone down.

At the point of acquisition, the library must also decide if it wishes to purchase any backfile years and what the cost versus benefit to patrons will be. Since some titles on CD-ROM, such as the *Monthly Catalog of Government Publications*, are distributed by more than one company, it is prudent to investigate the differences in price, coverage, and indexing to determine which is the better choice for an individual library. Many companies also offer a quantity discount so that a large institution that receives more than one CD subscription may be entitled to a 5 or 10 percent discount on the second and subsequent subscriptions. Additionally, some regional OCLC networks and consortiums are able to offer their members a small discount, generally 5 percent, on any CD title that they order through the network, since the network is ordering titles in quantity. These are all useful ways to help reduce the high cost of CD titles.

Cataloging and Classification of CDs

For many library collections, there will be no debate over whether or not to catalog CD-ROM titles. With an increased emphasis on having all the titles a library owns reflected in its catalog of holdings, it will be apparent that cataloging CD-ROM titles makes good sense; they are in the library collection and the best way to make them easy to locate and accessible is to provide appropriate bibliographic records. The next question is which format takes precedence in the cataloging; the fact that the CD-ROM title can be both a computer file and a serial means that a case could be made for cataloging them either as machine-readable datafiles or as serials. Several years ago, it was this author's observation that many CD-ROM titles were cataloged in RLIN as serials; the Library of Congress records were mainly, if not exclusively, serials format records. The CONSER policy at that time was that these datafile serials were to be cataloged as serials. A more recent search of selected titles resulted in about equal numbers cataloged as datafiles as cataloged as serials.

When one considers that the MDF (machine-readable datafile) format allows for a title to be either a serial or a monograph and provides extra fixed fields, as well as unique variable fields to detail the physical format and the system requirements, then it is fairly straightforward to contend that the MDF format is the more appropriate one. The datafile format also allows for the inclusion of both ISSN and continued and continuing title fields (780 and 785). Examples of records from each of these formats are shown in Figures 7.2 and 7.3. Given the dual nature of many CD-ROM titles, they are machine files but they often have periodicity, one can see the advantages of MARC format integration when both aspects will be able to be conveyed more easily. Recently, CONSER reversed its earlier policy and announced that, beginning with the implementation of the second phase of format integration in March 1996, the primary format indicator for CD-ROMs and other computer files would be the computer file, and the seriality of CD-ROMs that are periodicals in frequency would be expressed as the secondary format indicator. This reversal of past CONSER practice, while not popular in all quarters, makes good sense to a number of serials librarians and serials catalogers who have cataloged these titles as computer files all along.

The issue of call numbers for CD-ROM titles is purely a local option and will depend, to some extent, on whether or not the disks are placed on a shelf that patrons access, whether they are kept next to the workstations, or whether they are at a service desk. A library might want to assign a call number, merely to be able to establish a shelflist file of CD-ROM titles, or to keep a count of

Figure 7.2
CD-ROM Serial Cataloged in MDF Format

NOTIS CATALOGING
UP-AGP5939 FMT D RT m BL s DT 05/24/89 R/DT 05/24/89 STAT mc E/L ?
DCF a D/S D SRC d PLACE mau LANG eng MOD T/AUD D/CODE c DT/1
1986 DT/2 9999 DF/TYP d MACH a FREQ q REG r GOVT

035/1: : |a (CStRLIN)PAUG89-D6
035/2: : |a (CaOTULAS)185161704
040: : |a PU-Med |c PU-Med |d PU
090/1: : |a CD-ROM |b 7 |p 1 |i 05/24/89 CT
245:00: |a PsycLIT |h [computer file]
260: : |a Wellesley Hills, MA : |b SilverPlatter Information Services, |c1986-
300/1: : |a computer laser optical disks ; |c 4 3/4 in. |e computer floppy disks +
template.
315: : |a Quarterly
362/1:0 : |a 1986-
440/1: 0: |a SilverPlatter information system
500/1: : |a Title from label on disk.
500/2: : |a Each new disk is cumulative from 1983.
500/3: : |a Accompanied by installation diskettes and manual.
520/4: : |a Summaries of the world's serial literature in psychology and related
diskiplines compiled from the PsyINFO online database and Psychological
abstracts, published by the American Psychological Association.
538/5: : |a System requirements: IBM PC, XT or AT or compatible; 512 K; PC or
MS DOS 2.1 or higher; 1 floppy disk drive or hard disk drive; CD-ROM drive.
650/1: 0: |a Psychology |x Abstracts |x Software.
650/2: 0: |a Psychology |x Indexes |x Software.
710/1:20: |a American Psychological Association.
710/2:20: |a SilverPlatter Information, Inc.
730/3:02: |a Psychological abstracts.
730/4:01: |a PsycINFO (Data base)
740/5:01: |a Psyc Lit.
950: : |l REF |e 104\\Current.\rec'd\Ref.Room\ |z Currently received |i05/24/89 C

the number of these titles in the collection. One example of a local classification decision is the assignment of a call number that consists of a format prefix plus a sequential number as in: CD-ROM 2. Another possible approach is to assign the same type of call number, Library of Congress classification number, for example, to CDs as to print material. This gives the library the opportunity to integrate these materials on the open shelves, if desired, but may also facilitate their retrieval by call number in the OPAC. If every branch library uses a separate sequence of cardinal numbers, then searching for CD-ROM 25 may result in a list that contains five instances of CD-ROM 25 in five different locations for five completely different titles.

It will be worth watching in the future what happens with the various proposals for dealing with multiple versions of the same title on one record, and what the ramifications will be for dealing with CD-ROMs and print versions. This will only be an issue if the contents of the paper version and the CD-ROM

Figure 7.3
CD-ROM Title Cataloged in Serial Format

```
ID:DCLCSN9238138-S RTYP:c  ST:p  FRN:  MS:c EL:     AD:04-27-89 CC:9110 BLT:as
DCF:a CSC:d MOD:  SNR:  ATC:     UD:06-06-93
CP:mau L:eng SL:0 GPC:  CPI:0 ALPH: ISDS:     TYP:
PSC:c  D:198u/9999 FRQ:q REG:r PHY:  REP:    CNC:abi  IS:
MMD:    OR:  POL:  DM:  RR:     COL:    EML:    GEN: BSE:
    010    sn9238138
    035    (OCoLC)19613770
    042    lcd
    050 1  BF1$b.P92
    245 04 The PsycLit database$h[computer file].
    246 10 PsycLit
    246 10 Psyc lit
    260    Boston :$bSilverPlatter,
    300    computer laser optical disks ;$c4 3/4 in.
    310    Quarterly (cumulative)
    500    Title on disk label: PsycLit.
    500    System requirements: (Minimum) DOS-compatible PC; 640K RAM, including 500K free;
DOS 3.1 or higher; Microsoft Extensions, version 2.0 or higher (version 2.1 or higher with DOS
version 4.0 or higher); floppy disk drive; hard disk, with 650K available for SPIRS software and
2.5MB available for temporary storage of data; ISO 9660-compatible CD-ROM drive with cables
and interface card; monitor; printer (optional). (Recommended) 386 CPU with 80MB hard disk;
4MB RAM; DOS 5.0; Microsoft Extensions, version 2.1 or higher; high-density floppy disk drive;
CD-ROM drive; color VGA monitor; printer.
    500    Accompanied by user's guide (1 v. (loose-leaf)) and SPIRS software on 3 1/2 in. or 5 1/4 in.
disk.
    500    Also usable with a comparable Macintosh system when accompanied by MacSPIRS
software and other Macintosh-related accompanying materials.
    500    Description based on: Jan. 1974-Dec. 1982; title from title screen.
    515    Consists of an archival disk, updated and reissued irregularly; and a current disk, reissued
quarterly.
    520    Contains summaries of the world's serial literature in psychology and related disciplines,
compiled from the PsycInfo database; current disk <1987-Sept. 1992-> contains also a separate
database of summaries of the world's English-language chapters and books: PsycLit book
chapters & books on SilverPlatter.
    550    Issued by: American Psychological Association.
    580    CD-ROM ed. of: Psychological abstracts.
    580    Also available online, from 1967, as: PsycInfo (DIALOG File 11); and, for current material,
as: PsycAlert (DIALOG File 140).
    650 0  Psychology$xAbstracts$xData bases.
    650 0  Psychology$xIndexes$xData bases.
    710 20 American Psychological Association.
    730 00 PsycLit book chapters & books on SilverPlatter.
    775 1  $tPsychological abstracts$x0033-2887$w(DLC)   29023479$w(OCoLC)1763052
```

version are truly the same; often the machine-readable publication has additional material or extra files, or the print and the CD-ROM do not cover the same time periods while the print title has been changed or modified for the CD version. This variation between the two formats is a consideration when a library is making the decision on whether or not to cancel print versions of a title. Often, a good CD vendor's catalog will provide enough specific information on coverage and the source of the original data to help libraries in making selection and cancellation decisions for CD-ROM and print titles, respectively.

Receipt of CD-ROMs

Once the initial CD disks have been received on the subscription and someone has verified that all of the appropriate search software and users' manuals are included, it is appropriate to set up an ongoing receipt routine for the subsequent disks. There are advantages to performing the same sort of check-in routines for CD titles that are done for periodical issues. CD titles that are serials are usually issued quarterly or semiannually and there are individual units to be recorded and occasionally claimed. Therefore, an online receipt record or a manual check-in record is a good way to track the receipt. If the title is cumulative (each disk supersedes the previous one), and it is being received in an online record, it is reasonable to reflect just the period of time covered by the latest disk. Instructions about returning superseded disks can be made in the receipt record. Many libraries stamp a property or receipt date stamp on journal issues after they are checked in; it is not as easy to do this with a CD disk, since it is generally encased in plastic, but one can stick on a plain label and stamp that.

Duplication of Formats

For many libraries, at least initially, a CD-ROM subscription to an index or abstract is an additional subscription and not a replacement for the print copy. This means greater expense for the serials budget in a time of shrinking resources. In a study of CD-ROM use in Western Europe, libraries reported that the print version was used less when the library also held a CD-ROM subscription and that the CD-ROMs saved staff and users' time. About half of the respondents reported a willingness to cancel print subscriptions for some titles, but in some instances, the print subscription to be cancelled was the second print copy for the institution (Raitt and Chen 1990, 18–19). There can also be differences in coverage between the CD version and the print title and often fewer years represented in the CD-ROM version. In some libraries, a "wait-and-see" approach is the norm, and CD-ROM titles have been added and no print subscriptions cancelled until the reference staff evaluates the use of the titles on CD-ROM. It is quite possible that the more stringent acquisitions budgets of the late 1990s, the massive serials cancellation projects that many libraries are being forced to undertake, and the mushrooming of both free and paid journal titles on the Internet will make canceling print subscriptions for titles also held in CD-ROM an inevitability. As with any serials purchase which represents a commitment of dollars over many years, library staff will want to carefully weigh the benefits of each new CD-ROM title against the rather high subscription price and the possibility of needing to add more workstations. To help justify the costs of CDs received on subscription rather than through licensing, libraries may want to forward earlier disks to a branch library each time a new disk is received. It is possible to do this for titles in which the library retains all disks.

Users at another site benefit from having access to the title even though they do not have the very latest disk, while the library gets additional use from the disk for the same price.

Networking CD-ROMs

The CD-ROM title, like the paper journal titles, arrives as a single physical piece. Initially, most libraries mounted their CD titles one title to a given workstation. Only a single user could be using the title at any one time. The technology now exists, and has for several years, to network or link CD workstations to allow multiple access to a certain title from more than one workstation. For heavily used titles such as *Psychological Abstracts*, offering a title at more than one station is a definite advantage and reduces waiting time and user frustration. Several vendors such as SilverPlatter and Novell offer options for networking CD-ROM workstations in a Local Area Network (LAN) or for taking advantage of the newer client/server technology with databases loaded on a server and then accessed remotely by a group of clients.

COMPUTER TAPE FILES

Although computer tapes of index databases are not a new concept, current uses are more sophisticated and more powerful for the user than previously. A number of integrated system vendors market software that links the titles cited in commercial indexes (such as the Wilson indexes) to the library's own bibliographic file. The patron searching *Readers' Guide* online with a hit for a citation from *Southern Literary Review* will see that the library owns *Southern Literary Review* and then will be given the option to display its call number and library location. While the cost of a database on computer tape far exceeds that of a CD subscription and may be as high as $10,000–$15,000 per year, the immediate advantage of the database is that it can be accessed simultaneously by many users. Serials librarians and subject bibliographers are now being asked to grapple with the issues of deciding which computer databases to load into their online systems. In addition to the subscription cost, there is the cost of the initial software that provides the so-called "hook to holdings" as well as the time and expense of creating or obtaining and then testing the load program for each database to be mounted. Local tape loading is a high maintenance activity for the library systems staff and often includes: developing and/or customizing the load programs, loading tapes or FTPing in files, and running index regeneration programs. Depending on the sophistication of the existing product, there will be an ongoing effort for the loading of subsequent tapes and index regeneration that will need to be integrated into the systems staff's regular work flow. Patrons need the latest information and for any information to have been indexed in a timely fashion; one advantage of locally loading database tapes is that the information is more current than can ever be possible with a quarterly CD-ROM product. Some vendors now provide these database files through FTP (File Transfer Protocol) rather than on tape; this facilitates loading the data, since it eliminates the manual steps of tape handling and mounting. Nonetheless, a staff member must still be designated to retrieve and bring in the file to the library's local system at the appointed time.

Since the cost and maintenance issues surrounding the local loading of database files are considerable, some libraries have created special task forces or standing committees drawing on individuals from collection development, reference, and other public service areas to debate the issues and to make recommendations on which databases are most appropriate for the library's collection. This type of access to multiple databases, offered in conjunction with the library's online catalog and at the same workstation, greatly extends access to the library's own collection and makes more readily available a wealth of other periodical and monograph literature. The library patron is able, in one online session, to mine the riches of several database and catalog resources.

THE FUTURE

Microforms and newspapers will continue to exist and to be used; microforms because they fill a storage and preservation niche that will not quickly be subsumed or replaced by the alternative electronic technologies, and newspapers because they recognize that they need an online presence which many of them have already begun to create and market and because individuals will for some time to come prefer to sip their morning brew with paper, not screen, in hand. The publications of governments and international organizations are an important public record of the issues of the day; their publication is of value to scholars both present and future, whether they come to light in paper, on fiche, on CD, or on the Web.

The CD-ROM medium will also be with us for some time to come, as it does have definite advantages for the compression of large quantities of information into a compact, portable form. It was probably the breakthrough technology in terms of putting workstations at the users' fingertips and also represented, for some libraries, the early stages in the concept of the scholar's workstation. Even networked CDs, however, are bounded and limited by the limits of the network itself. Computer tapes and files available via FTP provided easy access across the campus with the tie-in to local holdings, a very powerful feature, yet required a library commitment to system maintenance and, at times, a very staff-intensive effort. All of these formats will receive competition from the various online offerings on the Internet. Therefore, in the future, the emphasis will be on information widely dispersed in time and space and format, and yet, available wherever the information seeker is and whenever he or she wishes.

REFERENCES

Bosch, Stephen, Patricia Promis, and Chris Sugnet. 1994. *Guide to Selecting and Acquiring CD-ROMS, Software and Other Electronic Publications*. Chicago and London: American Library Association (ALCTS Acquisitions of Library Materials Section, Publications Committee).

"CD-ROM Update." 1990. *Library Systems Newsletter* 10, no. 8: 63–65.

Farrington, Jean Walter. 1981. "Out of the Dungeon: Mainstreaming Microforms." *Serials Librarian* 5, no. 4: 37–40.

GPO 2001: Vision for a New Millennium. 1991. Washington, DC: U.S. Government Printing Office.

Hernon, Peter, and Charles R. McClure. 1992. "Dissemination of U.S. Government Information in CD-ROM and Other Forms." *CD-ROM Professional* 5, no. 2: 67–71.

Nissley, Meta. 1989. "CD-ROM in Libraries: Revolution or Revolt." *CD-ROM Librarian* 4, no. 9: 20–21.

Nicholls, Paul, and Patricia Sutherland. 1993. "The State of the Union: CD-ROM Titles in Print 1992." *CD-ROM Professional* 6, no. 1: 60–64.

Raitt, David, and Ching-chih Chen. 1990. "Use of Optical Products in Libraries and Information Centres in Western Europe." *Electronic Library* 8, no. 1 (February): 15–25.

Schwartz, Candy. 1992. "The CD-ROM Journal Literature: Where Do You Look?" *CD-ROM Professional* 5, no. 1: 42–46.

Study to Identify Measures Necessary for a Successful Transition to a More Electronic Federal Depository Library Program: Report to the Congress. June 1996. Washington, DC: U.S. Government Printing Office.

Warro, Edward A. 1994. "What Have We Been Signing? A Look at Database Licensing Agreements." *Library Administration and Management* 8, no. 3: 173–177.

8

The Electronic Explosion: From E-Mail to World Wide Web

The emergence of integrated digital communications systems appears to be rapidly undermining previous commitments to the print-on-paper communication system. The scholar-producers of library collections are increasingly recognizing digital systems as the new "core" or "defining" technology of the post-industrial era, and it is quite apparent that they are shifting knowledge production to this new medium with great rapidity.

Harris and Hannah (1996, 4)

INTRODUCTION

In the past several years, electronic mail has transformed the way many Americans and other people around the world work, communicate, and correspond for business and pleasure. With this surge in the use of the Internet for e-mail, it is not surprising that the electronic journal, along with other forms of electronic text, is gaining in popularity as a fast and easy way to make current information available to many individuals at low cost. Until very recently, there were only a handful of electronic journal titles, all published from academic institutions, and nearly all free of charge. Over the past year, a significant number of commercial publishers have begun to develop and implement plans for their own online journals using the latest in technology and distribution. "Traditional practices for buying, storing, and accessing journals are being challenged by the advent of electronic journals and electronic full-text periodical

products that are stored remotely and delivered on demand via the Internet''
(Ketcham and Born 1996, 45).

EARLY ELECTRONIC PUBLICATIONS

The earliest handful of online or electronic journals were scholarly in nature
and grew out of communications and related disciplines. Some examples of these
early titles are: *Ejournal, Electronic Journal of Communication, Journal of the
International Academy of Hospitality Research, New Horizons in Adult Education, Postmodern Culture*, and *Psycoloquy*. The oldest of these, *Psycoloquy*,
began publication in 1985 as an electronic bulletin board, while *Ejournal* started
in April 1991 as a forum for discussing the problems and advantages of electronic text. Only a few years ago, the prevalent format for e-journals was ASCII
files which were distributed over the Internet or Bitnet or on floppy disks; the
onus was then on the local site or library to receive or load the data on a
workstation, verify the contents, and then post it on the local system (Litchfield
1991, 83). The files could be single files sent to an individual or departmental
e-mail account or multiple files represented by a table of contents which the
recipient (in many cases, library staff) had to download or request from the
remote location and then load or post onto the local system.

It is easy to see that the local storage and retrieval of e-journals opens a Pandora's box
of new activities for library systems and technical services personnel. In the past, journal
processing consisted of receiving, marking, binding and shelving of hard copy materials
with only bibliographic data stored online. With e-journals, all of this activity will occur
online, requiring a higher level of computer sophistication than may currently exist in
most serials receiving units. (Litchfield 1991, 84)

It is critical to note that since this statement was made in 1991, technology has
leapfrogged forward, and the future for serials processing that Litchfield and
others predicted did not come to pass and probably will not.

Just as scholars found the Internet to be fast and efficient for disseminating
information, so, too, did the library profession take early advantage of the Internet as a means of keeping its constituents informed about library activities
and developments in the publishing world. Several library-related newsletters
and journals were inaugurated which took advantage of e-mail, including several
lists of potential interest to serials librarians. SERIALST, ACQNET, and
GOVDOCS-L are all active listservs whose subscribers in some cases number
in the thousands, and each has an editor or editorial board who reads all incoming messages and then groups and posts messages on a frequent, if not daily,
basis. Initially, SERIALST was an unedited list. With time and the maturing of
the medium, editorial control has been tightened somewhat, making the contents
more relevant and better organized with multiple comments on the same issue
grouped together. Examples of other online newsletter publications are: *Newsletter on Serials Pricing Issues* and *ALCTS Network News*. The serials pricing

newsletter actively solicits contributions and comment, and can be the site for a lively exchange of views between publishers and librarians. The *ALCTS Network News*, informally dubbed AN2, is an official publication of the Association for Library Collections and Technical Services, a division of the American Library Association, and is somewhat more structured in nature and includes news of ALCTS and ALA that is relevant to its members. Thus far, there is no subscription fee to subscribe to these lists and newsletters; they show up in one's e-mail box as they are distributed. Another example is the ACQNET Newsletter for monograph and serials acquisitions, which is also an edited newsletter. An annotated list of discussion lists and e-journals for technical services staff recently appeared in LRTS (Reich et al. 1995, 303–319). Individuals wishing to access these titles used to have to subscribe to these titles themselves or through their institutions, which would probably load the issues on some sort of server. Today, they may still choose to receive them through their personal e-mail accounts, but also have the option of reading them on one of the many news readers which a number of colleges and universities also provide.

Libraries today can choose to bypass entirely this process of intensive in-house manipulation of files that are requested and then locally loaded. What has made this possible is the coming of age of the World Wide Web and the relative ease with which colleges and universities and their libraries are able to mount local Web servers. With a Web server, a library no longer needs to retrieve and mount e-journals and other files locally unless the library decides to act as the publisher or distributor for the publication. (The University of Pennsylvania Library, for example is the distributor for the publication *The Scientist*.) Instead, all that is required is that the library provide the links on the home server to point to the files or data on whatever machine it is located, wherever. Setting up a local Web server does involve some work for systems staff, but the work involved is fairly straightforward. Creating the links can be handled by either systems staff or often by librarians who have the requisite knowledge of HTML. Creating the link for any given electronic publication or site, for example, only needs to be done once, and there is no longer any need to bring in files to the local system every time an issue or article is published or released. What is essential, however, is regular checking of the link to make certain that it is still an active one; it may be possible to automate some of this checking.

RECENT DEVELOPMENTS

In the Web environment, all the parts of a document are encoded using a standard called Hypertext Markup Language (HTML). HTML allows for the various parts of the text and the graphics to be linked to each other and to other documents and other sites. In order to navigate or use material that has been formatted in HTML, there are special software packages called Web clients or browsers. Examples are Lynx (a character-based client using VT100 terminal emulation that only deals with text) and Mosaic and Netscape, two graphical

Web browsers that allow for the full range of text, images, sound, and video. The number of Web sites has proliferated rapidly, and many universities and libraries that had installed gopher clients are quickly moving to the newer, more powerful Web servers, if they haven't already.

Many libraries now use the capabilities of HTML in conjunction with Web servers to provide easy links to electronic journals and other materials. The electronic journal resides on its home location and the local library points to it and then the user is automatically connected to it upon clicking. Each resource available through the WWW has its own unique code called a "Uniform Resource Locator" or URL. If an individual knows the URL for an electronic journal or other source, he or she can quite easily access it using Netscape or some other graphical browser, or even Lynx; if the library provides the linkages using HTML, then the user need only click on the name or picture of the resource and the computer does the rest. The user does not have to worry about knowing the URL, and all sorts of links upon links can be created by the library and followed by the user. More recently, commercial firms have begun providing sophisticated search engines which allow the Netscape or Lynx user to search various portions of the Internet's content. Searches can be phrase searches or keyword searches and the results usually employ some form of relevancy ranking with sites that have more of the words in the search occurring first. Examples of these new search tools are: Alta Vista, Lycos, InfoSeek, and Yahoo.

In 1989, one author was decidedly lukewarm about the future of electronic text: "the transformation from print to electronic is likely to be a slow process, and it is hard to visualize electronic transmission as the sole medium for more popular magazines. Electronic publishing may in fact continue as a parallel rather than a substitute technology" (Piternick 1989, 96). As it has turned out, Piternick was both right and wrong. Interest in the electronic format has surged, and there is a small number of journals that exist only in electronic format. Other titles, from popular ones like *MacUser* and *Newsweek*, to more scholarly journals have a presence on the Internet as full standalone publications, as part of the Electronic Newsstand (http://www.enews.com), or as simply tables of contents and abstracts. In addition, new electronic publications that exploit the graphic capabilities of the WWW are appearing daily in a wide variety of fields. One need only open a magazine or newspaper or watch the television screen to see or hear a reference to that publication's or broadcast's Web site. These rapid developments in multimedia publications have been made possible by the widespread use of the World Wide Web and the ready availability of the graphical browsers (Netscape, Mosaic, and the proprietary ones developed for subscribers to CompuServe, America Online, etc.), which make it possible for readers all over the world to access, read, print, and mark up these titles from their own desktops. As a consequence, the Internet is "perhaps the most democratic medium in history. Serious publishers, even corporate ones, carry no more weight on the World Wide Web than bored college students who publish on the Web in their spare time" (Ferguson 1995, 37).

FROM GOPHER TO WEB

The migration in technology from paper titles only to paper and Internet access through a gopher was relatively fast; the transformation from gopher title to Web presence was lightning speed in comparison. Although new paper journals are still being born each year, there is a steadily increasing cadre of electronic journals on the Internet which are beginning to change the complexion of serials collection development and to make inroads into the traditional serials selection process. Electronic journals have existed for several years now; in the earliest stages, a library would most likely make the decision to subscribe to the online title and the issues, as they were prepared and distributed, would be sent via e-mail to an individual or a department account. The receiving individual or department then would decide how best to make them available to its user community; one scenario was to mount the issues on a library computer and provide appropriate listings and pointers so that users could freely access them. With the use of gopher software at individual libraries, software allowing one computer to point and link to resources loaded elsewhere, it became possible for the interested library to link to many electronic journals without having to load them locally. This development expanded the scope of electronic journals (and other materials) that could be made easily available to the local user community. It no longer mattered where the text was stored, as the links were almost transparent to the user. The combination of electronic journals plus gopher software was a powerful one and is a concrete example of being able to take advantage of access rather than ownership of material. Gopher software became commonplace, and many colleges and universities had their own gopher servers; subsequently, many libraries also set up gophers with links to electronic journals and other scholarly and bibliographic resources that were thought to be of interest to their patrons. Gopher software was always limited by the fact that it only accommodates text; consequently, gophers have all but faded away, their appeal diminishing with the rapid development of the World Wide Web, a graphical, multimedia Internet environment that allows for the linking of documents that may include text, images, and sound. The possibilities for connecting all kinds of material are now unlimited (Ratzan 1994, 66).

With a gopher client or a Web server and without the need for local maintenance of large files, the selection decision for many electronic journals (those that are free for the linking) is divorced from economic or price considerations and is reduced to the most basic questions: what is the value of this material to this library's users and what is the advantage of having this resource readily accessible with such a link? There are many hundreds of free electronic journals, and they run the gamut of disciplines and include everything from *Academe This Week* (the online *Chronicle of Higher Education*) to *Journal of Buddhist Ethics, Essays in Medieval Studies*, and *Electronic Journal of Combinatoric*, to such refereed titles as: *Complexity International*, a computer science journal, *Educational Policy Analysis Archives, Journal of Artificial Intelligence Re-*

search, *Music Theory Online* (begun in 1993), *Flora Online*, and *Architronic: The Electronic Journal of Architecture.*

COMMERCIAL ELECTRONIC JOURNALS

As the Web has become the Internet publishing place of choice, and as an increasing number of individual users have high-end machines at their desks, both commercial and society publishers are positioning themselves as active players in the electronic arena. OCLC was one of the first providers of online journals with its *Online Journal of Current Clinical Trials.* Commercial and society publishers have also begun to make the transition to the digital format; by late 1996, both Academic Press and ACM (Association for Computing Machinery) had made virtually all of their titles available online, while Elsevier announced its intention to test the initial release of ScienceDirect (300 titles online in early 1997) with additional titles to be added throughout the year. This is a dramatic shift and has the potential to greatly impact on in-library use of print journal collections and the library's need or desire to acquire titles in a tangible (non-digital) format. OCLC, for example, has been a leader in making sci-tech electronic journals available with complete text and tables, charts, and other illustrative material using their own Windows-based graphical user interface. In 1992, the first *commercial* e-journal was introduced in a shared venture between OCLC and the American Association for the Advancement of Science (AAAS). This journal, *Online Journal of Current Clinical Trials*, is unique in that it is interactive; it incorporates Hypertext features which enable the user to scroll, to see references at any time, and to search on particular words. It is available online during selected hours, and publication is continuous and updated daily during the week. Initially, *Online Journal of Current Clinical Trials* carried the modest subscription fee of $100. According to one serials librarian, "it represents a new aspect of serials management. We now have a journal without the traditional volume numbers and issue numbers. It adds to the dynamic unpredictability of serials at the same time that it reduces the delay in getting important scientific information out into the field" (Schieber 1992, 33). Subsequently, AAAS sold the *Online Journal* to Elsevier, and there is now a choice of access and interfaces available. Other e-journals are now also available by subscription from OCLC, and the subscriber receives issues which are complete and finished and put out on a regular basis. These titles include: *Online Journal of Knowledge Synthesis for Nursing*, and *Electronics Letters Online* published by the Institute of Electrical and Electronics Engineers (IEEE). In each case, there is a subscription fee for the title, which can include the Guidon (graphical user interface) software or some other mode of access, unlimited connect time, and the ability to print locally and to download documents (Keyhani 1994).

Since the introduction of OJCCT, the number of e-journals has continued to proliferate to the extent that the 1994 edition of *Internet World's On Internet* listed more than 300 electronic journals and newsletters. In the short time since that edition was published, the number has probably tripled or quadrupled. Elsevier, publisher of more than 1,100 journals, also has entered this electronic playing field with its Elsevier Electronic Subscriptions service which gives libraries the choice of complete electronic editions either instead of or in addition to paper journals. The journal files are provided to libraries to be used with their own or commercial software such as OCLC's SiteSearch system or their Guidon graphical interface, and are handled through a licensing agreement.

For the OCLC online journals, the library is making a collection decision analogous to deciding to subscribe to a print journal; there is an annual fee and this gives the library unlimited access 23 hours a day. One difference, however, is that the library has the option of merely notifying users of the availability of this title to them for use on their own office or home workstations as well as of providing it on-site in the library. For the mostly free online journals, a library can decide to subscribe by receiving each issue on its own machine or by pointing to the journal through gopher software or via a Web server.

Other large publishers are entering the arena, and one other noteworthy example is Academic Press, which is offering full text of its complete list of journal titles to library consortia; the libraries in the consortium will have online access to all of the journals for which their members now hold current print subscriptions.

One issue that nags at the scholarly world and that has not yet been fully resolved is the value placed on an article published only online and not coexisting or solely existing in print form. Many faculty authors and those individuals who evaluate them for academic tenure and promotion are having difficulty arriving at standards for assessing online publication. Other individuals have carefully delineated all of the functions that an electronic journal must satisfy in order to be accepted as a substitute for print (Schaffner 1994).

SPECIAL PROJECTS

E-Journals

Several consortia are also making electronic journals available either in local online catalogs or over the Internet. The Red Sage project is a cooperative effort between AT&T Bell Laboratories and the University of California at San Francisco for making medical journals available online. A number of large universities and Elsevier recently completed a five-year pilot project for the distribution of electronic journals in materials science called The University Licensing Project (TULIP). In the final report on this project, one of the conclusions from the studies of users is that "there is enthusiasm about the concept of desktop access to electronic information, but the end of paper products seems to be far away still. Besides some practical benefits of paper products, there also seem to be *'emotional' ties* with paper and the library" (Hunter 1996). Other experimental approaches to distributing electronic journals involve cooperative efforts between foundations or university presses and libraries. Two examples are Project Muse and JSTOR. Project Muse is a joint effort of the Johns Hopkins University Press and the Johns Hopkins library and academic computing center to make the content of all of the press's 42 scholarly journals available over the World Wide Web. It is a combined effort involving the university press, librarians, computing staff, and others to make the full text of three journals published by Johns Hopkins Press accessible in the library and eventually over the Internet (DeLoughry 1994, A23). To date, Project Muse incorporates the full text of fifteen journals. One hallmark of this project is the involvement of the library from the beginning as a primary distributor, if not publisher, of faculty research. This, according to the library's representative on the project, has altered the role of the librarian: catalogers are tagging the information in the tables of contents and supplying the Library of Congress with subject headings, but more important, "librarians now view themselves as having a more direct involvement in the scholarly communication process—right from the beginning. They have agreed to be 'publisher's agents'—actively seeking and developing electronic scholarly publishing projects" (Cochenour 1995, 77). The Mellon Foundation, in conjunction with the University of Michigan and now several other university libraries, is developing a digital collection for the arts and sciences called the Journal Storage Project, or JSTOR. Initially, there will be ten titles in economics and history available through Michigan's Web site. Lastly, another project, based in Britain and called the Open Journal Project, brings together publishers and several professional societies (British Computer Society) for the purpose of publishing electronic journals in a network environment to provide maximum access to them.

In some of these projects, there is usually the requirement that the software at the individual user's desktop include a browser such as Netscape, Mosaic, or some other World Wide Web program rather than the basic VT100 emulation in order to get the full benefit of images as well as text. As the technology associated with providing access to electronic journals changes, the role of the publisher, the role of the university press, and the role of the librarian intersect and in some instances blur.

Newspapers

In addition to journals online, there is also a swell of interest among newspaper publishers in making their titles available both through the commercial online services such as America Online, CompuServe, and Prodigy, and now directly on the Internet where the costs to the publisher are less. Details of this trend are cited by Resnick (1994, 69–73) in a recent article, and key examples are the *San Jose Mercury News* which was put up on America Online in 1993, and the *Palo Alto Weekly* and the *Raleigh News and Observer*, both of which opted to publish directly on the Internet. The Palo Alto newspaper is free to those with Internet access; the Raleigh paper has both a free version available to all North Carolina public schools and a commercial version which it aims to sell to print subscribers at a price that is competitive with the paper copy. The *Wall Street Journal* is another newspaper that is experimenting with multiple forms of information delivery of some or all of the paper's contents over phone lines, via e-mail, and by fax (Montgomery 1993, 25–26). For the publishers of newspapers, "the fabric of a newspaper changes on the World Wide Web, where hot links, discussion forums, sounds, movies, and other features add new dimensions to news delivery. Moreover, new types of custom news delivery services are emerging" (Goldsborough 1995, 40). One commercial site called Commercial Newspaper Services includes details about approximately 200 newspaper sites that already exist or are in development (Goldsborough 1995, 40).

Since these ventures are relatively new, academic libraries are just beginning to deal with them, but as the number of newspapers proliferates and as the access becomes simpler, libraries will certainly want to reevaluate their print newspaper collections. It may be possible ultimately to provide access to a greater number of newspapers using the Internet than the cost of print subscriptions, since there are no mailing costs. The *New York Times* and the *Philadelphia Inquirer* and *Daily News*, and now a whole host of foreign newspapers, have Web sites which offer a portion of the day's news and sometimes supplemental material.

COMMERCIAL EFFORTS

Commercial publishers are also making much greater use of the Internet for creating awareness of their products and journals as well as offering paid subscriptions online. Examples of free titles include the Electronic Newsstand (table of contents and sample articles from a host of more popular news and sports magazines) and *Academe This Week* (the latest week's *Chronicle of Higher Education* online). Other publishers are offering the table of contents as a teaser with perhaps some free full text available, but not everything. For example, "*High Performance Computing* (HPC) sends free one-line summaries of articles to anyone who has previously sent e-mail to the subscription address. Interested readers then order articles by sending e-mail addresses to a designated electronic address. The full text of the desired item is then relayed back to the reader within minutes. Paid subscribers may select any article in the weekly index. Nonpaid subscribers have a limited choice" (Ratzan 1994, 64).

Another publisher who has demonstrated a readiness to move rapidly with the changing times is UMI. Its CD-ROM product, ProQuest Periodicals, is a cross between a CD-ROM index and abstract and a commercial document delivery service. These CDs include an index database to the publications and then full-text images (scanned) of the journals' contents. They provide the ease of sophisticated indexing along with the article as it appeared in the original publications with all of the photographs, charts, and other visual material. Fur-

thermore, the article or selected pages can then be laser-printed at the workstation. Examples of ProQuest titles are: Business Periodicals Ondisc, General
Periodicals Ondisc, and Social Sciences Full Text. These databases are expensive, but provide the contents of many, many journals. For smaller libraries,
Magazine Express offers cover-to-cover contents of about 80 journals with indexing of well over 100 titles. UMI, like many other vendors, also has plans
for a Web version of its journal offerings.

In the past year, Web software has made it possible for libraries to point to
a number of electronic journals without subscribing to them. This has been
particularly true for scholarly journals published or produced out of universities
and for some of the more popular news magazine titles. The commercial publishers of scientific and technical journals have gradually been beginning to
address how best to take advantage of this new medium. For them, there are
real issues related to pricing and the need to continue to make a profit. Elsevier
Science recently announced that its more than 1,100 journals will all be available
in electronic form in addition to or in lieu of paper, and that it will sell them
through an electronic subscription license. This project is seen as a logical suc-
cessor to TULIP, an Elsevier experiment in which the full text of more than 40
materials science journals was made available to nine research libraries. Elsevier
has billed this as an experiment and has indicated that it ''wants to be with its
clients at the forefront of electronic publishing by starting now to develop an
open electronic journal infrastructure'' (Dietz 1995). In early 1996, Elsevier's
presence on the Web included four journals, several conference proceedings,
and tables of contents called ESTOC, Elsevier Science Tables of Contents Service. The service is updated weekly and provides coverage of about 900 journals
(www.elsevier.nl/cas/estoc/). Another full-text title on the Elsevier Web page is
Immunology Today, which is available directly on the WWW or through OCLC
using its special Guidon software. One of the selling points of this version is
that it includes items not found in the print title such as job trends, a bookstore,
and a company directory.

The Association of Computing Machinery (ACM), a society publisher, several
years ago boldly announced that it would reinvent itself solely as an electronic
publisher. In an aggressive statement, ACM detailed the breakdown in the traditional cycle of authoring, submission, and publication of journal articles in
favor of release of material to the Internet, acceptance of critical comments from
colleagues and other researchers, and the appending or incorporating of these
comments into a document that is dynamic and not archived. As an answer to
this disintegration, ACM proposed to create its own digital library of all of its
literature which would be online and accessible by all society members in spring
1995 (Denning 1994). Although it did not meet its timetable, ACM today provides access to the tables of contents, abstracts, and reviews of all papers published in its journals since 1985, and this archive can be searched by keyword.
Thus, ACM offers a breadth of coverage (although not yet the depth) not seen
with some other electronic journal services (www.ac.org/pubs./toc). Other com-

mercial publishers are making their titles available as well, either directly or through a third-party distributor. For example, Chapman and Hall mounted all of its journals on the WWW in 1996; access, however, is only offered in conjunction with a subscription to a print version of the title. With the print subscription, the library can arrange for all of the registered users within that institution to have access. Not only is the user able to search tables of contents for all issues in a volume, but the electronic version will be searchable up to four weeks before the print title is in the library. An example of one such journal is the *Journal of Materials Science*, which, for the 66 issues of the several titles that comprise this title, costs $3,595 for the print version and $4,150 for the print plus Internet access, an additional cost of only about 15 percent.

Based in the United Kingdom, CatchWord is one example of a distributor which "specializes in the re-publishing or parallel publishing of printed scholarly journals on the Internet. . . . Access is controlled, allowing either subscription based or pay-per-page access" (CatchWord Ltd. 1996). CatchWord maintains multiple servers around the world and exists as a service provider to publishers and collects no money from clients. The access is controlled by the publisher, not by CatchWord, but this firm does offer document delivery to the user's desktop. Carfax is one publisher that is making use of CatchWord as its distributor.

Yet another commercial enterprise is JOURNALS.At-HOME, a WWW site that contains a selection of tables of contents and abstracts for eighteen scientific and medical journals. Developed by Cadmus Digital Solutions, JOURNALS.At-HOME allows journal publishers to begin small and then expand their online offerings from just tables of contents to abstracts and eventually full contents. Cadmus will also offer document delivery service on its journals through a partnership with UnCover (Padmus 1996, 1). Also in the UK, the Institute of Physics, in collaboration with the large network provider SuperJANET and eight other scientific publishers, has the requisite material for electronic journals and the ability to offer graphics and moving images all quickly and with a new degree of manipulability (Pullinger and Baldwin 1996). Today, all of the Institute of Physics journals are available to print subscribers through a special licensing agreement.

Costs

As more libraries broaden their collection development policies to include electronic journals, it will be interesting to see what happens to the costs associated with these titles. These are the early days of electronic journals for a fee, and while libraries weigh the benefit of online publications in addition to or instead of print subscriptions (mainly the former at this point in time), publishers gingerly approach the delicate matter of setting prices for this new format. In many cases, the cost for access to the online version is a percentage added on to the cost of the print journal, and in some, but not all cases, a subscription to the print title is a prerequisite. For those publishers who wish to restrict use not just to the patrons of a particular library or campus but to limit the number of users who are logged on at any one time, the library may be required to pay access fees based on the number of simultaneous users or the number of passwords that are needed. Just as some libraries have already broken out the cost of other electronic media (computer tapes, CD-ROMs, floppy disk titles) from the rest of the serials budget, it is probable that the costs of electronic journals will be tracked separately from print journals, either as part of an overall electronic information budget and/or by subject category within the computer formats budget line.

PROCESSING ISSUES

Serials librarians were early and enthusiastic subscribers to the various professionally related listservs and newsletters. At that time, being an individual subscriber was simple and straightforward; the real questions arose when the library wanted to make electronic newsletters and journals available to patrons at a time when not every library terminal was a PC and not every student had high-powered computing at his or her desk. In one of the first articles to be published on the topic, Gail McMillan and her colleagues at Virginia Polytechnic Institute raised questions about the format itself and then detailed the various issues to be resolved before deciding to make e-journals available on the campus IBM mainframe computer (McMillan et al. 1991, 77–86). First, the issue of format: is the term "electronic journal" an oxymoron when the basic unit of information is no longer the journal or even the journal article, but rather "the electronic document or 'compuscript.' It (the electronic journal) will increasingly lose its resemblance to the journal article. It won't require numbering or check-in and it won't be limited by a style sheet. Over time it will incorporate unique features of the electronic medium such as hypertext links, interactive capabilities, and multimedia'' (McMillan et al. 1991, 81). Indeed, the electronic journal has all of the above today and is flourishing.

Also five years ago, many librarians (like McMillan et al.) foresaw a whole host of technical services issues surrounding electronic journals and these included: ordering, receiving, and cataloging of these electronic materials. Librarians wondered if serials clerks would need to receive issues of e-journals by e-mail and if so, how would they be checked in? Or would the serials clerk open the mailbox, request the issue or article and then forward it to systems staff who would actually upload or load it onto the mainframe? Happily, the rapid development from electronic journals available via e-mail to gopher server, and soon thereafter Web server, has meant that most of these questions have become moot. Libraries decide to point to the sites they wish to provide for their patrons and do not have to get involved in elaborate retrieval and receipt procedures for online material.

Providing full MARC cataloging records for electronic journals is another matter, however, and is viewed as essential by a majority of academic libraries. Cataloging electronic journals and newspapers ensures that the titles are represented in the online catalog like every other format in the library's collection. Serials catalogers and multimedia catalogers are assisted in their cataloging efforts by the existence of OCLC's InterCat Project, which was one of the first systematic attempts to catalog Internet resources. When the trial period was over in the spring of 1996, OCLC allocated funding for the project and it remains a starting point for cataloging these resources. The mere fact that libraries are cataloging electronic journals for the library's online catalog demonstrates a healthy trend to treat all serial formats equally and to make processing of any format as much a part of the mainstream work flow as possible.

THE LIBRARY'S ROLE AS INTERMEDIARY

With nearly every member of an academic community hooked up to the Internet and able to tap into electronic journals through the use of campus-wide information systems, gopher software and now Web servers, a fundamental question is whether there is a need for the library to play the role of information intermediary in making these e-journals available. On some campuses, the library has its own Web or gopher server and decides which electronic journals it would like to point to and make available based on its own curriculum and faculty's research interests. This policy of local selectivity provides direction to the users on a particular campus and saves them the trouble of wading through a plethora of lists or having to call up multiple Web sites to identify one title of interest. The increasing dilemma of Internet resources today is not a paucity of resources but an overabundance and not knowing exactly where to begin.

Although e-journals are said to be moving toward the mainstream, there are some in the field who predict that this is just a transitory phenomenon which will be replaced by documents on demand or some other form of article on request service or the provision of full text. Nonetheless, the number of refereed scholarly electronic journals is increasing, and publication here is being accepted by some universities as part of the tenure evaluation (Ratzan 1994, 64).

DOCUMENT DELIVERY AND FULL TEXT

The other significant development that is altering how serials librarians perform their daily tasks is the emergence and, some might say, burgeoning of document delivery services and full-text options. In addition to the journal publishers who are providing access to all of their titles as a package (Academic Press, Institute of Physics, for example), there are other vendors who provide indexing and abstracts of titles from a variety of publishers with full text for an increasing number of the titles. These title lists are dynamic and growing in size, but every few years the distributor must renegotiate the rights to the distribution of that title. Several examples of these products are: EBSCOHost from

EBSCO, *Expanded Academic Index* from Information Access Company, and ProQuest Direct from UMI. Increasingly, these products are moving to the Web and taking advantage of its superior graphic capabilities. These services have great appeal for students and other researchers because they enable the individual to locate so much more information onscreen without having to go anywhere. A key concern of serials librarians is the archiving of these journals and who will take responsibility for it. If the library cancels its subscription to the online version after several years, what happens in terms of that backfile of issues for the library's users: the library paid for five years' worth of coverage, will it be left with no paper issues and no online file to access either, or will there be ongoing access privileges to that portion of the file in which they have invested? Librarians also worry that the publishers or distributors of full text have not yet fully committed to long-term archiving and storage of this material. These are the early stages of delivery of full text and these and many other questions need to be and will be addressed in the next five years. In that period, serials librarians may find themselves spending more time on licensing and price negotiations than on completing paper volumes for binding. At the same time, serials librarians and others must continue to carve out and create a role for the library so that it remains an active player in this electronic circus.

REFERENCES

"Cadmus Debuts JOURNALS.At-HOME, Teams with UnCover Co. for Document Delivery." 1996. *Information Today* 13, no. 1: 1, 6.

CatchWord World Wide Web home page. 1996. (http://www.catchword.co.uk)

Cochenour, Donnice. 1995. "Project Muse: A Partnership of Interest." *Serials Review* 21, no. 3: 75–81.

Denning, Peter J., and Bernard Rous. 1994, November 30. "The ACM Electronic Publishing Plan." [E-mail to P. Renfro, forwarded to J. Farrington] [Online], November 30.

Dietz, Roland D.J. 1995. "Press Release: Elsevier Announces: Electronic Subscriptions, The Next Step after TULIP." SERIALST, February 23. Posted by John Tagler.

DeLoughry, Thomas J. 1994. "Journals Via Computer." *Chronicle of Higher Education* (March 9): A23–24.

Ferguson, Paul. 1995. "On the Cyber Racks." *Internet World* (September): 37–39.

Goldsborough, Reid. 1995. "News Paperless." *Internet World* (September): 40–44.

Harris, Michael H., and Stan A. Hannah. 1996. " 'The Treason of the Librarians': Core Communication Technologies and Opportunity Costs in the Information Era." *Journal of Academic Librarianship* 22, no. 1: 3–9.

Hunter, Karen. 1996, July 18. "TULIP Final Report: Executive Summary" [Online]. Available World Wide Web (http://www.elsevier.nl/locate/tulip).

Internet World's on Internet 94. 1994. Westport, CT: Mecklermedia.

ISI's Electronic Library Update. 1995. Vol. 1, no. 1 (April).

Ketcham, Lee, and Kathleen Born. 1996. "Projecting the Electronic Revolution While Budgeting for the Status Quo." *Library Journal* 121 (April 15): 45–51.

Keyhani, Andrea. 1994. "Building an Electronic Journal." In National Online Meeting (15th: New York, NY). New York: Learned Information, 257–61.

Langshied, Linda. 1991. "The Changing State of the Electronic Journal." *Serials Review* 17, no. 3: 7–14.

Litchfield, Charles A. 1991. "Local Storage and Retrieval of Electronic Journals: Training Issues for Technical Services Personnel." *Serials Review* 17, no. 4: 83–84.

McMillan, Gail et al. 1991. "Electronic Journals: Considerations for the Present and the Future." *Serials Review* 17, no. 4: 77–86.

Montgomery, Margot J. 1993. "Document Supply in a Changing World." *Interlending and Document Supply* 21, no. 4: 24–37.

Nicholls, Paul, and Patricia Sutherland. 1993. "The State of the Union: CD-ROM Titles in Print 1992." *CD-ROM Professional* 6, no. 1: 60–64.

Okerson, Ann. 1991. "The Electronic Journal: What, Where and When?" *Public Access Computer Systems Review* 2, no. 1: 5–24.

Piternick, Anne B. 1989. "Serials and the New Technology: The State of the 'Electronic Journal.' " *Canadian Library Journal* (April): 93–97.

Pullinger, David, and Christine Baldwin. 1996. "SuperJournal: A Project in the UK to Develop Multimedia Journals." [Online] *D-Lib Magazine*, January. Available on the World Wide Web (www.dlib.org/dlib/january96/briefings/01super.html).

Raitt, David, and Ching-chih Chen. 1990. "Use of Optical Products in Libraries and Information Centres in Western Europe." *Electronic Library* 8, no. 1: 15–25.

Ratzan, Lee. 1994. "The Internet Cafe: Network Incunabula." *Wilson Library Bulletin* 68 (May): 64–66.

Reich, Vicky, Connie Broos, Willy Cromwell, and Scott Wicks. 1995. "Electronic Discussion Lists and Journals: A Guide for Technical Services Staff." *Library Resources and Technical Services* 39, no. 3: 303–319.

Resnick, Rosalind. 1994. "Newspapers on the Net." *Internet World* 5, no. 5: 69–73.

Schaffner, Ann C. 1994. "The Future of Scientific Journals: Lessons from the Past." *Information Technology and Libraries* 13, no. 4: 239–247.

Schieber, Phil. 1992. "Online Journal of Current Clinical Trials Begins Electronic Publication." *OCLC Newsletter* no. 198: 33–34.

University of Pennsylvania Library home page. 1996. *Electronic Journals & News Sources* (http://www.library.upenn.edu/ej/xej-news-index.html).

9

Serials Cataloging in the Twenty-First Century: A Multiplicity of Challenges

INTRODUCTION

Change is sweeping through the cataloging world; radically different ways of approaching the process of cataloging are being introduced in many academic libraries, and library managers and practitioners are working to reverse the somewhat dull image cataloging conjures up in some individuals' minds. This change has been primarily focused on the cataloging of monographs, but serials cataloging, too, is now getting its share of attention and close scrutiny. The potent combination of local online catalogs and access to other libraries' catalogs through the Internet, coupled with shrinking library budgets, is forcing a reevaluation of the entire cataloging process and its intrinsic goals. In addition, the availability of cataloging services in the form of books ready for the shelf sent accompanied by machine-readable bibliographic records from OCLC, from firm order book dealers, and from several of the monograph approval plan vendors is prompting more libraries to outsource some or all of their cataloging and processing.

Opinions about the desirability of outsourcing are strong and divergent; two articles espousing contradictory views appeared recently in *Library Journal* (Gorman 1995; Waite 1995). Prior to this, writers in the field have been bemoaning in general the negatives associated with cataloging. One article bluntly acknowledged that "cataloging has a negative image to overcome [since] it is associated with the application of arcane rules rather than with the interesting problems in information retrieval, database design, or with managing in a dynamic environment'' (Gregor and Mandel 1991, 44). These same authors, nonetheless, proposed some specific areas in which change in the cataloging arena would be beneficial. These ranged from a reexamination of how patrons search catalogs and the trend toward linking several local catalogs together, to suggestions for simpler descriptive cataloging, a reduction in the number of LC rule interpretations, and changes in the way subject terms are applied. Indeed, since this article appeared there have been positive developments toward simplification, and one of these concepts, the core serials record, will be addressed later in the chapter.

As academic libraries in particular have migrated their cataloging processes from cataloging on one of the national utilities to cataloging in their own local systems, there has been a reduction in the amount of member copy available from the utilities. This lack of easily shared copy and the strictures of library budgets in general have made it imperative that library technical services units reexamine their cataloging practices and justify what they are doing. The old school of ''cataloging as perfect as possible'' is perhaps slowly giving way to a more pragmatic approach. How much detail is necessary in a cataloging record and what degree of authority control is essential? As one author aptly stated, ''Local administrative practice should emphasize lean records in the interest of both local and more general cost saving and service enhancement'' (P. Graham 1990, 217). This is a new age where less may indeed be more.

Serials cataloging traditionally serves several purposes, one of which is to detail a publication's history with linking notes to past titles and subsequent titles. Over the years, there have been differing opinions on the best way to deal with the complexities of a journal's changing titles. There has also been revived interest in minimal or core records for some serial titles, most especially those that are in esoteric, often non-Roman alphabet, languages. This chapter will focus on these and other developments in the way cataloging is carried out in academic libraries, the reasons for and against the cataloging and classification of serials, as well as trends in the cataloging of electronic publications.

CHANGES IN THE CATALOGING PROCESS

Effect of Local System

For many libraries, making the switch to local processing, that is, cataloging on the library's own online system, has forced a reexamination of the entire searching, ordering, and cataloging work flow. Although the cataloging is being handled locally, there is still a need for a bibliographic resource database for cataloging copy, whether it be Library of Congress weekly tapes, or the RLIN, or OCLC databases. This resource database can be both a source of cataloging copy from the Library of Congress and a way for individual libraries to share their records with other participating libraries in the United States and Canada and elsewhere. The library's local online system, comprised of the online public catalog (OPAC), circulation files, serials check-in records, and acquisitions orders as well as authority files, nonetheless takes precedence over any external resource datafile and, in this automated age, assumes great importance, since it is where the cataloging activity takes place. Furthermore, the most accurate and complete picture of the library's holdings from bound volumes to most recently received current issues will usually be found in the library's local system. When the local system is also where the cataloging actually takes place, then the initial acquisitions order record takes on greater significance. Typically, the acquisitions or source record is created in one of three ways: (1) by downloading a bibliographic record from an LC file or one of the utilities using special software, (2) by tape loading records from LC or some other source such as MARCIVE for U.S. government publications, or (3) by keying in a brief or full record from scratch.

In many libraries, the availability of large and comprehensive databases of MARC records together with the technology to easily import these records have made it possible to establish a rather complete bibliographic record at the time of ordering. Consequently, the online order record becomes the basis for the full cataloging record. This means that a greater emphasis is placed on making this initial acquisitions record the best record possible. Following this to its logical conclusion, this close attention to the caliber of the initial order record paves the way for a clerk in acquisitions to both receive the item and then to finish cataloging it. Some libraries have developed internal codes for indicating the quality of the acquisitions record based on its original source; these codes indicate to the receipt clerk whether he or she is able to go ahead and catalog the item upon receipt, whether it will have to be referred to one of the cataloging units, or whether or not it will be routed to delay shelves to be re-searched in the bibliographic utilities at a later date.

Cataloging upon Receipt

The concept of cataloging upon receipt in acquisitions is a radical departure from past practice for many libraries and one that requires adjustments on the part of staff at all levels. Ownership, either wholly or in part, of the cataloging process is being transferred out of the cataloging department and being shared with acquisitions staff. For this to work well, there needs to be good communication across department or division lines as well as appropriate training for all staff involved in cataloging. Nonetheless, in a time when the costs of cataloging an item have become ever greater and harder to justify, efficiencies in the work flow and reductions in the number of times an item is handled between receipt and getting to the shelf have to be seriously explored and tried. To date, this author is aware of this kind of transition taking place for monographs, but not necessarily for serials. The number of serials departments with cataloging backlogs of any size may be smaller than original cataloging departments with backlogs, and serials staff have long been conscious of the need to get serials items cataloged very quickly and the records available for the public due to the time-sensitive nature of much of the material. One might make the argument, and probably be convincing, that the rules governing serials title fields and the complexities of serials holdings records and the like mitigate against having the whole cataloging process done by a clerk upon receipt.

Staffing for Serials Cataloging

There is a whole category of monographic material that is cataloged by support staff, generally material that has good bibliographic records from the Library of Congress or some other source and that does not require much modification or the assignment of call numbers. Likewise, it is not unreasonable to expect that much of the straightforward serials cataloging for items with some sort of copy, including title changes, can be handled by a well-trained support staff person. Cataloging for unusual formats such as computer files and electronic journals, the assignment of call numbers, and true original cataloging (cataloging from scratch, as it were) are most often the responsibility of a cataloger librarian. Serials material may also be divided by language with titles in non-Roman alphabets in particular being routed to and then cataloged by specialized staff, but there are indeed some academic libraries where serials cataloging support staff and serials cataloger librarians handle all serials in all formats no matter what the language.

The location of serials cataloging staff on the library's organization chart has long been one of the biggest variables among serials departments in different libraries. There is a tendency today to move serials catalogers back into the cataloging department if they have been separated and part of a separate serials department, and this practice seems to be gaining in acceptance. The reasons can be traced to the intertwined nature of online files and online records, the existence of e-mail for intralibrary communication, and perhaps also a renewed recognition that separation by format is no longer necessary, particularly since format integration has now been achieved. All catalogers must now deal with added title fields (246s) for books as well as serials, and with the concept of the primary and secondary nature of the material to be cataloged.

Whether the serials cataloging staff is located in a separate serials department, however, or is considered a part of a larger cataloging department (an issue that is explored more fully in another chapter), they should have close interaction with the staff who are responsible for checking in periodicals and other serials. This promotes consultation between the check-in staff and the catalogers on possible title changes, on how to handle special supplemental publications, and the like. It can also work to reduce problems later on caused by missing title changes or classed separately supplements.

It is fairly typical for serials cataloger librarians to perform original cataloging and also to work closely with paraprofessional or high-level clerical staff who handle titles for which there is Library of Congress copy or acceptable records from another library. The bibliographic utilities load cataloging records from the Library of Congress weekly and between these records and cataloging contributed by member libraries, the amount of true original cataloging of newly published serials has certainly decreased, most definitely for English-language materials and the key Western European languages. For a time, many large academic libraries were engaged in massive retrospective conversion projects of all of their current (and sometimes even their ceased and non-current) serials titles, and contributed records for these older titles to RLIN and OCLC. With the more recent trend toward local processing and cataloging on one's own system, there has been a decline in the number of shared records available on RLIN, or at best a delay in their being available as quickly as in the past. The records from a library's local cataloging process must now be tape loaded into the utility database before they are there for use by other libraries, and some libraries, unfortunately, have stopped contributing their records altogether. This means that in some cases, there are fewer member records that can be used and modified by non-professional serials cataloging staff.

Despite the greater availability of cataloging copy for some serials titles, there are still categories of material that will often require original cataloging done by a librarian. Examples are: titles in esoteric or non-Roman alphabet languages, rare serials, serials in electronic formats such as CD-ROM or computer disks, and special collections of material that need extra notes or somewhat different treatment. Sometimes original cataloging for a serial needs to be done because the library cannot afford to wait for someone else to do the work. The immediacy of information in an online system and the need to check in successive periodical issues upon receipt add an element of urgency to the serials cataloging process. It does not seem appropriate to deny patrons access to five issues of a weekly waiting to be received, all for lack of a cataloging record. It is also accepted practice in many libraries that the original cataloger be the one responsible for assigning call numbers and doing any necessary authority work, while paraprofessional serials catalogers can be expected to search the database, select the cataloging record, do some modifications to the copy chosen, and then add the location and holdings information and any notes about shelving or retention. Many title changes can also be handled by paraprofessional staff.

Serials Cataloging Practices

Individual libraries' cataloging and classification practices for serials are more varied than for monographs, due in part to the dynamic nature of serials, the different possibilities for shelving them, and their very transience. Cataloging treatment for some types of serials may be linked to decisions made on how and where to shelve these serials. For example, periodicals may be handled differently from annuals and monographic series volumes, and newspapers may get briefer cataloging than periodicals or perhaps no call number. Titles that are only retained for a limited period of time and then discarded may not warrant the expense of staff time for full cataloging. If these titles are shelved alphabetically, they may not require call numbers either.

In some smaller library collections, patrons might be adequately served by having popular and general periodicals shelved by title and represented in an online or printed list. The list would simply provide access by title and include the range of volumes held. Undergraduates having citations to specific issues would merely need to know whether or not the library owned the title. Even bound volumes that were retained permanently could be shelved by title. This is consistent with the practice at some libraries of cataloging, but not classifying, their serials and periodicals, and shelving them by title or main entry. Even science and engineering collections, which assign call numbers to their journals, often shelve both the bound volumes and the unbound issues by title or main entry.

What is lost in only providing a list of titles held is the publication history of any given title as well as subject access. Without this publication history, identical, but different, titles are not as easily distinguished, and it may be necessary to add a place of publication beside like titles in such a list. In addition, the lack of subject headings means that a beginning researcher will not be able to determine as easily which periodical titles are relevant to a given topic. If, as is the case for many students, the greatest number of searches are for known items, then the lack of subject access would not pose real difficulties. Since most libraries have access to one of the large utilities (OCLC, RLIN, WLN), cataloging copy is readily available for the majority of periodical and serial titles. Cataloging these titles provides the library user with a complete description of the title as well subject access. If the library is a member of a union list of serials of any sort, being able to report titles and holdings according to prescribed conventions is often desirable, if not mandatory. Furthermore, cataloging the serials in the library's collection provides tracking for the numerous and inevitable title changes that occur over the spectrum of the collection.

It is this author's opinion that, given the wealth of resources available for obtaining bibliographic records, there is little reason or justification for not cataloging, that is, describing and providing subject access to the serials collection. Cataloging all serials further ensures that these titles are given full or equal status in the library's collection and represented in the same fashion in the library's online or card catalog as are books, and are thus recognized as an equally important part of the total collection.

Sources of Cataloging Records

If a library does decide to catalog and classify its periodicals and serials, there are good sources of bibliographic data available. In addition to the utilities which load Library of Congress cataloging tapes weekly, there are several CD-ROM products, such as Bibliofile and LaserQuest, which contain LC cataloging records. These CD-ROM products can be a good starting point for libraries that have never cataloged their serials or are in the process of converting manual cataloging records to online format. Bibliofile and LaserQuest are updated on a regular basis.

Both OCLC and RLIN contain a wealth of older serials records, due in large part to the CONSER Program. The CONSER Project, now CONSER Program, was begun in 1975, and was a major effort to create a database of serials records for the United States and Canada. This resulted in serials cataloging records being created for many hundreds of thousands of titles (O'Neill 1991). In addition to the CONSER records, the utilities grew with the addition of member cataloging records for unique titles not already represented in the database. The 1970s and 1980s represented the heyday of the cataloging utility, both as bibliographic resource and as precursor to the local online catalog; during this time most academic libraries migrated their cataloging from strictly manual, in-house card production operations to online cataloging on OCLC, RLIN, or WLN. Although OCLC records contain a local data field, it was not really possible to maintain ongoing volume holdings online. With RLIN, libraries could show all volumes received online and both update the online cataloging record and then get a replacement shelflist card which would show this added volume. Until the late 1980s, the bibliographic utility was truly multipurpose and was used as a card production machine, a resource database for cataloging copy, and a resource for interlibrary loan for items not held locally. In no way, however, was either RLIN or OCLC a local online catalog, although RLIN came closer for those libraries who chose to update their holdings online. With the creation of local online catalogs, beginning in the late 1980s, many libraries began working toward fully integrated systems for all library functions. Total local processing became the goal for cataloging and for many libraries has already become a reality. Simultaneous with this change, the role of the utility has evolved and continues to evolve and both OCLC and RLIN are evaluating their place in libraries and beginning to offer new services. OCLC, for example, offers contract cataloging, access to journal article databases, and assistance with CJK cataloging, while RLIN is exploring providing bibliographic records using FTP (File Transfer Protocol) and provides a public interface (Eureka) to its bibliographic records as well as access to a host of citation databases.

Serials Holdings and Standards

From the patron's perspective, it is not merely enough to know if the library owns the title he or she needs, but more important, does the library hold the particular issue or volume in which the desired article resides. Consequently, over the years, serials librarians have put a lot of time and effort into discussing the form of serials holdings statements and into the creation and maintenance of said holdings statements. In December 1989, the USMARC Format for Holdings Data was published; it was the third USMARC communications format, the other two being the format for bibliographic data and the format for authority data. This new format applies to not only serial items but also single and multipart items in almost any other format. The first update to the format was issued in April 1991. As of this writing, the major utilities have not yet made the necessary modifications to enable libraries cataloging on them to make use of the holdings format. Several of the vendors of integrated systems, such as NOTIS, Innovative Interfaces, and Endeavor Information Systems, have software releases which do support MARC holdings. This MARC standard, like the standards for bibliographic and authority records, is a communication format designed to transmit data electronically in a systematic way. Hence, the holdings data is put into numbered fields and lettered subfields in a way that can be parsed by a computer.

The standard that governs how this data is encoded, the ANSI Standard Z39.44–1986 for serials holdings, has significant implications for libraries, since this is where the decisions are made about how the library's holdings are to be recorded. How detailed the holdings should be, how much preservation and individual piece information will be noted, and what changes or training are required to integrate this new requirement into the existing serials cataloging work flow are some of the issues that need to be addressed. There is also a separate standard for non-serial holdings (ANSI/NISO Z39.57–1989), but in 1995 a new standards committee was formed to explore the feasibility of creating one single standard for both types of holdings. This committee has endorsed the concept of one single standard, in part because of the number of publications that could be treated as either serials or monographs, and also, more important, because "the digitization of information and the storage of data in electronic format are also calling into question long-standing definitions of 'serial' and 'non-serial.' Standards Committee AL believes each library should make this determination for itself rather than have it either stated or implied in a holdings statement" (Bloss 1995, 9). If indeed, in several years' time, there is one standard for all of these publications, it will simplify the training of library staff and allow for greater local flexibility in setting up holdings statements.

Classifying Serials

Deciding whether or not to classify serials, that is, to assign them call numbers, can be arrived at on plainly pragmatic grounds (how the library wishes to shelve them) or based on some theoretical ideal that all material should be classified in order to locate it with like materials. Speaking practically, whether or not a library decides to classify its serials and periodicals may depend on how it views the material being used. Generally, serials (annuals, reference titles, monographic series volumes) are shelved with the monographs in the library's collection, and therefore, they are most often cataloged and classified and shelved in the regular stacks. The real choice comes with periodical titles. Here, the considerations are several: the shelving arrangement for bound and unbound issues and volumes, retention and binding policy, and the types of patrons being served. A discussion of periodicals arrangement on SERIALST several years ago brought out the fact that while more libraries shelve their unbound current periodical issues alphabetically by title (or main entry) than by call number, the number of libraries that shelved by call number was only slightly less than those that shelved alphabetically. The chief advantage of the alphabetical arrangement is that patrons do not need to consult any other source to locate a journal on the shelves; this promotes easy browsing of current material, but does not group like subjects together. Those libraries that use the call number arrangement find that some of their patrons like having all of the philosophy journals in one spot and all of the chemistry journals together, even though, to find a particular title, they would need to have the call number first. Obviously, frequent users of the collection will know where their titles are located on the shelves and will not have to check first for browsing of the latest issues. One processing disadvantage of the call number approach is that the check-in clerk either has to write a call number on the piece or print or type up a call number label before the issue can go to the shelf. One can also argue that it probably takes longer to shelve by call number than by title. Most individuals would be able to alphabetize a stack of journals faster than they could put them in Library of Congress or Dewey call number order.

The size of the unbound periodical collection is also a factor if a library has the luxury of starting from scratch and deciding which approach to take. In a departmental or branch library whose collection is only one or two subjects, the number of titles may be quite small, and therefore shelving by title is easy to do and still preserves browsability, since all the titles are most likely in the same discipline anyway. When the title changes, however, and the shelving is an alphabetic arrangement, then a decision has to be made whether or not to shelve all of the unbound issues together under the new title or to leave them in two separate places until they are bound. Most libraries will probably put all of the loose issues under a label for the new title with a shelf marker or notation in the old title location. In the call number scheme, the alphabetic vagaries of changed titles become a moot point, since the basic call number will usually remain the same (if the numbering continues), or only the cutter line will be modified slightly with the new title.

Format Integration

Format Integration is the term used to describe the bringing together of all of the MARC bibliographic formats into one format, with the result being that bibliographic fields that were previously limited to a single format (serials, machine data files, scores, etc.) may now be used interchangeably across all formats or types of material. Instead of seven different MARC formats, there is one MARC format, and a MARC bibliographic record now has a primary format type, but the material being described may also have elements of a secondary format. Format integration will allow for the coding and reflection of these different aspects of the work in the one bibliographic record. The classic example for serials is an index or abstract title issued on CD-ROM; the work is a serial in terms of frequency, but is also an electronic file. Before format integration, the serials cataloger had to explicitly choose between either the MARC serials format and the computer file format, or else just accept LC's guidance as to which was the accepted or standard . The first phase of format integration which involves changes in the variable fields was implemented in 1995. The second phase, the integration of fixed fields, was adopted in March 1996, and both OCLC and RLIN implemented it for their users shortly thereafter. For serials catalogers, many of whom are already accustomed to working in more than one MARC format, the adjustment to format integration will be a relatively simple one and will allow for greater flexibility in bringing out all of the elements of a particular work.

SERIALS CATALOGING ISSUES

For serials catalogers, several issues have required attention and even generated debate and discussion in recent years. With the installation of local online catalogs, libraries became more concerned about having all of their bibliographic records in machine form, and hence, the retrospective conversion industry was born. Other issues which have been the focus of attention in the serials cataloging arena include: the handling of title changes and what constitutes a title change, the question of multiple versions and whether they must have separate bibliographic records, and most recently, the emergence of electronic publications and how these do or do not fit the traditional definitions of serials and monographs.

Retrospective Conversion

Serials cataloging traditionally serves several purposes, one of which is to provide details on a title's publishing history as well as linking notes to past and continuing titles. As libraries have installed online catalogs, there has been pressure from users and administrators alike to represent all of the library's serials holdings in the online catalog. Over the past decade, many serials departments have engaged in specially funded retrospective conversion projects designed to make a machine-readable record available for every serial title. Generally, the first priority is to create records for all currently received titles and their associated previous titles and then to convert titles that are dead or no longer received. Serials librarians have several options for handling retrospective conversion of the titles in their collection. For some libraries, the process of retrospective conversion is best done using the services of their utility (OCLC or RLIN); other libraries will prefer to contract with a commercial firm such as MARCIVE or RLA (now a part of the Research Libraries Group) that specializes in this area. The conversion source will probably give the library several options, one of which would be to receive only Library of Congress bibliographic records; another option is to receive both LC records and also records from other libraries that meet certain standards. It is always useful to supply some sample data to any conversion vendors under consideration and then to see the results of their searching and the kind of output that will be supplied. This gives the library manager a sense of what the vendor's hit rate for acceptable records is and allows the vendor the opportunity to assess the complexity and difficulty of the collection to be converted and the amount of work involved. In addition to the results of a sample file, the serials manager needs to determine the mechanics and the scope of the project: (1) what fields is the vendor searching and what are the match points for determining a hit, (2) how many searches are done, (3) what kind of data is the firm working from (photocopies of shelflist cards, or printed list, for example) , (4) what kind of reports can the library expect to receive, (5) how the records will be supplied (tape, FTP file, for example), (6) what is the per record cost for searching, for supplying the record when there is a match, and (7) is there any provision for subsequent searches after some elapsed time. Depending on the service selected, there may be more or less time and involvement required of the library staff in preparing titles to be searched and in doing follow-up as the reports and records are provided.

For libraries with complex holdings statements, it may be simpler and more efficient if the entire serials retrospective conversion process is handled completely by staff in the library. If the holdings information is not all in one place, on the shelflist card, for example, and some consulting of the stacks or of other files such as a Kardex file will be necessary, then there may be merit in doing the work in-house. Getting the basic bibliographic record from a conversion vendor is relatively straightforward, but the question of multiple holding statements for multiple locations is more complicated, especially if the local cataloging was done before the introduction of successive entry cataloging and the library wishes, as much as possible, to convert all records under the new rules. Many libraries contract out the conversion of their monograph collections, but prefer to handle the conversion of serials themselves, even though they may still be using RLIN or OCLC as the source of their records.

Title Changes

One thing that never varies with serials is that they change titles frequently. Over time, the rules for dealing with title changes have changed. Until 1971, the Library of Congress followed the principle of latest entry cataloging. Every time the title of the piece changed, the existing bibliographic record was changed and the latest title became the main entry and a "title varies" note was added or expanded upon. This "title varies" note gave all of the earlier titles of the work with their relevant publication dates. Each of these earlier titles was cited as an added entry so that a patron had access to the entire history of the title.

The *Anglo-American Cataloging Rules* (AACR), which were adopted in 1967, provided for the implementation of successive entry cataloging; the Library of Congress, however, continued to update older records until it could no longer stay current and finally, in 1971, adopted successive entry. In successive entry cataloging, each new title of a serial is given its own bibliographic record and linking note fields are included to show the previous title and the later title if the title changes again. While this has resulted in many more serials records, and lengthy discussions about what exactly constitutes a title change, it has meant that patrons searching any title in a periodical's history can expect to find a record under that specific title with an indication of when it was published, and what came before, and what came after. The disadvantage of separate records for each title is that there can often be multiple entries in an online index display for different portions of a title, and a patron without a specific citation may not know which title record is the appropriate one, and may have to look at several records before finding the relevant one.

Although most librarians feel the practice of successive entry has worked reasonably well in the machine environment, there have been a few libraries, most notably Northwestern University, that returned to the practice of latest entry cataloging. One of its rationales for doing this was a very pragmatic one related to order records in the online system. By continuing with latest entry cataloging, the order record attached to the existing (or older title) bibliographic record could continue to be used, and the vendor did not have to informed of a new system order number. Details of the Northwestern experience have been documented in *Cataloging and Classification Quarterly* (Case et al. 1988). Although a few other libraries followed Northwestern University's lead, most librarians have been reluctant to do so, since this practice is so clearly against the accepted cataloging standards as promulgated by the Library of Congress (Bernhardt 1988). For libraries that report their holdings to union lists or who are committed to a certain standard of cataloging on a utility, such deviation is either not allowed or results in their cataloging records being substandard and not as usable by other libraries. Some might even go so far as to say this practice violates the spirit of cooperative cataloging.

Just as there are those few libraries that have gone back to latest entry cataloging, so are there some proponents of yet another alternative, earliest entry cataloging. Flaspeter and Lomker's article "Earliest Online . . ." presented the relative advantages and disadvantages of latest entry, successive entry, and earliest entry cataloging for serials (Flaspeter and Lomker 1985). Chief among the advantages of earliest entry cataloging is the ability to do a title change online upon receipt of the new title; the existing bibliographic record would be updated with a field labeled "Later title," which would include the new title and the beginning publication date. Doing the title change immediately in this manner would save the time of doing a complete new bibliographic record for each title change and would still provide access to all the titles in a publication's history.

Despite the rationality of this proposal, there is no indication that this has been adopted by libraries.

A related concern in the past ten years has been the evolving definition of what constitutes a title change. In the first edition of the *Anglo-American Cataloguing Rules*, the definition of what constituted a title change (Rule 6D1) was all-encompassing and broadly included any change in title, corporate body, or person listed as author in the main entry (AACR 1967, 22). This rule resulted in numerous title changes for very minor variations in the title, variations that often denoted no change in scope, format, or content of the publication, and yet resulted in the creation of seemingly unnecessary new bibliographic records. With the publication of the second edition of the cataloging rules, the definition of a title change (Rule 21.2A1), as it applied to serial publications, was both tightened and explicitly stated (AACR2 1988, 314–315). A title change included any change in the first five words of the title except a change in the initial article, or any change (addition, deletion, or modification) to important words in the title including changes in their spelling. In addition, a whole series of "do not consider the title to have changed if" statements was added which in essence ruled out title changes due to abbreviated forms of words, differences in spelling, singular versus plural forms, and differences in punctuation in the title. Also eliminated as title changes were changes in the words after the first five which did not change the meaning of the title or broaden or change the subject of the publication, and also the addition or deletion of the issuing body at the end of the title. The overriding principle, after all of the emendations and interpretations of the rule, is that "in case of doubt, consider the title proper to have changed" (AACR2 1988, 315).

The most recent rule interpretations for title changes add several more categories of slight changes that can be ignored and also provide guidance on situations where the publication uses two or more titles on an occasional basis (fluctuating titles), but it seems clear that the publisher did not intend to change the title (*Library of Congress Rule Interpretations* 1990). Overall, this ongoing debate and discussion about what constitutes a title change has had the ultimate and beneficial effect of cutting down on the number of titles that were perceived to have changed title, and thus reduced the amount of work for serials catalogers everywhere.

Multiple Versions

Another issue confronting serials catalogers is the issue of multiple versions and the suitability of one bibliographic record for these multiple versions. Two committees, the CONSER Multiple Versions Task Force and the Library of Congress Multiple Versions Committee, have been working on identifying situations in which one bibliographic record might suffice for multiple formats of the same basic work. In the case of serials, a classic case would be one in which the library owns both the paper and the microform of a periodical title. The content is the same, but the physical format is different. Current cataloging practice dictates that there be two separate records, one for the paper and one for the microform. AACR2 clearly stated that the bibliographic record should describe the work in hand, regardless of the physical format, and that microforms be described as microforms whether or not they were original publications in microform or reproductions of paper titles. This meant that the publishing information for the piece in hand was what was to be included in the imprint area of the bibliographic record, even if this was publishing information for something other than the original work. Librarians, catalogers in particular, objected so strongly to this that the Library of Congress issued a rule interpretation reinstating the earlier practice of describing the original (usually the paper copy) in the body of the record, and then using a note for the particulars of the microform. This rule interpretation has become, in effect, the current standard. "Unfortunately, LC's rule interpretation did not go far enough. It reversed the principle of emphasizing description of the physical piece in hand, but it failed to address the consequence of that principle: the requirement to create separate bibliographic records" (C. Graham 1990, 22). The net result has been that most larger libraries that follow the national standards are creating multiple bibliographic records for the same title in different forms: one for the paper copy, one for the microfilm or microfiche, and perhaps an additional one or more for CD-ROMs, floppy disks, or online files. Much of the impetus of the work of these two committees has been to streamline the cataloging process and to reduce the number of lengthy records taking up space in online systems. To that end, the proposal to adopt multiple version cataloging had been targeted for adoption in late 1993. However, this adoption has not happened.

While the issues surrounding the proposal of a single record have not been fully resolved, CONSER did recently allow for an interim compromise in one specific area only, and that is the area of online or remote access versions of printed journals. This compromise allows "CONSER catalogers to provide access to the online version THROUGH the paper record without separately cataloging the online version. . . . we are not cataloging the electronic version on the paper record, only noting its existence. This is not a 'single record cataloging approach,' as many have wanted to call it" (Hirons 1996). This interim approach will be evaluated in six months' time or sometime in spring 1997. CONSER overall still states that in most cases, a separate record should be created for each version of a title.

In addition to questions about what constitutes versions of the same work, there are issues related to the implementation and use of the new MARC format for holdings and locations. The questions of what are the same work and what are different editions have ramifications for books, sound recordings, musical scores, as well as serials. One new case for consideration is, when is the CD-ROM version of an index the same work as the paper index and when is it not? In many instances, the CD-ROM product covers different time periods and may have added material not found in the paper index. Therefore, it may, in fact, be a different work, not a different version of the same title, and so not subject to this new treatment. For detailed discussion of these and other specific serials cataloging issues, there is a regular column in each issue of *Serials Review*.

Other Electronic Publications

With the proliferation of electronic titles on the Internet, many of which are serial in nature, there are those who question whether or not "such changes in serials publishing made possible by the Internet are so profound as to demand new bibliographic terminology" (Duranceau 1996, 69). There are others who argue for flexibility in interpreting the definition of a serial as evidenced in the electronic environment, but state that these new serials do still have periodicity and issue numbers and dates. Two who feel more strongly offer the thesis that the electronic arena has spawned a new form of publication, neither monograph nor serial, but with elements of both, that they would call "bibliographic hermaphrodites" (Graham and Ringler 1996, 73). These new forms of publication are complete in one part, are able to be updated, and have the "potential to continue indefinitely" (Graham and Ringler 1996, 73). Whereas serials are intended to continue indefinitely, that is not the case for the hermaphrodites; rather, their defining characteristic as posited by Graham and Ringler is their "updatability." Furthermore, they would include in this category not only World Wide Web pages, online abstracting services, and libraries' OPACs, but also looseleaf publications. This is probably only the first of other proposals yet to come on how to deal with the complex new forms of publication on the Web; despite its seeming radicalness, it is motivated by the desire to preserve the principles of serials cataloging as it is known. To stay current with the latest thinking on these and other topics, many serials librarians find both CONSERLine and AUTOCAT (both online listservs) valuable sources of information and debate for issues specifically related to the cataloging of serials. Another source of information, primarily cataloging copy, is InterCat, OCLC's cataloging project for Internet resources. What has happened with the tools of the trade for serials catalogers (but also for serials managers in general), is that just as new publication in non-library fields has gone electronic, cataloging tools (LC classification schedules, geographic names, rule interpretations) are being provided on CD and on local area networks as well as on the Web (the aforementioned InterCat and also other libraries' cataloging policies and procedures).

CATALOGING SIMPLIFICATION

Core Serials Record

Another area of concern for serials catalogers and serials librarians is the movement toward cataloging simplification or cataloging modification, as it has been called, spearheaded by the Library of Congress. Specific proposals were outlined in a white paper distributed in 1992 (Avram 1992). Many of the proposals related most directly to monographic cataloging, but one proposal regarding series treatment decisions did affect serials. In the short term, LC proposed simplifying what is required on series authority records and in the long term, incorporating series decision information into a future online check-in record. The impetus for the reform was primarily economic, since cataloging costs are high and often difficult to justify to budget administrators.

With the increased emphasis on cost savings in all areas of library operations, the resulting reexamination of cataloging records led to the concept of a minimal level cataloging record in addition to the traditional full cataloging record. Subsequently, proposals were made and a standard adopted for core records for monographs, audio-visual materials, and serials. In 1993, the Cooperative Cataloging Council defined a core record level for monographs which was in the middle between the full and the minimal level records. In early 1994, CONSER members began exploring the desirability of a core record for serials, and by late in the year, the first proposal for which fixed and variable fields should constitute such a record level was distributed for comments (Schottlaender 1994). With the adoption of the core serials record in 1996, it will be possible for serials catalogers to more accurately code the level of the cataloging and for libraries sharing cataloging copy to know from the coding what fields will be in the record. The addition of this new record level offers serials librarians greater flexibility in dealing with materials in esoteric languages, publication types such as working papers that may not merit the time and expense of full cataloging, and other local special serials, by providing a recognized and accepted record that can be clearly labeled as meeting the core level.

Cataloging of Computer Files

With the proliferation of serial titles published on CD-ROM and on floppy disk, until recently, libraries have had to address the question of whether to catalog those CD-ROMs that are indexes or abstracts or full-text journals or collections of journals using the MARC serials format, or to catalog them with the MARC computer files format (Leathem 1994). Until format integration, using the serials format meant that some of the specific note fields for computer files were not present, while the computer files format did not include all serials fields. The ISSN and some other key fields, however, were subsequently added to the computer files format; nonetheless, until spring 1996, CONSER dictated that these titles were to be cataloged as serials in order that they could be authenticated (Hirons 1993, 10). In 1996, with the adoption of the second phase of format integration, CONSER reversed itself, as was noted earlier, in favor of the machine-readable datafile as the primary format designator.

With the reality of format integration, the primary format of any bibliographic record is less important, since the cataloger will be able to designate that something is both a computer file and yet a serial and also be able to include other information, such as frequency and a previous title.

OUTSOURCING OF CATALOGING AND STAFFING

Before the cataloging utilities existed, every library had to do almost all of its own original cataloging, and technical services divisions and units were often heavily staffed with lots of original catalogers and clerks to create original records, to search print National Union Catalog volumes or microfiche for copy to be photographed or copied, and to order the necessary catalog cards from the Library of Congress. Typists were also needed to create the basic catalog card for titles for which no LC cards were available. Cataloging was a labor-intensive process which, with the advent of OCLC and RLIN more than twenty years ago, became less so. In the present climate of needing to exercise even greater economies, of ensuring that every step taken is essential, and of stressing customer service to one's patrons, libraries are reexamining their cataloging costs, struggling to reduce their backlogs, and rethinking the need to perform all cataloging on site. It is important to appreciate ahead of time that although contracting out cataloging of materials may offer the advantages of timeliness and a reduction in some staffing costs, there will generally be staff time required to administer the process and to ensure that appropriate measures are taken when the material is received to monitor the overall quality of the work being done. These and other considerations are covered in detail in a recent ALA publication (Kascus and Hale 1995). Several of the large, domestic monograph approval vendors now offer the option of receiving cataloging records on tape or in an FTP file for all of the books that are shipped to the library each week. Others, like OCLC with its TECHPRO service, will provide cataloging done to the library's specifications either for current materials, to clear up backlogs, or to deal with materials in a special language or particular format. The materials are shipped to the cataloging contractor and returned ready for the shelf in accordance with the specifications in the library's profile. The advantages of such outsourcing or contract cataloging is that the library can save money on staff costs, reduce the time it takes to get a book cataloged, and may even reduce cataloging backlogs. Although one may think of this kind of outsourcing as being most appropriate for monographic material, there are libraries that have included serials in the profile for this kind of treatment (Duranceau 1994, 71). It seems clear that in the next five to ten years there will be an increase in the use of outside sources for cataloging, possibly for new serials or for serials in specific languages, and this development will affect the shape and scope of technical services operations in general and of serials departments in some measure.

THE FUTURE

The traditionalists among us can be reassured that there will be paper serials to catalog for many years to come (as well as microfilms and microfiche, and probably even floppy disks and CD-ROMs for the foreseeable future) and the ongoing maintenance associated with title changes and ceased and suspended titles. The excitement and dazzle generated by the latest publishing ventures on the World Wide Web are testament to the increasing popularity of this new format and surely mean that serials librarians will continue to be challenged not only by cataloging and providing access to e-journals and other Web sites, but also by grappling with the larger issues of what is the definition of a serial (do hermaphrodites really exist?), do all forms need their own bibliographic records, and ultimately, how many versions of a title does a library need to own and maintain? Of all of the times in which to be a serials cataloger, this ranks as one of the most dynamic and interesting since the introduction of MARC in the 1960s and the inception of the utilities in the 1970s.

REFERENCES

Anglo-American Cataloguing Rules (AACR). North American ed. 1967. Chicago: American Library Association.

Anglo-American Cataloguing Rules (AACR2). 2d ed. 1988. Chicago: American Library Association.

Avram, Henriette. 1992. "Cataloging Modifications at the Library of Congress Collections Service" (January 2). Unpublished paper.

Bernhardt, Melissa. 1988. "Dealing with Serial Title Changes: Some Theoretical and Practical Considerations." *Cataloging and Classification Quarterly* 9, no. 2: 25–39.

Bloss, Marjorie. 1995. "Development of a Single National Standard for Holdings Statements for Bibliographic Items." *Information Standards Quarterly* 7, no. 4: 8–9.

Case, Mary M., Elisabeth Janakiev, Kevin M. Randall, and Bradley D. Carrington. 1988. "Rules for Latest Entry Cataloging: Northwestern University Library Supplement to AACR2." *Cataloging and Classification Quarterly* 9, no. 2: 41–54.

Duranceau, Ellen, ed. 1994. "Vendors and Librarians Speak on Outsourcing, Cataloging, and Acquisitions." *Serials Review* 20, no. 3: 69–83.

Duranceau, Ellen Finnie, ed. 1996. "Old Wine in New Bottles? Defining Electronic Serials." *Serials Review* 22, no. 1: 69–79.

Flaspeter, Marjorie, and Linda Lomker. 1985. "Earliest Online. . . ." *Serials Review* 11, no. 2: 63–70.

Gorman, Michael. 1995. "The Corruption of Cataloging." *Library Journal* (September 15): 32–34.

Graham, Crystal. 1990. "Definition and Scope of Multiple Versions." *Cataloging and Classification Quarterly* 11, no. 2: 5–32.

Graham, Crystal, and Rebecca Ringler. 1996. "Hermaphrodites & Herrings." *Serials Review* 22, no. 1: 73–77.

Graham, Peter S. 1990. "Quality in Cataloging: Making Distinctions." *Journal of Academic Librarianship* 16, no. 4: 213–218.

Gregor, Dorothy, and Carol Mandel. 1991. "Cataloging Must Change!" *Library Journal* 116, no. 6 (April 1): 42–47.

Hirons, Jean L. 1996, August 27. E-Serials and CONSER. Internet Cataloging Project [Online]. Available e-mail (INTERCAT@oclc.org).

Hirons, Jean L., ed. 1993. *CONSER Cataloging Manual*. Washington, DC: Library of Congress.

Kascus, Marie A., and Dawn Hale. 1995. *Outsourcing Cataloging, Authority Work, and Physical Processing: A Checklist of Considerations*. Chicago and London: American Library Association.

Leathem, Cecilia A. 1994. ''An Examination of Choice of Formats for Cataloging Nontextual Serials.'' *Serials Review* 20, no. 3: 59–67.

Library of Congress Rule Interpretations. 1990. Washington, DC: Library of Congress, Cataloging Distribution Service.

O'Neill, Rosanna M. 1991. ''CONSER: Cons . . . and Pros, or, What's in It for Me.'' *Serials Review* 17, no. 2: 53–62, 76.

Schottlaender, Brian E.C. 1994, September 25. CONSER Proposal: Core Record for Serials. Serials List [Online]. Available e-mail (SERIALST@uvmvm.uvm.edu).

Waite, Ellen J. 1995. ''Reinvent Catalogers!'' *Library Journal* (November 1): 36–37.

Selected Bibliography

Anders, Vicki, Colleen Cook, and Roberta Pitts. 1992. "A Glimpse into a Crystal Ball: Academic Libraries in the Year 2000." *Wilson Library Bulletin* 67, no. 2: 36–40.

"Annual Survey of Automated Library System Vendors: Integrated, Multi-User, Multi-Function Systems Running on Mainframes, Minis, and Micros That Use a Multi-User Operating System." 1994. *Library Systems* 14, nos. 3/4: 17–32.

Astle, Deana. 1994, February 24. Periodical use studies [e-mail to J. Farrington] [Online]. Available e-mail (jfarring@pobox.upenn.edu).

Bailey, Charles W., Jr. 1994. "Scholarly Electronic Publishing on the Internet, the NREN, and the NII: Charting Possible Futures." *Serials Review* 20, no. 3: 7–16.

Bloss, Alex. 1992. "Serials Management Is Not for Sissies." *ALCTS Newsletter* 3, no. 2: 14–15.

Bluh, Pamela. 1993. "Document Delivery 2000: Will It Change the Nature of Librarianship?" *Wilson Library Bulletin* 67, no. 6: 49–51, 112.

Bridge, Frank R. 1993. "Automated System Marketplace 1993: Part I: Focus on Minicomputers." *Library Journal* 118 (April 1): 52–64.

Broadway, Rita, and Jane Qualls. 1990. "Periodicals Public Service: A Staff Training Program." *Serials Review* 16, no. 3: 51–54.

Burckel, Nicholas C. 1992. "Electronic Dissemination of Full-Text Journal Articles." *C&RL News* 53, no. 5: 322–323.

Butler, Brett. 1991. "The Electronic Library Program: Developing Networked Electronic Library Collections." *Library Hi-Tech* 9, no. 2: 21–30.

Butler, Brett. 1992. "Electronic Editions of Serials: The Virtual Library Model." *Serials Review* 18, nos. 1–2: 102–136.

Butler, H. Julene, ed. 1994. "Abstracts of Papers Presented at the International Conference on Refereed Journals, October 1993." *Serials Review* 20, no. 4: 21–30.

Caswell, Jerry V. et al. 1995. "Importance and Use of Holdings Links between Citation Databases and Online Catalogs." *Journal of Academic Librarianship* 21, no. 2: 92–96.

Chappell, Mary Ann. 1993. "Meeting Undergraduate Literature Needs with ILL/Document Delivery." *Serials Review* 19, no. 1: 81–86.

Chiou-sen, Dora Chen. 1995. *Serials Management: A Practical Guide.* Chicago and London: American Library Association.

Christ, Ruth, and Selina Lin. 1992. "Serials Retrospective Conversion: Project Design and In-House Implementation." *Cataloging and Classification Quarterly* 14, nos. 3/4: 51–73.

Christensen, John O. 1992. "Cost of Chemistry Journals to One Academic Library, 1980-1990." *Serials Review* 18, no. 3: 19–34.

Christensen, John O. 1993. "Do We Know What We Are Paying For? A Comparison of Journal Subscription Costs." *Serials Review* 19, no. 2: 39–61.

Christensen, John O., and Howard B. Christensen. 1995. "Application of a Sampling Method in Journal Cost Studies." *Serials Review* 21, no. 2: 17–28.

Clack, Mary Elizabeth, and John F. Riccick. 1990. "The Future of Serials Librarianship: Part 2." *Serials Review* 16, no. 3: 61–67, 80.

Cochenour, Donnice. 1993. "Establishing a Current Periodicals Room: Colorado State's Experience." *Serials Review* 19, no. 2: 13–22.

Creth, Sheila D. 1994. "The Information Arcade: Playground for the Mind." *Journal of Academic Librarianship* 20 (March): 22–23.

Culbertson, Michael. 1992. "Analysis of Searches by End-Users of Science and Engineering CD-ROM Databases in an Academic Library." *CD-ROM Professional* 5, no. 2: 76–79.

Davenport, Elizabeth. 1993. "The Journal at the Crossroads: A One-Day Seminar for Librarians, Publishers, Subscriptions Agents and the Readers of Serials." *NASIG Newsletter* 8, no. 5.

Degener, Christie T., and Marjory A. Waite. 1991. "Using an Automated Serials System to Assist with Collection Review and Cancellations." *Serials Review* 17, no. 1: 13–20.

DeLoughry, Thomas J. 1994. "Journals Via Computer." *Chronicle of Higher Education* (March 9): A23–24.

Dijkstra, Jan Willem. 1992. "Factors in Setting Prices of Journals." *Collection Management* 15, nos. 3/4: 533–548.

Dougherty, Richard M. 1989. "Turning the Serials Crisis to Our Advantage: An Opportunity for Leadership." *Library Administration and Management* 3, no. 2: 59–64.

Drabenstott, Jon, ed. 1989. "Truth in Automating: Case Studies in Library Automation." *Library Hi-Tech* 7, no. 25: 95–111.

Drabenstott, Karen. 1994. *Analytical Review of the Library of the Future.* Washington, DC: Council on Library Resources.

Duranceau, Ellen, ed. 1994. "Vendors and Librarians Speak on Outsourcing, Cataloging, and Acquisitions." *Serials Review* 20, no. 3: 69–83.

Duranceau, Ellen Finnie, ed. 1995. "Cataloging Remote-Access Electronic Serials: Rethinking the Role of the OPAC." *Serials Review* 21, no. 4: 67–77.

Duranceau, Ellen Finnie, ed. 1996. "Old Wine in New Bottles? Defining Electronic Serials." *Serials Review* 22, no. 1: 69–79.

Dykeman, Amy, and Julia Zimmerman. 1991. "The Georgia Institute of Technology Electronic Library: Issues to Consider." *Cataloging and Classification Quarterly* 13, nos. 3/4: 211–221.

Emtag, Alan. 1994. "The Whys and What of URLs and URNs." *Serials Review* 20, no. 4: 32–34.

Erkkila, John E. 1990. "CD-ROM vs. Online: Implications for Management from the Cost Side." *Canadian Library Journal* (December): 421–28.

Farrington, Jean Walter. 1981. "Out of the Dungeon: Mainstreaming Microforms." *Serials Librarian* 5, no. 4: 37–40.

Farrington, Jean Walter. 1985. "Automated Serials Control: How to Get There or As Many Questions as Answers." *Drexel Library Quarterly* 21, no. 1: 77–86.

Farrington, Jean Walter. 1986. "The Serials Visible File: Observations on Its Impending Demise." *Serials Review* 12, no. 4: 33–36.

Farrington, Jean Walter. 1988. "Selecting a Serials System: The Technical Services Perspective." *Library Resources and Technical Services* 32, no. 3: 402–406.

Farrington, Jean Walter. 1990. "*In Medias Res*: A Serials Department in Transition." *Serials Librarian* 19, nos. 1/2: 31–42.

Fisher, Janet H., and John Tagler. 1993. "Perspectives on Firm Serials Prices." *Serials Review* 19, no. 4: 63–72.

Fuseler, Elizabeth. 1994. "Providing Access to Journals—Just in Time or Just in Case?" *C&RL News* 55, no. 2: 130–132, 148.

George, Lee Anne. 1993. "Fee-Based Information Services and Document Delivery." *Wilson Library Bulletin* 67, no. 6: 41–44, 112.

Gorman, Michael. 1994. "The Treason of the Learned: The Real Agenda of Those Who Would Destroy Libraries and Books." *Library Journal* (February 15): 130–131.

Gorman, Michael. 1995. "The Corruption of Cataloging." *Library Journal* (September 15): 32–34.

Gossen, Eleanor A., and Suzanne Irving. 1995. "Ownership versus Access and Low-Use Periodical Titles." *Library Resources and Technical Services* 39, no. 1: 43–52.

Graham, Peter S. 1995. "Requirements for the Digital Research Library." *College and Research Libraries* 56, no. 4: 331–339.

Grant, Marilyn A., and John C. Stalker. 1989. "The Multiplatter CD-ROM Network at Boston College." *Laserdisk Professional* 2, no. 5: 12–18.

Gyeszly, Suzanne D., Marifran Bustion, and Jane Treadwell. 1990. "Infrequently Used Serials: A Space Utilization Project." *Collection Management* 12, nos. 1/2: 109–123.

Harloe, Bart, and John M. Budd. 1994. "Collection Development and Scholarly Communication in the Era of Electronic Access." *Journal of Academic Librarianship* 20, no. 2: 83–87.

Harrison, Teresa M., Timothy Stephen, and James Winter. 1991. "Online Journals: Disciplinary Designs for Electronic Scholarship." *Public Access Computer Systems Review* 2, no. 1: 18–27.

Hawbaker, A. Craig, and Cynthia K. Wagner. 1996. "Periodical Ownership Versus Online Access: A Cost-Benefit Analysis." *Journal of Academic Librarianship* 22, no. 2: 105–130.

Hawks, Carol Pitts. 1994. "Building and Managing an Acquisitions Program." *Library Acquisitions: Practice and Theory* 18, no. 3: 297–308.

Huesmann, James. 1991, November 14. Journal cataloging, classification and location, a preliminary analysis of alternatives. Serials List [Online]. Available e-mail (SERIALST@uvmvm.uvm.edu).

Keating, Lawrence R. II, Christian Easton Reinke, and Judi A. Goodman. 1993. "Electronic Journal Subscriptions." *Library Acquisitions: Practice and Theory* 17: 455–463.

Kilpela, Raymond. 1968. "Administrative Structure of the University Library." *College and Research Libraries* 29, no. 6: 511–516.

Kirshan, K. 1991. "Organization of Serials in the University Libraries in Canada." *Canadian Library Journal* (April): 123–126.

Kutz, Myer. 1992. "Distributing the Costs of Scholarly Journals: Should Readers Contribute?" *Serials Review* 18, nos. 1–2: 73–84.

LaGuardia, Cheryl. 1995. "Virtual Dreams Give Way to Digital Reality." *Library Journal* (October 1): 42–44.

Landoni, Monica, Nadia Catenazzi, and Forbes Gibbs. 1993. "Hyper-books and Visual Books in an Electronic Library." *Electronic Library* 11, no. 3: 175–186.

Langschied, Linda. 1994. "Electronic Journal Forum: VPIEJ-L: An Online Discussion Group for Electronic Journal Publishing Concerns." *Serials Review* 20, no. 1: 89–94.

Lesk, Michael. 1992. "Pricing Electronic Information." *Serials Review* 18, nos. 1–2: 38–44.

Lowell, Felice K. 1989. "From Kardex to INNOVACQ: Serials Control Online." *Serials Librarian* 16, nos. 1/2: 17–28.

Lowry, Charles B. 1995. "Managing Technology: Putting the Pieces Together—Essential Technologies for the Virtual Library." *Journal of Academic Librarianship* 21: 297–300.

Lynch, Clifford A. 1991. "Serials Management in the Age of Electronic Access." *Serials Review* 17, no. 1: 7–12.

Marks, Kenneth E., and Steven P. Nielsen. 1991. "A Longitudinal Study of Journal Prices in a Research Library." *Serials Librarian* 19, nos. 3/4: 105–135.

Martin, Susan K. 1993. "Librarians on a Tightrope: Getting from Here to There and Loosening Up in the Process." In *After the Electronic Revolution, Will You Be the First to Go?*, ed. Arnold Hirshon. Chicago: American Library Association, 39–49.

Martin, Sylvia, and Judith Ricke. 1989. "Implementation of Online Serials Control: Two Approaches within the Same Library System." *Serials Review* 15, no. 3: 7–17.

McCoy, Patricia Sayre. 1995. "Technical Services and the Internet." *Wilson Library Bulletin* 69, no. 7: 37–40.

McKay, Sharon Cline, and Betty Landesman. 1991. "The SISAC Bar Code Symbol." *Serials Review* 17, no. 2: 47–51.

McMillan, Gail et al. 1991. "Electronic Journals: Considerations for the Present and the Future." *Serials Review* 17, no. 4: 77–86.

Meiseles, Linda, and Sue Feller. 1994. "Training Serials Specialists: Internships as an Option." *Library Administration and Management* 8, no. 2: 83–86.

Miller, Tim. 1994. "Online in 1999: Ten Predictions." *Information Today* 11: 55–57.

Miller, Tim. 1995. "How to Become an Electronic Librarian." *Information Today* (February): 40–41.

Moothart, Tom. 1995. "Migration to Electronic Distribution Through OCLC's Electronic Journals Online." *Serials Review* 21, no. 4: 61–65.

Naylor, Maiken. 1990. "Assessing Current Periodical Use at a Science and Engineering Library: A dBASE III+ Application." *Serials Review* 16, no. 4: 7–19.

Naylor, Maiken. 1993. "A Comparison of Two Methodologies for Counting Current Periodical Use." *Serials Review* 19, no. 1: 27–34, 62.

Nelson, Robert, and Melissa Kummerer. 1993. "EBSCO, A Ten-Year Retrospective and View Toward the Future." *Library Hi-Tech* 11, no. 3: 37–49.

Nelson, Theodor Holm. 1993. "You, The Guardians of Literature Still." In *After the Electronic Revolution, Will You Be the First to Go?*, ed. Arnold Hirshon. Chicago: American Library Association, 9–17.

"New Roles for Publishers in an Electronic World." 1992. *Publishers Weekly* 239, no. 41 (September 14): 527–532.

Niles, Judith. 1988. "Technical Services Reorganization in an Online Integrated Environment." *Cataloging and Classification Quarterly* 9, no. 1: 11–17.

Peters, Paul Evan. 1995. "Digital Libraries Are Much More Than Digitized Collections." *EducomReview* (July/August): 11–15.

Pioness, Geraldine F. 1990. "Serials Replacement Orders: A Closer Look." *Serials Review* 16, no. 1: 65–80.

Presely, Roger L. 1993. "Firing an Old Friend, Painful Decisions: The Ethics between Librarians and Vendors." *Library Acquisitions: Practice and Theory* 17: 53–59.

Racine, Drew. 1992. "Access to Full-Text Journal Articles: Some Practical Considerations." *Library Administration and Management* 2, no. 2: 100–104.

Rein, Laura O. et al. 1993. "Formula-Based Subject Allocation: A Practical Approach." *Collection Management* 17, no. 4: 25–48.

Resnick, Rosalind. 1994. "Newspapers on the Net." *Internet World* 5, no. 5: 69–73.

Roes, Hans, and Joost Dijkstra. 1994. "Ariadne: The Next Generation of Electronic Document Delivery Systems." *Electronic Library* 12, no. 1: 13–19.

Rooks, Dana. 1993. "The Virtual Library: Pitfalls, Promises, and Potential." *Public-Access Computer Systems Review* 4, no. 5: 22–29.

Rooks, Dana C. 1993. "Electronic Serials: Administrative Angst or Answer." *Library Acquisitions: Practice and Theory* 17: 449–454.

Rosen, Linda. 1993. "The Information Professional as Knowledge Engineer" (Part I). *Information Today* 10, no. 4: 57–60.

Rush, James E. 1988. "The Library Automation Market: Why Do Vendors Fail? A History of Vendors and Their Characteristics." *Library Hi-Tech* 6, no. 3 (23): 7–21.

Rush, James E. 1995. "Electronic Publishing—The Future Is Today." *PALINET News*, no. 112: 2, 6.

Schlabach, Martin L., and Susan J. Barnes. 1994, March. "The Mann Library Gateway System." *Public-Access Computer Systems Review* [Online], 5 (1), 5–19. Available e-mail (listserv@uhupvm1.uh.edu). Message: GET SCHLABAC PRV5N1 F=MAIL.

Sellberg, Roxanne. 1995. "Managing the Cataloging Enterprise in an Academic Library: An Introduction." *Wilson Library Bulletin* 69, no. 7: 33–36.

Stern, Barrie T., and Robert M. Campbell. 1989. "ADONIS: Delivering Journal Articles on CD-ROM" (Part II). *CD-ROM Librarian* 2, no. 2: 15–22.

Swan, John. 1993. "The Electronic Straitjacket." *Library Journal* (October 15): 41–46.

Taylor, Arlene G. "The Information Universe: Will We Have Chaos or Control?" *American Libraries* 25, no. 7: 629–632.

Ten Have, Elizabeth Davis. 1993. "Serials in Strategic Planning and Reorganization." *Serials Review* 19, no. 2: 7–48.

Tenopir, Carol. 1993. "Electronic Access to Periodicals." *Library Journal* (March 1): 54–55.

Treloar, Andrew. 1996. "Electronic Scholarly Publishing and the World Wide Web." *Journal of Scholarly Publishing* 27, no. 3: 135–150.

Tuttle, Marcia. 1994. "Serials Management." In *Guide to Technical Services Resources*, ed. Peggy Johnson. Chicago: American Library Association, 120–135.

Waite, Ellen J. 1995. "Reinvent Catalogers!" *Library Journal* (November 1): 36–37.

Ward, Martin. 1975. "Observations of Serials Management in Seventeen London Libraries." *Library Association Record* 77, no. 10: 247–255.

Weigel, Friedemann. 1996. "EDI in the Library Market: How Close Are We?" *Library Administration and Management* 10, no. 3: 141–146.

Wiggins, Richard. 1995. "The Word Electric." *Internet World* (September): 31–34.

Willis, Katherine et al. 1994. "TULIP—The University Licensing Program: Experiences at the University of Michigan." *Serials Review* 20, no. 3: 39–47.

Winke, R. Conrad. 1993. "Discarding the Main Entry in an Online Cataloging Environment." *Cataloging and Classification Quarterly* 16, no. 1: 53–70.

Wise, Suzanne. 1993. "Making Lemonade: The Challenges and Opportunities of Forced Reference Serials Cancellations; One Academic Library's Experience." *Serials Review* 19, no. 4: 15–26, 96.

Woodward, Hazel, and Cliff McKnight. 1995. "Electronic Journals: Issues of Access and Bibliographic Control." *Serials Review* 21, no. 2: 71–78.

Woodsworth, Anne. 1992. "In the Midst of a Paradigm Shift: The Ownership Dilemma." *Library Issues* 12, no. 4: 3–4.

Young, Ian R. 1992. "The Use of a General Periodicals Bibliographic Database Transaction Log as a Serials Collection Management Tool." *Serials Review* 18, no. 4: 49–60.

Index

About the Author

JEAN WALTER FARRINGTON is Head of Materials Acquisitions at the University of Pennsylvania library. She is an active member of the American Library Association, is a frequent guest lecturer at the College of Information Science and Technology, Drexel University, and has been involved in a number of library automation projects at Penn.